Introduction to Machine Learning

Introduction to Machine Learning

Jacob Pearson

MURPHY & MOORE
www.murphy-moorepublishing.com

Published by Murphy & Moore Publishing,
1 Rockefeller Plaza,
New York City, NY 10020, USA

ISBN: 978-1-63987-333-3

Cataloging-in-Publication Data

Introduction to machine learning / Jacob Pearson.
p. cm.
Includes bibliographical references and index.
ISBN 978-1-63987-333-3
1. Machine learning. 2. Cybernetics. 3. Computers. 4. Machine theory.
5. Artificial intelligence. I. Pearson, Jacob.
Q325.5 .I58 2022
006.31--dc23

For information on all Murphy & Moore Publications
visit our website at www.murphy-moorepublishing.com

⋈ MURPHY & MOORE

Contents

Permissions

Index

Preface

The study of computer algorithms which aim to improve automatically through experience is defined as machine learning. It is considered as a part of artificial intelligence. Machine learning algorithms build models based on sample data or training data, in order to make predictions without being explicitly programmed to do so. They are used in a wide variety of applications, such as email filtering and computer vision. They are also used in conditions wherein it is difficult or unfeasible to develop conventional algorithms to perform the needed tasks. The discipline of machine learning allows computers to discover how they can perform tasks without the need of any explicit programing. It focuses on computers learning from the data provided allowing them to carry out certain tasks. This book presents the complex subject of machine learning in the most comprehensible and easy to understand language. While understanding the long-term perspectives of the topics, it makes an effort in highlighting their impact as a modern tool for the growth of the discipline. This book will provide comprehensive knowledge to the readers.

A detailed account of the significant topics covered in this book is provided below:

Chapter 1- Machine learning is an application of artificial intelligence where a machine, using software applications, learns to predict and act without being explicitly programmed. There are different types of machine learning with varying designs and components. This chapter aims to introduce machine learning and its accompanying fields to the reader in a simple and easy to understand manner.

Chapter 2- Clustering is a type of unsupervised learning method where the machine learns to draw up conclusions from datasets on the basis of similarities and dissimilarities. This chapter delves into the subject of clustering, the various types of clustering, and their analysis and validity for a thorough understanding of the subject.

Chapter 3- Dimensionality reduction is the process through which the number of input variables in a dataset is reduced while still retaining the meaningful properties of the original data. Feature selection, feature reduction, principal component analysis, Fisher linear discriminant analysis, generalized discriminant analysis, singular value decomposition, etc. are a few concepts which are elaborated in this chapter for a better understanding.

Chapter 4- There are various types of classification techniques in machine learning, each suited to a specific task and role, and is a part of the supervised machine learning approach. This chapter touches upon the various classification techniques like statistical classification, probabilistic classification, multiclass classification and linear classifier to provide an extensive understanding on the topic.

Chapter 5- Many theories on machine learning have been put forward to determine the best approach to develop complex artificially intelligent systems which can learn and perform tasks without any human intervention. Theories like the computational learning theory, statistical learning theory, adaptive resonance theory, Hebbian theory, etc. are all part of this endeavor and are thoroughly covered in this chapter.

Chapter 6- Machine learning algorithms are programs that adjust themselves to perform better as they are exposed to more data. They automatically create models of data and change how they process data over time. There are many types of machine learning algorithms and each one is thoroughly examined and analyzed to provide a complete understanding of this subject.

It gives me an immense pleasure to thank our entire team for their efforts. Finally in the end, I would like to thank my family and colleagues who have been a great source of inspiration and support.

Jacob Pearson

Basics of Machine Learning

Machine learning is an application of artificial intelligence where a machine, using software applications, learns to predict and act without being explicitly programmed. There are different types of machine learning with varying designs and components. This chapter aims to introduce machine learning and its accompanying fields to the reader in a simple and easy to understand manner.

In present times, giving a computer to carry out any task requires a set of specific instructions or the implementation of an algorithm that defines the rules that need to be followed. The present day computer system has no ability to learn from past experiences and hence cannot readily improve on the basis of past mistakes. So, giving a computer or instructing a computer controlled programme to perform a task requires one to define a complete and correct algorithm for task and then programme the algorithm into the computer.

Such activities involve tedious and time consuming effort by specially trained teacher or person. Jaime et al also explained that the present day computer systems cannot truly learn to perform a task through examples or through previous solved task and they cannot improve on the basis of past mistakes or acquire new abilities by observing and imitating experts. Machine Learning research endeavors to open the possibility of instruction the computer in such a new way and thereby promise to ease the burden of hand writing programmes and growing problems of complex information that get complicated in the computer.

When approaching a task-oriented acquisition task, one must be aware that the resul-tant computer system must interact with human and therefore should closely match human abilities. So, learning machine or programme on the other hand will have to interact with computer users who make use of them and consequently the concept and skills they acquire- if not necessarily their internal mechanism must be understandable to humans. Also Alpaydin stated that with advances in computer technology, we currently have the ability to store and process large amount of data, as well as access it from physically distant locations over computer network. Most data acquisition devices are digital now and record reliable data. For example, a supermarket chain that has hundreds of stores all over the country selling thousands of goods to millions of customers. The point of sale terminals record the details of each transaction: date, customer identification code, goods bought and their amount, total money spent and so forth, this typically amounts to gigabytes of data every day. This store data becomes useful only when it is analyzed and tuned into information that can be used or be predicted.

We do not know exactly which people are likely to buy a particular product or which author to suggest to people who enjoy reading Hemingway. If we knew, we would not need any analysis of the data; we would just go ahead and write down code. But because we do not, we can only collect data and hope to extract the answers to these and similar question from data. We can construct a good and useful approximation. That approximation may not explain everything, but may still be able to account for some part of data. We believe that identifying the complete process may not be possible; we can still detect certain patterns or regularities. This is the niche of machine learning. Such patterns may help us understand the process, or we can use those patterns to make predictions: Assuming that the future, at least the near future, will not be much different from the past when the sample data was collected, the future predictions can be expected to be right.

Machine learning is not just a database problem; it is a part of artificial intelligence. To be intelligent, a system that is in a changing environment should have the ability to learn. If the system can learn and adapt to such changes, the system designer need not foresee and provide solutions for all possible situations. Machine learning also help us find solutions to may problems in vision, speech recognition and robotics. Let's take the example of recognizing of faces: This is a task we do effortlessly; we recognize family members and friends by looking their faces or from their photographs, despite differences in pose, lighting, hair, style and so forth. But we do consciously and are able to explain how we do it. Because we are not able to explain our expertise, we cannot write the computer program. At the same time, we know that a face image is not just a random collection of pixel: a face has structure, it is symmetric. There are the eyes, the nose, the mouth, located in certain places on the face. Each person's face is a pattern that composed of a particular combination of these. By analyzing sample face images of person, a learning program captures the pattern specific to that person and then recognizes by checking for the pattern in a given image. This is one example of pattern recognition.

Machine learning is programming computers to optimise a performance criterion using example data or past experience. We have a model defined up to some parameters, and learning is the execution of a computer program to optimise the parameter of the model using the training data or past experience. The model may be predictive to make predictions in the future, or descriptive to gain knowledge from data, or both. Machine learning uses the theory of statistics in building mathematical models, because the core task is making inference from sample. The role of learning is twofold: First, in training, we need efficient algorithms to solve the optimised problem, as well as to store and process the massive amount of data we generally have. Second, once a model is learned, its representation and algorithmic solution for inference needs to be efficient as well. In certain applications, the efficiency of the learning or inference algorithm, namely, its space and time complexity may be as important as its predictive accuracy.

Over the years, Jaime et al elaborated that research in machine learning has been pursued with varying degrees of intensity, using different approaches and placing emphasis on different, aspects and goals. Within the relatively short history of this discipline, one may distinguish three major periods, each centered on a different concept:

- Neural modelling and decision-theoretic techniques.

- Symbolic concept-oriented learning.

- Knowledge-intensive approaches combining various learning strategies.

The Neural Modelling (Self Organised System)

The distinguishing feature of the first concept was the interest in building general purpose learning systems that start with little or no initial structure or task-oriented knowledge. The major thrust of research based on this approach involved constructing a variety of neural model-based machines, with random or partially random initial structure. These systems were generally referred to as neural networks or self-organizing systems. Learning in such systems consisted of incremental changes in the probabilities that neuron-like elements (typically threshold logic units) would transmit a signal. Due to the early computer technology, most of the research under this neural network model was either theoretical or involved the construction of special purpose experimental hardware systems, such as perceptrons, pandemonium. The groundwork for this paradigm was laid in the forties by Rashevsky in the area of mathematical biophysics, and by McCulloch, who discovered the applicability of symbolic logic to modeling nervous system activities, related research involved the simulation of evolutionary processes, that through random mutation and "natural" selection might create a system capable of some intelligent, behavior. Experience in the above areas spawned the new discipline of pattern recognition and led to the development of a decision-theoretic approach to machine learning. In this approach, learning is equated with the acquisition of linear, polynomial, or related discriminant functions from a given set of training examples. One of the best known successful learning systems utilizing such techniques was Samuel's checkers program. Through repeated training, this program acquired master-level performance somewhat; different, but closely related, techniques utilized methods of statistical decision theory for learning pattern recognition rules.

The Symbolic Concept Acquisition Paradigm

A second major paradigm started to emerge in the early sixties stemming from the work of psychologist and early AI researchers on models of human learning by Hunt. The paradigm utilized logic or graph structure representations rather than numerical or statistical methods Systems learned symbolic descriptions representing higher level knowledge and made strong structural assumptions about the concepts to be acquired.

Examples of work in this paradigm include research on human concept acquisition and various applied pattern recognition systems. Some researchers constructed task oriented specialized systems that, would acquire knowledge in the context of a practical problem. Ryszard learning system was an influential development in this paradigm. In parallel with Winston's work, different approaches to learning structural concepts from examples emerged, including a family of logic-based inductive learning programs.

The Modern Knowledge-Intensive Paradigm

The third paradigm represented the most recent period of research starting in the mid-seventies. Researchers have broadened their interest beyond learning isolated concepts from examples, and have begun investigating a wide spectrum of learning methods, most based upon knowledge-rich systems specifically, this paradigm can be characterizing by several new trends, including:

- Knowledge-Intensive Approaches: Researchers are strongly emphasizing the use of task-oriented knowledge and the constraints it provides in guiding the learning process One lesson from the failures of earlier knowledge and poor learning systems that is acquire and to acquire new knowledge a system must already possess a great deal of initial knowledge.

- Exploration of alternative methods of learning: In addition to the earlier research emphasis on learning from examples, researchers are now investigating a wider variety of learning methods such as learning from instruction, learning by analogy and discovery of concepts and classifications.

In contrast to previous efforts, a number of current systems are incorporating abilities to generate and select tasks and also incorporate heuristics to control their focus of attention by generating learning tasks, proposing experiments to gather training data, and choosing concepts to acquire.

Importance of Machine Learning

These are benefits of machine learning and these are why research in machine learning is now what could not be avoided or neglected. Using machine learning techniques make life easier for computer users. These are the importance of machine learning. They are:

- Some tasks cannot be defined well except by example; that is we might be able to specify input and output pairs but not a concise relationship between inputs and desired outputs. We would like machines to be able to adjust their internal structure to produce correct outputs for a large number of sample inputs and thus suitably constrain their input and output function to approximate the relationship implicit in the examples.

- It is possible that hidden among large piles of data are important relationships and correlations. Machine learning methods can often be used to extract these relationships (data mining).

- Human designers often produce machines that do not work as well as desired in the environments in which they are used. In fact, certain characteristics of the working environment might not be completely known at design time. Machine learning methods can be used for on the job improvement of existing machine designs.

- The amount of knowledge available about certain tasks might be too large for explicit encoding by humans. Machines that learn this knowledge gradually might be able to capture more of it than humans would want to write down.

- Environments change over time. Machines that can adapt to a changing environment would reduce the need for constant redesign. New knowledge about tasks is constantly being discovered by humans. Vocabulary changes. There is a constant stream of new events in the world. Continuing redesign of AI systems to conform to new knowledge is impractical. But machine learning methods might be able to track much of it.

Machine Learning Varieties

Research in machine learning is now converging from several sources and from artificial intelligent field. These different traditions each bring different methods and different vocabulary which are now being assimilated into a more united discipline. Here is a brief listing of some of the separate disciplines that have contributed to machine learning:

- Statistics: A long-standing problem in statistics is how best to use samples drawn from unknown probability distributions to help decide from which distribution some new sample is drawn. A related problem is how to estimate the value of an unknown function at a new point given the values of this function at a set of sample points. Statistical methods for dealing with these problems can be considered instances of machine learning because the decision and estimation rules depend on a corpus of samples drawn from the problem environment. We will explore some of the statistical methods later in the book. Details about the statistical theory underlying these methods can be found in Orlitsky.

- Brian Models: Nonlinear elements with weighted inputs have been suggested as simple models of biological neurons. Networks of these elements have been studied by several researchers. Brain modelers are interested in how closely these networks approximate the learning phenomena of living brain. We shall see that several important machine learning techniques are based on networks of nonlinear elements often called neural networks. Work inspired by this school is sometimes called connectionism, brain-style computation or sub-symbolic processing.

- Adaptive Control Theory: Control theorists study the problem of controlling a process having unknown parameters which must be estimated during operation. Often, the parameters change during operation and the control process must track these changes. Some aspects of controlling a robot based on sensory inputs represent instances of this sort of problem.

- Psychological Models: Psychologists have studied the performance of humans in various learning tasks. An early example is the EPAM network for storing and retrieving one member of a pair of words when given another. Related work led to a number of early decision tree, and semantic network, methods. More recent work of this sort has been influenced by activities in artificial intelligence which we will be presenting. Some of the work in reinforcement learning can be traced to efforts to model how reward stimuli influence the learning of goal seeking behaviour in animals. Reinforcement learning is an important theme in machine learning research.

- Artificial Intelligence: From the beginning, AI research has been concerned with machine learning. Samuel developed a prominent early program that learned parameters of a function for evaluating board positions in the game of checkers. AI researchers have also explored the role of analogies in learning and how future actions and decisions can be based on previous exemplary cases. Recent work has been directed at discovering rules for expert systems using decision tree methods and inductive logic programming another theme has been saving and generalizing the results of problem solving using explanation based learning.

- Evolutionary Models: In nature, not only do individual animals learn to perform better, but species evolve to be better fit in their individual niches. Since the distinction between evolving and learning can be blurred in computer systems, techniques that model certain aspects of biological evolution have been proposed as learning methods to improve the performance of computer programs. Genetic algorithms and genetic programming are the most prominent computational techniques for evolution.

Components of Machine Learning

There is tremendous promise from machines that can make decisions for themselves. Routine business decisions on things such as pricing, time estimates, and category choices can now be automated and scaled ad infinitum. Advanced pattern recognition algorithms serve as intelligent helpers, improving the effectiveness and focus of your specialized knowledge workers many times over. Algorithmic "pre-screens" of potential drug combinations, patient documents, contracts or images can speed-up the discovery and review process when the volume of data becomes too great to manually look through. Examples like these hint at powerfully intelligent algorithms that can offer new capabilities in a business setting. But in practice, the algorithms alone are not enough. Deployed, they may serve as an integral decision-making unit of a larger system; however these algorithms make up a small part of the system design and engineering efforts.

Data Sources

Traditionally, the task of computing an answer (or output) from incoming information was written by your Software Engineer. To oversimplify things, their job has been to synthesize an explicit set of instructions that a computer can repeatedly execute. As far as algorithmic development goes, the Software Engineer may require only a few examples (and perhaps few more "edge-cases") to determine these steps. Machine Learning algorithms functionally do this, but the approach is more statistical. As data is fed in, the algorithms transform the information into a probable output. They then make very minor self-corrections each time the prediction is wrong. To reach the point where these algorithms begin responding correctly on a wide gamut of possible incoming information, they require far more than a few examples. To make matters a bit more complicated, features deemed useful for predicting the correct outcome may come from disparate sources. Understanding what it takes to extract and then combine the necessary data from multiple sources will give you an idea of the engineering effort involved. Collecting data is an essential step for training, making predictions, and re-training as the outside world changes.

In a deployed setting, the notion of concept drift comes into play. If you train your model on data of a certain characteristic, then it will only perform well on new data of the similar characteristics. This refers to the algorithms capacity to generalize to new information. Your data source may change over time; either smoothly, abruptly, or cyclically (in the case of seasonality). There are several approaches to address this, but as the relationship from your inputs to outputs have changed, your model or your data preparation should change too. You will extract features from your data sources and use these as features to train a model. Features curated from data sources for training must be available for inference on new, unseen and unlabeled items. Missing data is a common occurrence in the real world, but this needs to be closely monitored as information moves from your data sources into your model. Often times it helps to assign ownership over each data source or processed feature, so changes in business logic, data collection or data organization will not silently disrupt your models performance.

Data Storage

Since the available signals for the machine learning system come from a variety of sources and may be reused or processed further, often times a good solution is to create an intermediate storage system that will hold these extracted "features". Some companies choose to design a repository of extracted features commonly referred to as a "data lake". This unstructured data store can be continuously updated and used to generate features for a variety of machine learning systems. This structure is useful because it is not as rigidly bound to a schema as traditional relational databases, and can allow for you to more easily adapt changes as new features are engineered. When there is a large amount of data that ultimately needs to be ingested and joined together for the machine learning system, it may also make sense to establish a structured data warehouse that holds the prepared data. Deformalized tables of pre-joined datasets help speed up processing for your analytics and machine learning algorithms. If you have a database that supports your business processes, it is most likely intended for fast transactions that support customer activity, but for analytics you should setup a database that supports analytical queries. Establishing these intermediary databases is necessary because it is unwise to run taxing analytical queries against your production database every time the machine learning system executes a prediction or a query is processed.

Data Pipeline

The discussion of extracting data from a variety of sources, transforming it into appropriate signals for a machine learning algorithm and loading it into places where it's needed falls under the umbrella of ETL processes. Modern paradigms of these data workflows take a functional approach to data transformations, and the ecosystem of tools have begun to support code as a means for defining these pipelines.

Where the data comes from, how it is getting transformed, and where it ends up going is an integral part of the machine learning system, but it can also become the most complex. Pipelines can be created to extract data from a source; others can pass the data through functions that clean, normalize or check for missing values. Additional pipelines can process data to feed it into charts, visualizations, and into and out of a multitude of machine learning systems. Keeping a handle on this data flow as more pipelines are added to the system can become a formidable challenge for growing organizations, and the technical debt in maintaining these systems are often overlooked by management.

For young companies, leveraging third party tools and providers for pipeline management is far more preferable than building pipelines from scratch, and as the machine learning systems mature, organizations will most likely require dedicated engineers to manage the infrastructure. In the early stages of implementing your data strategy, it may make the most sense to get an end-to-end pipeline in place before any model is deployed. Heuristics and traditional programming logic is still very useful, and these components can be converted into features themselves or replaced in your pipeline with a predictive model when the time is right.

Machine Learning Model

The machine learning model is your core system responsible for receiving in signals from your business and making decisions; whether classifying observations to be in one category or another, or by providing a quantified prediction of what the results should be. They are best built for routine decisions that are based on the same subset of information ones that require much of your valuable knowledge workers time to process.

To build one, you must have many historical examples that are labeled with the results you want to duplicate. Documents that failed or passed examination, images that have been flagged as appropriate or inappropriate, activity that has been recorded to be suspicious, price assignment based on descriptors, date assignment based on requirements. A machine learning algorithm will learn by example, finding subtle patterns in the many dimensions of the incoming data and learn how to make the decision for it. This class of algorithms is considered "supervised learning".

There are learning algorithms that do not require labeled "Truths" on your data. Referred to as "unsupervised learning", these machine learning algorithms are also excellent at finding patterns in the data; uncovering structures and groupings that are not immediately realized by manual analysis. Some use cases include determining the precise location of a new cell tower or chain-store based on geographical data, or even clustering and segmenting customer or market groups by considering many factors simultaneously. Often, these algorithms are best for intelligent grouping, but do have application in other domains.

Dashboards, Monitors and Interfaces

This can be considered the last mile of your machine learning system. How does the algorithm interface with your business? Who is the end user, and how will they interact with the outputs? A Software Engineer may want an API to call, while an Analyst may want tabulated results to query. A Product Manager may want a report or visualization sent to their email or accessible through a dashboard. Your customer may want to see the output in the form of an emoticon on the customer platform. Executives may want the predicted results in an info graphic that describes a high level view of the industry or business. The degree of automation and sophistication of delivery depend on these end user requirements. If you require the results on a frequent basis, then more engineering effort will be required to automate the delivery.

Monitors that keep track of the input signals and output predictions of the model also require a degree of consideration. Are the readings stored as log files somewhere on a server? Are they emailed to the maintainer in the case of abnormal behavior? Do they require their own dashboard? Are they aggregated and included in a report at each ingestion of data?

Recent demands of the market require for interpretability of the machine learning models themselves. Understanding which input signals contributed the most to your models prediction, or the reasoning behind a specific prediction require unique visualizations of the data, the predictions, and even the models inner workings. In one approach called "feature ranking", model predictions are run repeatedly while dropping portions of the incoming data, and the corresponding prediction accuracy is measured. The impact each missing feature has on predictions can be visualized, even as heat maps in the case of image data.

Design of Learning System

Basic Procedures in the Design of a Learning System

The steps in the design of a learning system can be listed as follows:

- Choose the training set X and how to represent it.

- Choose exactly what is to be learnt, i.e. the target function C.

- Choose how to represent the target function C.

- Choose a learning algorithm to infer the target function from the set.

- Find an evaluation procedure and a metric to test the learned function.

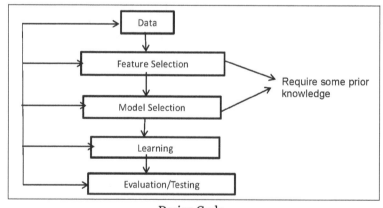

Design Cycle.

Design Cycle

The design cycle is shown in figure. The first step is the collection of data. The next step is the selection of features. This is an important step that can affect the overall learning effectiveness. In most cases, prior knowledge about the input data and what is to be learned is used in selecting appropriate features. The third step is model selection, which is essentially selection of a model that will be used to fit the training data. Here again prior knowledge about the data can be used to select the model. Once the model is selected, the learning step fine tunes the model by selecting parameters to generalize it. Finally the evaluation and testing step selects the parameters of the model, that fit the data and that also generalizes well.

Before we proceed, let us understand the meaning of learning in this context. We will explain learning using the example of the Hand-written character recognition problem. In this scenario we can define the problem as:

- Task T: Recognizing hand-written characters.

- Performance measure P: Percentage of characters correctly classified.

- Training experience E: A database of hand-written characters with their classifications.

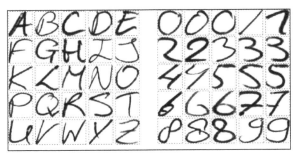
Handwritten Characters.

This example will be used throughout this module to explain the design steps.

Details of the Design of a Learning System

- Collection of Data: As already explained, the first step is the collection the data $D=\{d_1,d_2,...d_m,...d_n\}$ where each data point represents the input data and corresponding output.

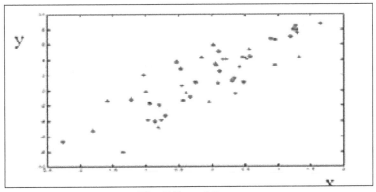
The Collected Data.

- Feature Selection: Feature Selection is essentially the process of selecting relevant features for use in model construction. The selection of features depends on the learning problem as given in Example.

Feature Selection

The students of a class have different attributes associated with them. Examples of such attributes include marks, native place, height etc. If the learning required is to find the association between native place and height, the marks feature should not be selected.

Feature Selection could be in two ways; one is by reducing the number of attributes considered for each data point. This type of feature selection is called dimensionality reduction as shown in Figure 3.4. The second method is to reduce the number of data points considered where the original $D=\{d_1,d_2,..d_m,...d_n\}$ is reduced to $D=\{d1....d_m\}$ where m<n.

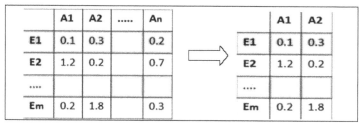

Reduction of Attributes.

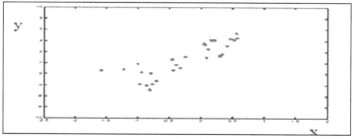

Reduction of Data Points.

1. Model Selection: The next step is the model selection where we select a model that would most likely fit the data points. A linear model is one of the simplest models we should try to fit to the data. A model (its hypothesis) has a set of parameters; for Example, a and b, the slope and the intercept in the simple linear model, show in figure below.

$$y = ax + b + \varepsilon \quad \varepsilon = N(0,\sigma)$$

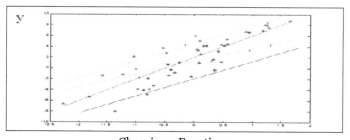

Choosing a Function.

An error function ε needs to be optimized. A simple example of an error function is the mean squared error given below:

$$\frac{1}{n}\sum_{i=1}^{n}\left(y_i - f(x_i)\right)^2$$

In this function n is the number of data points, y_i is the actual output obtained while $f(x_i)$ is the predicted output obtained by applying the function selected by the model. We will go into the details later on in future modules.

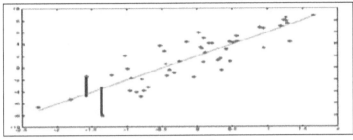

The Error Function.

2. The Learning step involves the finding values of the parameters that minimize the error.

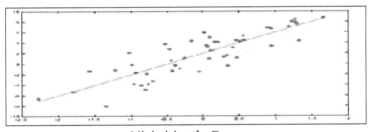

Minimizing the Error.

The final step is the application of the learnt model to apply (evaluate) the learned model for predicting ys for new hitherto unseen inputs x using learned function f(x).

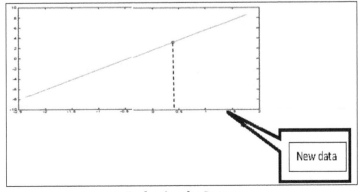

Evaluating the System.

Processing Data

The data given to the learning system may require a lot of cleaning. Cleaning involves getting rid of errors and noise and removal of redundancies.

Data Pre-processing

Data Pre-processing is another important process for effective learning. Pre-processing techniques include renaming, rescaling, discretization, abstraction, aggregation and introducing new attributes. Renaming or relabeling is the conversion of categorical values to numbers. However, this conversion may be inappropriate when used with some learning methods. Such an example is shown in Example where numbers impose an order to the values that is not warranted.

Example: Relabelling		
Categorical Values	Conversion to Numbers	Remarks
High, Normal, Low	2,1,0	Right
True, False, Unknown	2,1,0	Wrong
Red, Blue, Green	2,1,0	Wrong

Rescaling, also called normalization is the transferring of continuous values to some range, typically [-1,1] or [0,1]. Discretization or binning involves the conversion of continuous values to a finite set of discrete values. Another technique is abstraction where categorical values are merged together. In aggregation, actual values are replaced by values obtained with summary or aggregation operations, such as minimum value, maximum value, average, etc. Finally, sometimes new attributes that define a relationship with existing new data attributes are introduced. An example is replacing weight and height attributes by a new attribute obesity-factor which is calculated as weight/ height. These pre-processing techniques are used only when the learning is not affected due to such pre-processing.

Data Biases

It is important to watch out for data biases. For this, we need to understand the data source. It is very easy to derive "unexpected" results when data used for analysis and learning is biased (pre-selected). The results or conclusions derived for pre-selected data do not hold for general cases.

Example: Risks in pregnancy study.

Survey: The sample survey on risks in pregnancy was sponsored by DARPA at various military hospitals. The study was conducted on a large sample of pregnant woman.

Conclusion: The factor with the largest impact on reducing risks during pregnancy (statistically significant) is a pregnant woman being single. That is the conclusion that single woman has the least risk. What is wrong with this conclusion?

Feature Selection

Sometimes the size (dimension) of a sample collection can be enormous. The selection of features requires prior knowledge about the characteristics about the input data. A typical example is document classification, where the document corpus can be represented by 10,000 different words. The data can be counts of occurrences of different words. Such a data collection entails the learning of too many parameters but not provide enough samples to justify the estimation of the parameters of the model.

Feature selection reduces the feature sets. There are methods for removing input features. Such a technique is called dimensionality reduction. One method of dimensionality reduction is to replace inputs with features. Another method is to extract relevant inputs using a measure such as mutual information measure. Principal Component Analysis (PCA) is a method that mathematically reduces the dimension of the feature space. Another method of dimensionality reduction explained with an example of document classification is the grouping or clustering similar words using a suitable similarity measure and replacing the group of words with group label.

Model Selection

The next important step in the design of the learning system is model selection. Again, prior knowledge about the data collection would help in an effective model selection; however, only an estimate can be done. Initial data analysis and visualization can help to make a good guess about the form of the distribution or shape of the function. Independences and correlations among data points in the data collection can help in selecting a model. There may arise the over-fitting problem especially in the presence of bias and variance. Over fitting is the problem of selecting a function that exactly fits the data, where we are not able to generalize in order to make predictions about unseen data. In other words, a model over fits if it fits particularities of the training set such as noise orbias.

Avoiding Over-fitting

One method to avoid over-fitting is to ensure that there are sufficient number of examples in the training set. Another technique which will be later used for evaluation is the Hold Out method. In this method we hold some data out of the training set and train or fit on the training set (without data held out) and finally use the held out data for fine tuning the Model.

Another important mathematical technique is the use of the concept of regularization, which is the process of introducing additional information in order to prevent over-fitting. This information is usually of the form of a penalty for complexity. A model should be selected based on the Occam's razor principle (proposed by William of Ockham) which states that the explanation of any phenomenon should make as few assumptions as possible, eliminating, the observable predictions of the explanatory hypothesis or theory. In other words, the simplest hypothesis (model) that fits almost all the data is the best compared to more complex ones; therefore, there is explicit preference towards simple models.

Evaluation

There are simple methods for evaluation and more complex methods using different methods for splitting the data.

Hold Out Method

As already discussed the simplest evaluation method is the holdout method. In this method the data is divided into the training and test data sets.

Typically 2/3 of the data is used as training data and the other 1/3 is used as the testing set. If we want to compare the predictive performance on a classification or a regression problem for two different learning methods then we will need to compare the error results on the test data set and choose the method with better (smaller) testing error for better generalization error.

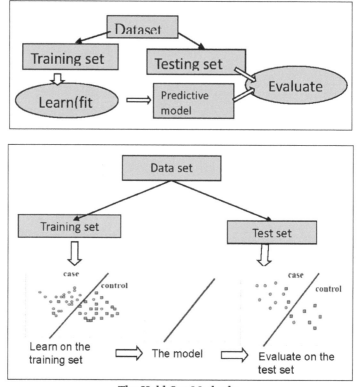

The Hold Out Methods.

Complex Methods

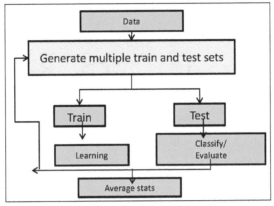

Complex Method.

The complex methods use multiple train/test sets based on various random resampling schemes such as cross-validation, random sub-sampling, and Bootstrap.

It is the generation of multiple training and test sets block that will change depending on the sampling method. In random sub-sampling, simple holdout method with random split of data into 70% for training and 30% for testing is repeated k times. In the case of cross-validation sub-sampling (k-fold), the data is divided into k disjoint groups and tested on kth group where the rest of the data has been used for training, that is leave one out cross-validation. Typically a 10-fold cross-validation is used. In the case of bootstrap, the training set of size N=size of the data D is used with sampling with replacement. These concepts are shown in figure below.

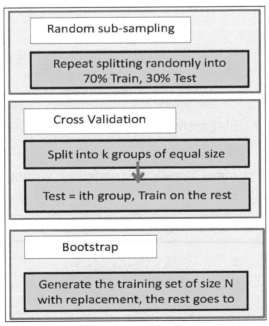

Sampling Methods.

Illustrative Example of the Process of Design

We use the example of handwritten character recognition as an illustrative example to explain to illustrate the design issues and approaches.

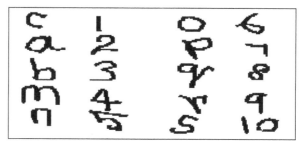
Set of Handwritten Characters.

We explain learning to perform a task from experience. Therefore, let us what is the meaning of task. Task can often be expressed through a mathematical function. In this case input can be x, output y and w the parameters that are "learned". In case of classification output y will be discrete E.g. class membership, posterior, probability, etc. For regression, y will be continuous. For the character recognition the task is as shown in figure below.

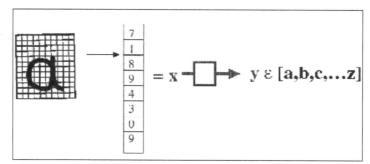
Character Recognition Task.

The following are the steps in the design process for character recognition.

Step 1: Let us treat the learning system as a black box; here we assume that the input a set of handwritten characters and the output is the letter q.

Step 2: Next we collect Training Examples (Experience). Without examples, our system will not learn as we are learning from examples.

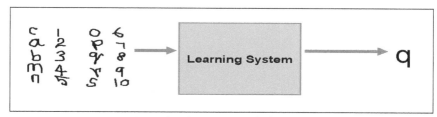
Learning System as a Black Box.

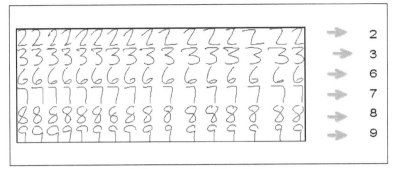

Collection of Training Data.

Step 3: Representing Experience: The next step is to choose a representation for the experience/examples. In our example the sensor input can represented by an n-dimensional vector, called the feature vector, $X = (x_1, x_2, x_3, ...,x_n)$. We can assume a 64-d vector to represent the 8X8 matrix of pixels.

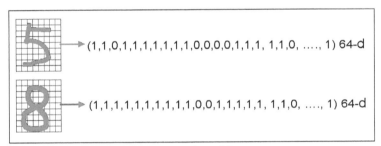

(1,1,0,1,1,1,1,1,1,1,0,0,0,0,1,1,1, 1,1,0, ..., 1) 64-d

(1,1,1,1,1,1,1,1,1,1,0,0,1,1,1,1,1, 1,1,0, ..., 1) 64-d

Representation of Data.

In order to represent the experience, we need to know what X is. Therefore we need a corresponding vector D, which will record our knowledge (experience) about X. The experience E is a pair of vectors E = (X, D). Now the question is how to represent D. Assuming our system is to recognise 10 digits only, then D can be a 10-d binary vector; each correspond to one of the digits.

D = (d0, d1, d2, d3, d4, d5, d6, d7, d8, d9)
e.g, if X is digit 5, then d5=1; all others =0
If X is digit 9, then d9=1; all others =0

10-d Binary Vector.

Step 4: Choose a Representation for the Black Box: The next step is the choosing of a representation for the black box. Here we need to choose a function F to approximate the black box and for a given X, the value of F would give the classification of X.

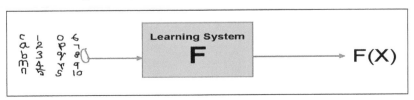

Learning System
F

F(X)

Choosing Function F.

Step 5: Learning/Adjusting the Weights: We need a learning algorithm to adjust the weights such that the experience from the training data can be incorporated into the system, where experience E is represented in terms of input X and expected output D. The function F(X) would be modified with weights W to obtain the learned output L as given in below.

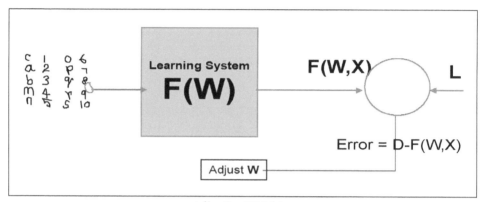

Adjusting Weights.

Step 6: Use/Test the System After learning is completed, all parameters are fixed and an unknown input X can be presented to the system for which the system computes its answer according to the function F(W,X).

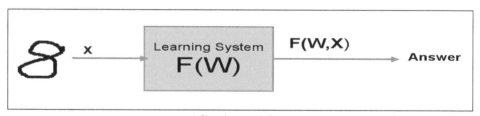

Adjusting Weights.

Types of Machine Learning

Machine learning algorithms are organized into taxonomy, based on the desired outcome of the algorithm. Common algorithm types include:

- Supervised learning: Where the algorithm generates a function that maps inputs to desired outputs. One standard formulation of the supervised learning task is the classification problem: the learner is required to learn (to approximate the behavior of) a function which maps a vector into one of several classes by looking at several input-output examples of the function.

- Unsupervised learning: Which models a set of inputs: labeled examples are not available.

- Semi-supervised learning: Which combines both labeled and unlabeled examples to generate an appropriate function or classifier.

- Reinforcement learning: Where the algorithm learns a policy of how to act given an observation of the world. Every action has some impact in the environment, and the environment provides feedback that guides the learning algorithm.

- Transduction: Similar to supervised learning, but does not explicitly construct a function: instead, tries to predict new outputs based on training inputs, training outputs, and new inputs.

- Learning to learn: Where the algorithm learns its own inductive bias based on previous experience.

The performance and computational analysis of machine learning algorithms is a branch of statistics known as computational learning theory. Machine learning is about designing algorithms that allow a computer to learn. Learning is not necessarily involves consciousness but learning is a matter of finding statistical regularities or other patterns in the data. Thus, many machine learning algorithms will barely resemble how human might approach a learning task. However, learning algorithms can give insight into the relative difficulty of learning in different environments.

Supervised Learning Approach

Supervised learning is fairly common in classification problems because the goal is often to get the computer to learn a classification system that we have created. Digit recognition, once again, is a common example of classification learning. More generally, classification learning is appropriate for any problem where deducing a classification is useful and the classification is easy to determine. In some cases, it might not even be necessary to give predetermined classifications to every instance of a problem if the agent can work out the classifications for itself. This would be an example of unsupervised learning in a classification context.

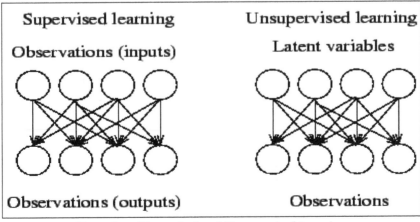

Examples of Supervised and Unsupervised Learning.

Supervised learning often leaves the probability for inputs undefined. This model is not needed as long as the inputs are available, but if some of the input values are missing, it is not possible to infer anything about the outputs. Unsupervised learning, all the observations are assumed to be caused by latent variables, that is, the observations is assumed to be at the end of the causal chain. Examples of supervised learning and unsupervised learning are shown:

Supervised learning is the most common technique for training neural networks and decision trees. Both of these techniques are highly dependent on the information given by the pre-determined classifications. In the case of neural networks, the classification is used to determine the error of the network and then adjust the network to minimize it, and in decision trees, the classifications are used to determine what attributes provide the most information that can be used to solve the classification puzzle. We'll look at both of these in more detail, but for now, it should be sufficient to know that both of these examples thrive on having some "supervision" in the form of pre-determined classifications. Inductive machine learning is the process of learning a set of rules from instances (examples in a training set), or more generally speaking, creating a classifier that can be used to generalize from new instances. The process of applying supervised ML to a real world problem is described in Figure. The first step is collecting the dataset. If a requisite expert is available, then s/he could suggest which fields (attributes, features) are the most informative. If not, then the simplest method is that of "brute-force," which means measuring everything available in the hope that the right (informative, relevant) features can be isolated. However, a dataset collected by the "brute-force" method is not directly suitable for induction. It contains in most cases noise and missing feature values, and therefore requires significant pre-processing according to Zhang et al.

The second step is the data preparation and data pre-processing. Depending on the circumstances, researchers have a number of methods to choose from to handle missing data. Hodge et al, have recently introduced a survey of contemporary techniques for outlier (noise) detection. These researchers have identified the techniques' advantages and disadvantages. Instance selection is not only used to handle noise but to cope with the infeasibility of learning from very large datasets. Instance selection in these datasets is an optimization problem that attempts to maintain the mining quality while minimizing the sample size. It reduces data and enables a data mining algorithm to function and work effectively with very large datasets. There is a variety of procedures for sampling instances from a large dataset. Feature subset selection is the process of identifying and removing as many irrelevant and redundant features as possible.

This reduces the dimensionality of the data and enables data mining algorithms to operate faster and more effectively. The fact that many features depend on one another often unduly influences the accuracy of supervised ML classification models. This problem can be addressed by constructing new features from the basic feature set. This technique is called feature construction/transformation. These newly generated features may lead to the creation of more concise and accurate classifiers. In addition, the discovery of meaningful features contributes to better comprehensibility of the produced classifier, and a better understanding of the learned concept. Speech recognition using hidden Markov models and Bayesian networks relies on some elements of supervision as well in order to adjust parameters to, as usual, minimize the error on the given inputs. Notice something important here: in the classification problem, the goal of the learning algorithm is to minimize the error with respect to the given inputs. These inputs, often called the "training set", are the examples from which the agent tries to learn. But learning the training set well is not necessarily the best thing to do. For instance, if I tried to teach you exclusive-or, but only showed you combinations consisting of one true and one false, but never both false or both true, you might learn the rule that the answer is always true. Similarly, with machine learning algorithms, a common problem is over-fitting the data and essentially memorizing the training set rather than learning a more general classification technique. As you might imagine, not all training sets have the inputs classified correctly. This can lead to problems if the algorithm used is powerful enough to memorize even the apparently "special cases" that don't fit the more general principles. This, too, can lead to over fitting, and it is a challenge to find algorithms that are both powerful enough to learn complex functions and robust enough to produce generalizable results.

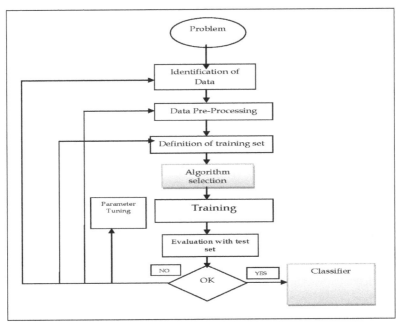

Machine Learning Supervise Process.

Unsupervised Learning

Unsupervised learning seems much harder: the goal is to have the computer learn how to do something that we don't tell it how to do! There are actually two approaches to unsupervised learning. The first approach is to teach the agent not by giving explicit categorizations, but by using some sort of reward system to indicate success. Note that this type of training will generally fit into the decision problem framework because the goal is not to produce a classification but to make decisions that maximize rewards. This approach nicely generalizes to the real world, where agents might be rewarded for doing certain actions and punished for doing others. Often, a form of reinforcement learning can be used for unsupervised learning, where the agent bases its actions on the previous rewards and punishments without necessarily even learning any information about the exact ways that its actions affect the world. In a way, all of this information is unnecessary because by learning a reward function, the agent simply knows what to do without any processing because it knows the exact reward it expects to achieve for each action it could take. This can be extremely beneficial in cases where calculating every possibility is very time consuming (even if all of the transition probabilities between world states were known). On the other hand, it can be very time consuming to learn by, essentially, trial and error. But this kind of learning can be powerful because it assumes no pre-discovered classification of examples. In some cases, for example, our classifications may not be the best possible. One striking example is that the conventional wisdom about the game of backgammon was turned on its head when a series of computer programs (neuro-gammon and TD-gammon) that learned through unsupervised learning became stronger than the best human chess players merely by playing themselves over and over. These programs discovered some principles that surprised the backgammon experts and performed better than backgammon programs trained on pre-classified examples. A second type of unsupervised learning is called clustering.

In this type of learning, the goal is not to maximize a utility function, but simply to find similarities in the training data. The assumption is often that the clusters discovered will match reasonably well with an intuitive classification. For instance, clustering individuals based on demographics might result in a clustering of the wealthy in one group and the poor in another. Although the algorithm won't have names to assign to these clusters, it can produce them and then use those clusters to assign new examples into one or the other of the clusters. This is a data-driven approach that can work well when there is sufficient data; for instance, social information filtering algorithms, such as those that Amazon.com use to recommend books, are based on the principle of finding similar groups of people and then assigning new users to groups. In some cases, such as with social information filtering, the information about other members of a cluster (such as what books they read) can be sufficient for the algorithm to produce meaningful results. In other cases, it may be the case that the clusters are merely a useful tool for a human analyst. Unfortunately, even unsupervised learning suffers from the problem of over fitting the training data. There's no silver bullet to avoiding the problem because any algorithm that can learn from its inputs needs to be quite powerful.

Unsupervised learning algorithms according to Ghahramani are designed to extract structure from data samples. The quality of a structure is measured by a cost function which is usually minimized to infer optimal parameters characterizing the hidden structure in the data. Reliable and robust inference requires a guarantee that extracted structures are typical for the data source, i.e., similar structures have to be extracted from a second sample set of the same data source. Lack of robustness is known as over fitting from the statistics and the machine learning literature. In this talk I characterize the over fitting phenomenon for a class of histogram clustering models which play a prominent role in information retrieval, linguistic and computer vision applications. Learning algorithms with robustness to sample fluctuations are derived from large deviation results and the maximum entropy principle for the learning process.

Unsupervised learning has produced many successes, such as world-champion calibre backgammon programs and even machines capable of driving cars! It can be a powerful technique when there is an easy way to assign values to actions. Clustering can be useful when there is enough data to form clusters (though this turns out to be difficult at times) and especially when additional data about members of a cluster can be used to produce further results due to dependencies in the data. Classification learning is powerful when the classifications are known to be correct (for instance, when dealing with diseases, it's generally straight-forward to determine the design after the fact by an autopsy), or when the classifications are simply arbitrary things that we would like the computer to be able to recognize for us. Classification learning is often necessary when the decisions made by the algorithm will be required as input somewhere else. Otherwise, it wouldn't be easy for whoever requires that input to figure out what it means. Both techniques can be valuable and which one you choose should depend on the circumstances--what kind of problem is being solved, how much time is allotted to solving it (supervised learning or clustering is often faster than reinforcement learning techniques), and whether supervised learning is even possible.

Algorithm Types

In the area of supervised learning which deals much with classification. These are the algorithms types:

Linear Classifiers:

- Logical Regression.
  - Naïve Bayes Classifier,
  - Perceptron,
  - Support Vector Machine,
  - Quadratic Classifiers.
- K-Means Clustering.
- Boosting.

- Decision Tree.

- Random Forest.

  ◦ Neural networks.

- Bayesian Networks.

Linear Classifiers

In machine learning, the goal of classification is to group items that have similar feature values, into groups. Timothy et al stated that a linear classifier achieves this by making a classification decision based on the value of the linear combination of the features. If the input feature vector to the classifier is a real vector $\vec{x}$, then the output score is:

$$y = f(\vec{w}.\vec{x}) = f\left(\sum_j w_j x_j\right)$$

Where $\vec{w}$ a real vector of weights and f is is a function that converts the dot product of the two vectors into the desired output. The weight vector $\vec{w}$ is learned from a set of labelled training samples. Often f is a simple function that maps all values above a certain threshold to the first class and all other values to the second class. A more complex f might give the probability that an item belongs to a certain class.

For a two-class classification problem, one can visualize the operation of a linear classifier as splitting a high-dimensional input space with a hyperplane: all points on one side of the hyper plane are classified as "yes", while the others are classified as "no". A linear classifier is often used in situations where the speed of classification is an issue, since it is often the fastest classifier, especially when $\vec{x}$ is sparse. However, decision trees can be faster. Also, linear classifiers often work very well when the number of dimensions in $\vec{x}$ is large, as in document classification, where each element in $\vec{x}$ is typically the number of counts of a word in a document. In such cases, the classifier should be well regularized.

Support Vector Machine: A Support Vector Machine as stated by Luis et al (SVM) performs classification by constructing an Ndimensional hyper plane that optimally separates the data into two categories. SVM models are closely related to neural networks. In fact, a SVM model using a sigmoid kernel function is equivalent to a two layer, perceptron neural network.

Support Vector Machine (SVM) models are a close cousin to classical multilayer perceptron neural networks. Using a kernel function, SVM's are an alternative training method for polynomial, radial basis function and multi-layer perceptron classifiers in which the weights of the network are found by solving a quadratic programming problem with linear constraints, rather than by solving a non-convex, unconstrained minimization problem as in standard neural network training.

In the parlance of SVM literature, a predictor variable is called an attribute, and a transformed attribute that is used to define the hyper plane is called a feature. The task of choosing the most suitable representation is known as feature selection. A set of features that describes one case (i.e., a row of predictor values) is called a vector. So the goal of SVM modelling is to find the optimal hyper plane that separates clusters of vector in such a way that cases with one category of the target variable are on one side of the plane and cases with the other category are on the other size of the plane. The vectors near the hyper plane are the support vectors. The figure below presents an overview of the SVM process.

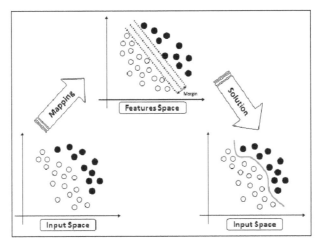

A Two-Dimensional Example

Before considering N-dimensional hyper planes, let's look at a simple 2-dimensional example. Assume we wish to perform a classification, and our data has a categorical target variable with two categories. Also assume that there are two predictor variables with continuous values. If we plot the data points using the value of one predictor on the X axis and the other on the Y axis we might end up with an image such as shown below. One category of the target variable is represented by rectangles while the other category is represented by ovals.

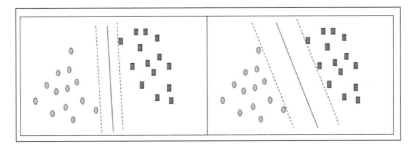

In this idealized example, the cases with one category are in the lower left corner and the cases with the other category are in the upper right corner; the cases are completely separated. The SVM analysis attempts to find a 1-dimensional hyper plane (i.e. a line) that separates the cases based on their target categories. There are an infinite number of possible lines; two candidate lines are shown above. The question is which line is better, and how do we define the optimal line.

The dashed lines drawn parallel to the separating line mark the distance between the dividing line and the closest vectors to the line. The distance between the dashed lines is called the margin. The vectors (points) that constrain the width of the margin are the support vectors. The following figure illustrates this.

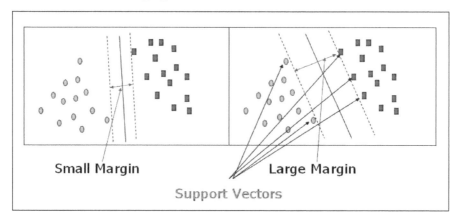

An SVM analysis finds the line (or, in general, hyper plane) that is oriented so that the margin between the support vectors is maximized. In the figure above, the line in the right panel is superior to the line in the left panel. If all analyses consisted of two-category target variables with two predictor variables, and the cluster of points could be divided by a straight line, life would be easy. Unfortunately, this is not generally the case, so SVM must deal with (a) more than two predictor variables, (b) separating the points with non-linear curves, (c) handling the cases where clusters cannot be completely separated, and (d) handling classifications with more than two categories. In this chapter, we shall explain three main machine learning techniques with their examples and how they perform in reality.

These are:

- K-Means Clustering.

- Neural Network.

- Self Organised Map.

K-Means Clustering

The basic step of k-means clustering is uncomplicated. In the beginning we determine number of cluster K and we assume the centre of these clusters. We can take any random objects as the initial centre or the first K objects in sequence can also serve as the initial centre. Then the K means algorithm will do the three steps below until convergence. Iterate until stable (= no object move group):

- Determine the centre coordinate.

- Determine the distance of each object to the centre.

- Group the object based on minimum distance.

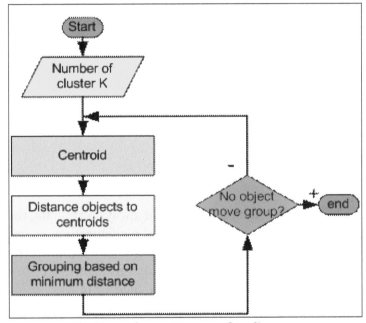

The Figure shows a K- means flow diagram.

K-means Iteration

K-means is one of the simplest unsupervised learning algorithms that solve the well known clustering problem. The procedure follows a simple and easy way to classify a given data set through a certain number of clusters (assume k clusters) fixed a priori. The main idea is to define k centroids, one for each cluster. These centroids should be placed in a cunning way because of different location causes different result. So, the better choice is to place them as much as possible far away from each other. The next step is to take each point belonging to a given data set and associate it to the nearest centroid. When no point is pending, the first step is completed and an early groupage is done. At this point we need to re-calculate k new centroids as barycenters of the clusters resulting from the previous step. After we have these k new centroids, a new binding has to be done between the same data set points and the nearest new centroid. A loop has been generated. As a result of this loop we may notice that the k centroids change their location step by step until no more changes are done. In other words centroids do not move any more.

Finally, this algorithm aims at minimizing an objective function, in this case a squared error function.

The objective function $J = \sum_{j=1}^{k} \sum_{i=1}^{m} \left\| x_i^{(j)} - c_j \right\|^2$ where $\left\| x_i^{(j)} - c_j \right\|^2$ is a chosen distance measure between a data point $x_i^{(j)}$ and the cluster center, c_j is an indicator of the distance of the n data points from their respective cluster centers. The algorithm in figure 4 is composed of the following steps:

- Place K points into the space resented by the objects that are being clustered. These points represents initial group centroids.

- Assign each object to the group that has the closest centroids.

- When all objects have been assigned, recalculate the positions of the K centroids.

- Repeat Steps 2 ans 3 until the centroids no longer move. This produces a sepration of the objects into groups from which the metric to be minimized can be calculated.

Although it can be proved that the procedure will always terminate, the k-means algorithm does not necessarily find the most optimal configuration, corresponding to the global objective function minimum. The algorithm is also significantly sensitive to the initial randomly selected cluster centers. The k-means algorithm can be run multiple times to reduce this effect. K-means is a simple algorithm that has been adapted to many problem domains. As we are going to see, it is a good candidate for extension to work with fuzzy feature vectors.

An example: Suppose that we have n sample feature vectors x_1, x_2,..., x_n all from the same class, and we know that they fall into k compact clusters, k < n. Let mi be the mean of the vectors in cluster i. If the clusters are well separated, we can use a minimum-distance classifier to separate them. That is, we can say that x is in cluster i if || x - m_i || is the minimum of all the k distances. This suggests the following procedure for finding the k means:

- Make initial guesses for the means m_1, m_2... m_k.

- Until there are no changes in any mean.

- Use the estimated means to classify the samples into clusters.

- For i from 1 to k.

- Replace m_i with the mean of all of the samples for cluster i.

- End_for.

- End_until.

Here is an example showing how the means m_1 and m_2 move into the centers of two clusters.

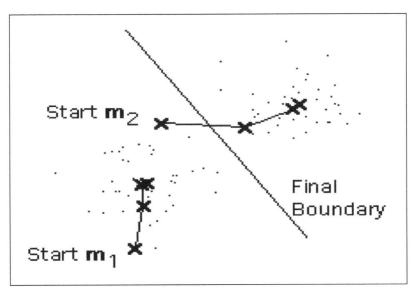

This is a simple version of the k-means procedure. It can be viewed as a greedy algorithm for partitioning the n samples into k clusters so as to minimize the sum of the squared distances to the cluster centers. It does have some weaknesses:

- The way to initialize the means was not specified. One popular way to start is to randomly choose k of the samples.

- The results produced depend on the initial values for the means, and it frequently happens that suboptimal partitions are found. The standard solution is to try a number of different starting points.

- It can happen that the set of samples closest to mi is empty, so that mi cannot be updated. This is an annoyance that must be handled in an implementation, but that we shall ignore.

- The results depend on the metric used to measure $|| x - m^i ||$. A popular solution is to normalize each variable by its standard deviation, though this is not always desirable.

- The results depend on the value of k.

This last problem is particularly troublesome, since we often have no way of knowing how many clusters exist. In the example shown above, the same algorithm applied to the same data produces the following 3-means clustering. Is it better or worse than the 2-means clustering?

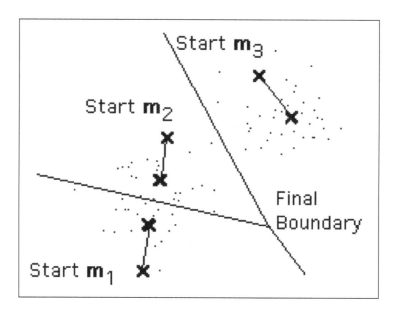

Unfortunately there is no general theoretical solution to find the optimal number of clusters for any given data set. A simple approach is to compare the results of multiple runs with different k classes and choose the best one according to a given criterion.

Neural Network

Neural networks can actually perform a number of regression and/or classification tasks at once, although commonly each network performs only one. In the vast majority of cases, therefore, the network will have a single output variable, although in the case of many-state classification problems, this may correspond to a number of output units (the post-processing stage takes care of the mapping from output units to output variables). If you do define a single network with multiple output variables, it may suffer from cross-talk (the hidden neurons experience difficulty learning, as they are attempting to model at least two functions at once). The best solution is usually to train separate networks for each output, then to combine them into an ensemble so that they can be run as a unit. Neural methods are:

Multilayer Perceptrons

This is perhaps the most popular network architecture in use today, due originally to Rumelhart and McClelland and discussed at length in most neural network textbooks. This is the type of network discussed briefly in previous sections: the units each perform a biased weighted sum of their inputs and pass this activation level through a transfer function to produce their output, and the units are arranged in a layered feed forward topology. The network thus has a simple interpretation as a form of input output model, with the weights and thresholds (biases) the free parameters of the model. Such networks can model functions of almost arbitrary complexity, with the number of layers, and the number of units in each layer, determining the function complexity. Important issues in Multilayer Perceptrons (MLP) design include specification of the number of hidden layers and the number of units in these layers.

The number of input and output units is defined by the problem (there may be some uncertainty about precisely which inputs to use, a point to which we will return later. However, for the moment we will assume that the input variables are intuitively selected and are all meaningful). The number of hidden units to use is far from clear. As good a starting point as any is to use one hidden layer, with the number of units equal to half the sum of the number of input and output units. Again, we will discuss how to choose a sensible number later.

Training Multilayer Perceptrons

Once the number of layers, and number of units in each layer, has been selected, the network's weights and thresholds must be set so as to minimize the prediction error made by the network. This is the role of the training algorithms. The historical cases that you have gathered are used to automatically adjust the weights and thresholds in order to minimize this error. This process is equivalent to fitting the model represented by the network to the training data available. The error of a particular configuration of the network can be determined by running all the training cases through the network, comparing the actual output generated with the desired or target outputs. The differences are combined together by an error function to give the network error. The most common error functions are the sum squared error (used for regression problems), where the individual errors of output units on each case are squared and summed together, and the cross entropy functions (used for maximum likelihood classification).

In traditional modeling approaches (e.g., linear modeling) it is possible to algorithmically determine the model configuration that absolutely minimizes this error. The price paid for the greater (non-linear) modeling power of neural networks is that although we can adjust a network to lower its error, we can never be sure that the error could not be lower still.

A helpful concept here is the error surface. Each of the N weights and thresholds of the network (i.e., the free parameters of the model) is taken to be a dimension in space. The $N+1$th dimension is the network error. For any possible configuration of weights the error can be plotted in the $N+1$th dimension, forming an error surface. The objective of network training is to find the lowest point in this many-dimensional surface. In a linear model with sum squared error function, this error surface is a parabola (a quadratic), which means that it is a smooth bowl-shape with a single minimum. It is therefore "easy" to locate the minimum. Neural network error surfaces are much more complex, and are characterized by a number of unhelpful features, such as local minima (which are lower than the surrounding terrain, but above the global minimum), flat-spots and plateaus, saddle-points, and long narrow ravines.

It is not possible to analytically determine where the global minimum of the error surface is, and so neural network training is essentially an exploration of the error surface. From an initially random configuration of weights and thresholds (i.e., a random point on the error surface), the training algorithms incrementally seek for the global minimum. Typically, the gradient (slope) of the error surface is calculated at the current point, and used to make a downhill move. Eventually, the algorithm stops in a low point, which may be a local minimum (but hopefully is the global minimum).

The Back Propagation Algorithm

The best-known example of a neural network training algorithm is back propagation. Modern second-order algorithms such as conjugate gradient descent and Levenberg-Marquardt (both included in ST Neural Networks) are substantially faster (e.g., an order of magnitude faster) for many problems, but back propagation still has advantages in some circumstances, and is the easiest algorithm to understand. We will introduce this now, and discuss the more advanced algorithms later. In back propagation, the gradient vector of the error surface is calculated. This vector points along the line of steepest descent from the current point, so we know that if we move along it a "short" distance, we will decrease the error. A sequence of such moves (slowing as we near the bottom) will eventually find a minimum of some sort. The difficult part is to decide how large the steps should be.

Large steps may converge more quickly, but may also overstep the solution or (if the error surface is very eccentric) go off in the wrong direction. A classic example of this in neural network training is where the algorithm progresses very slowly along a steep, narrow, valley, bouncing from one side across to the other. In contrast, very small steps may go in the correct direction, but they also require a large number of iterations. In practice, the step size is proportional to the slope (so that the algorithm settles down in a minimum) and to a special constant: the learning rate. The correct setting for the learning rate is application-dependent, and is typically chosen by experiment; it may also be time-varying, getting smaller as the algorithm progresses.

The algorithm is also usually modified by inclusion of a momentum term: this encourages movement in a fixed direction, so that if several steps are taken in the same direction, the algorithm "picks up speed", which gives it the ability to (sometimes) escape local minimum, and also to move rapidly over flat spots and plateaus. The algorithm therefore progresses iteratively, through a number of epochs. On each epoch, the training cases are each submitted in turn to the network, and target and actual outputs compared and the error calculated. This error, together with the error surface gradient, is used to adjust the weights, and then the process repeats. The initial network configuration is random, and training stops when a given number of epochs elapses, or when the error reaches an acceptable level, or when the error stops improving (you can select which of these stopping conditions to use).

Over-learning and Generalization

One major problem with the approach outlined above is that it doesn't actually minimize the error that we are really interested in - which is the expected error the network will make when new cases are submitted to it. In other words, the most desirable property of a network is its ability to generalize to new cases. In reality, the network is trained to minimize the error on the training set, and short of having a perfect and infinitely large training set, this is not the same thing as minimizing the error on the real error surface - the error surface of the underlying and unknown model. The most important manifestation of this distinction is the problem of over-learning, or over-fitting. It is easiest to demonstrate this concept using polynomial curve fitting rather than neural networks, but the concept is precisely the same. A polynomial is an equation with terms containing only constants and powers of the variables. For example:

$$y=2x+3$$

$$y=3x^2+4x+1$$

Different polynomials have different shapes, with larger powers (and therefore larger numbers of terms) having steadily more eccentric shapes. Given a set of data, we may want to fit a polynomial curve (i.e., a model) to explain the data. The data is probably noisy, so we don't necessarily expect the best model to pass exactly through all the points. A low-order polynomial may not be sufficiently flexible to fit close to the points, whereas a high-order polynomial is actually too flexible, fitting the data exactly by adopting a highly eccentric shape that is actually unrelated to the underlying function.

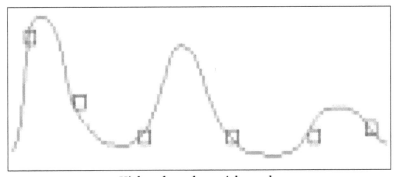

High-order polynomial sample.

Neural networks have precisely the same problem. A network with more weights models a more complex function, and is therefore prone to over-fitting. A network with less weight may not be sufficiently powerful to model the underlying function. For example, a network with no hidden layers actually models a simple linear function. How then can we select the right complexity of network? A larger network will almost invariably achieve a lower error eventually, but this may indicate over-fitting rather than good modeling.

The answer is to check progress against an independent data set, the selection set. Some of the cases are reserved, and not actually used for training in the back propagation algorithm. Instead, they are used to keep an independent check on the progress of the algorithm. It is invariably the case that the initial performance of the network on training and selection sets is the same (if it is not at least approximately the same, the division of cases between the two sets is probably biased). As training progresses, the training error naturally drops, and providing training is minimizing the true error function, the selection error drops too. However, if the selection error stops dropping, or indeed starts to rise, this indicates that the network is starting to overfit the data, and training should cease. When over-fitting occurs during the training process like this, it is called over-learning. In this case, it is usually advisable to decrease the number of hidden units and/or hidden layers, as the network is over-powerful for the problem at hand. In contrast, if the network is not sufficiently powerful to model the underlying function, over-learning is not likely to occur, and neither training nor selection errors will drop to a satisfactory level.

The problems associated with local minima, and decisions over the size of network to use, imply that using a neural network typically involves experimenting with a large number of different networks, probably training each one a number of times (to avoid being fooled by local minima), and observing individual performances. The key guide to performance here is the selection error. However, following the standard scientific precept that, all else being equal, a simple model is always preferable to a complex model, you can also select a smaller network in preference to a larger one with a negligible improvement in selection error. A problem with this approach of repeated experimentation is that the selection set plays a key role in selecting the model, which means that it is actually part of the training process. Its reliability as an independent guide to performance of the model is therefore compromised - with sufficient experiments, you may just hit upon a lucky network that happens to perform well on the selection set. To add confidence in the performance of the final model, it is therefore normal practice (at least where the volume of training data allows it) to reserve a third set of cases - the test set. The final model is tested with the test set data, to ensure that the results on the selection and training set are real, and not artifacts of the training process. Of course, to fulfill this role properly the test set should be used only once - if it is in turn used to adjust and reiterate the training process, it effectively becomes selection data.

This division into multiple subsets is very unfortunate, given that we usually have less data than we would ideally desire even for a single subset. We can get around this problem by resampling. Experiments can be conducted using different divisions of the available data into training, selection, and test sets. There are a number of approaches to this subset, including random (monte-carlo) resampling, cross-validation, and boot-strap. If we make design decisions, such as the best configuration of neural network to use, based upon a number of experiments with different subset examples, the results will be much more reliable. We can then either use those experiments solely to guide the decision as to which network types to use, and train such networks from scratch with new samples (this removes any sampling bias); or, we can retain the best networks found during the sampling process, but average their results in an ensemble, which at least mitigates the sampling bias. To summarize, network design (once the input variables have been selected) follows a number of stages:

- Select an initial configuration (typically, one hidden layer with the number of hidden units set to half the sum of the number of input and output units).

- Iteratively conduct a number of experiments with each configuration, retaining the best network (in terms of selection error) found. A number of experiments are required with each configuration to avoid being fooled if training locates a local minimum, and it is also best to resample.

- On each experiment, if under-learning occurs (the network doesn't achieve an acceptable performance level) try adding more neurons to the hidden layer(s). If this doesn't help, try adding an extra hidden layer.

- If over-learning occurs (selection error starts to rise) try removing hidden units (and possibly layers).

- Once you have experimentally determined an effective configuration for your networks, resample and generate new networks with that configuration.

Data Selection

All the above stages rely on a key assumption. Specifically, the training, verification and test data must be representative of the underlying model (and, further, the three sets must be independently representative). The old computer science adage "garbage in, garbage out" could not apply more strongly than in neural modeling. If training data is not representative, then the model's worth is at best compromised. At worst, it may be useless. It is worth spelling out the kind of problems which can corrupt a training set.

The future is not the past. Training data is typically historical. If circumstances have changed, relationships which held in the past may no longer hold. All eventualities must be covered. A neural network can only learn from cases that are present. If people with incomes over $100,000 per year are a bad credit risk, and your training data includes nobody over $40,000 per year, you cannot expect it to make a correct decision when it encounters one of the previously-unseen cases. Extrapolation is dangerous with any model, but some types of neural network may make particularly poor predictions in such circumstances. A network learns the easiest features it can. A classic (possibly apocryphal) illustration of this is a vision project designed to automatically recognize tanks. A network is trained on a hundred pictures including tanks, and a hundred not. It achieves a perfect 100% score. When tested on new data, it proves hopeless. The reason? The pictures of tanks are taken on dark, rainy days; the pictures without on sunny days. The network learns to distinguish the (trivial matter of) differences in overall light intensity. To work, the network would need training cases including all weather and lighting conditions under which it is expected to operate - not to mention all types of terrain, angles of shot, distances.

Unbalanced data sets: Since a network minimizes an overall error, the proportion of types of data in the set is critical. A network trained on a data set with 900 good cases and 100 bad will bias its decision towards good cases, as this allows the algorithm to lower the overall error (which is much more heavily influenced by the good cases). If the representation of good and bad cases is different in the real population, the network's decisions may be wrong. A good example would be disease diagnosis. Perhaps 90% of patients routinely tested are clear of a disease. A network is trained on an available data set with a 90/10 split. It is then used in diagnosis on patients complaining of specific problems, where the likelihood of disease is 50/50. The network will react over-cautiously and fail to recognize disease in some unhealthy patients. In contrast, if trained on the "complainants" data, and then tested on "routine" data, the network may raise a high number of false positives. In such circumstances, the data set may need to be crafted to take account of the distribution of data (e.g., you could replicate the less numerous cases, or remove some of the numerous cases), or the network's decisions modified by the inclusion of a loss matrix. Often, the best approach is to ensure even representation of different cases, then to interpret the network's decisions accordingly.

Semi-supervised Learning

Semi-supervised learning algorithms represent a middle ground between supervised and unsupervised algorithms. Although not formally defined as a 'fourth' element of machine learning (supervised, unsupervised, reinforcement), it combines aspects of the former two into a method of its own.

These algorithms operate on data that has a few labels, but is mostly unlabeled. Traditionally, one would either choose the supervised route or operate only on the data with labels, vastly reducing the size of the dataset; otherwise, one would choose the unsupervised route and discard the labels while keeping the rest of the dataset for something like clustering.

This is often the case in real world-data. Since labels are expensive, especially at the magnitude most datasets exist at, large datasets — especially for corporate purposes — may only have a few labels. For instance, consider determining if user activity is fraudulent or not. Out of one million users, the company knows this for ten thousand users, but the other ninety thousand users could either be malicious or benign.

Semi-supervised learning allows us to operate on these types of datasets without having to make the trade-offs when choosing either supervised learning or unsupervised learning.

In general, semi-supervised learning algorithms operate on this framework:

- A semi-supervised machine-learning algorithm uses a limited set of labelled sample data to train itself, resulting in a 'partially trained' model.

- The partially trained model labels the unlabeled data. Because the sample labelled data set has many severe limitations (for example, selection bias in real-world data), the results of labelling are considered to be 'pseudo-labelled' data.

- Labelled and pseudo-labelled datasets are combined, creating a unique algorithm that combines both the descriptive and predictive aspects of supervised and unsupervised learning.

Semi-supervised learning uses the classification process to identify data assets and clustering process to group it into distinct parts.

Algorithm: Semi-supervised GAN

The Semi-Supervised GAN, abbreviated as SGAN for short, is a variation of the Generative Adversarial Network architecture to address semi-supervised learning problems.

In a traditional GAN, a discriminator is trained to predict whether an image is real — from the dataset — or fake — generated by the generator model, allowing it to learn discriminating features from images, even without labels. Although most people usually use the generator in GANs, which has been trained to produce images that resemble those in the dataset, to produce realistically generated images, the discriminator can also be used through transfer learning as a beginning point to develop a classifier on the same dataset, allowing the supervised task to benefit from the unsupervised training. Since most of the image features have already been learned, the training time and accuracy to perform classification will be much better.

In an SGAN, however, the discriminator is trained simultaneously in two modes: unsupervised and supervised:

- In unsupervised, the discriminator needs to differentiate between real images and generated images, like in a traditional GAN.

- In supervised, the discriminator needs to classify an image into the several classes in a prediction problem, like in a standard neural network classifier.

In order to train these two modes simultaneously, the discriminator must output values for 1 + n nodes, in which 1 represents the 'real or fake' node and n is the number of classes in the prediction task.

In the Semi-Supervised GAN, the discriminator model is updated to predict K+1 classes, where K is the number of classes in the prediction problem and the additional class label is added for a new "fake" class. It involves directly training the discriminator model for both the unsupervised GAN task and the supervised classification task simultaneously. The entire dataset can be passed through the SGAN — when a training example has a label, the discriminator's weights are adjusted, otherwise, the classification task is ignored and the discriminator adjusts its weights to better distinguish between real and generated images.

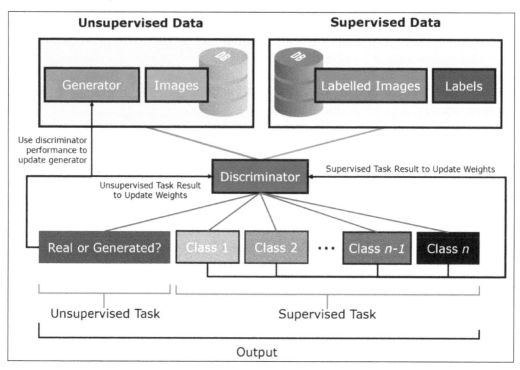

While allowing the SGAN to train unsupervised allows the model to learn very useful feature extractions from a very large unlabeled dataset, supervised learning allows the model to utilize the extracted features and use it on a classification task. The result is a classifier that can achieve incredible results on standard problems like MNIST even when trained on very, very few labeled examples (tens to hundreds).

The SGAN cleverly combines aspects of unsupervised and supervised learning to strengthen each other, allowing for the best of both worlds to work together to produce incredible results with minimal labels.

Use Cases and the Future of Machine Learning

In an era where the amount of data available is constantly growing exponentially, unsupervised data simply cannot stop and wait for labels to catch up. Countless real-world data scenarios appear like this — for instance, YouTube videos or website content. Semi-supervise learning is applied everywhere from crawling engines and content aggregation systems to image and speech recognition.

The ability of semi-supervised learning to combine the over fitting and 'under fitting' tendencies of supervised and unsupervised learning (respectively) creates a model that can perform classification tasks brilliantly while generalizing, given a minimal amount of labeled data and a vast sea of unlabeled data. Besides classification tasks, there exist other a wide host of purposes of semi-supervised algorithms, such as enhanced clustering and anomaly detection. Although the field itself is relatively new, algorithms are continually being created and perfected as they find a huge demand in today's digital landscape. Semi-supervised learning is, indeed, the future of machine learning.

Reinforcement Learning

Reinforcement learning is the training of machine learning models to make a sequence of decisions. The agent learns to achieve a goal in an uncertain, potentially complex environment. In reinforcement learning, an artificial intelligence faces a game-like situation. The computer employs trial and error to come up with a solution to the problem. To get the machine to do what the programmer wants, the artificial intelligence gets either rewards or penalties for the actions it performs. Its goal is to maximize the total reward.

Although the designer sets the reward policy–that is, the rules of the game–he gives the model no hints or suggestions for how to solve the game. It's up to the model to figure out how to perform the task to maximize the reward, starting from totally random trials and finishing with sophisticated tactics and superhuman skills. By leveraging the power of search and many trials, reinforcement learning is currently the most effective way to hint machine's creativity. In contrast to human beings, artificial intelligence can gather experience from thousands of parallel gameplays if a reinforcement learning algorithm is run on a sufficiently powerful computer infrastructure.

Examples of Reinforcement Learning

Applications of reinforcement learning were in the past limited by weak computer infrastructure. However, as Gerard Tesauro's backgamon AI super player developed in 1990's shows, progress did happen. That early progress is now rapidly changing with powerful new computational technologies opening the way to completely new inspiring applications.

Training the models that control autonomous cars is an excellent example of a potential application of reinforcement learning. In an ideal situation, the computer should get no instructions on driving the car. The programmer would avoid hard-wiring anything connected with the task and allow the machine to learn from its own errors. In a perfect situation, the only hard-wired element would be the reward function:

- For example, in usual circumstances we would require an autonomous vehicle to put safety first, minimize ride time, reduce pollution, offer passengers comfort and obey the rules of law. With an autonomous race car, on the other hand, we would emphasize speed much more than the driver's comfort. The programmer cannot predict everything that could happen on the road. Instead of building lengthy "if-then" instructions, the programmer prepares the reinforcement learning agent to be capable of learning from the system of rewards and penalties. The agent (another name for reinforcement learning algorithms performing the task) gets rewards for reaching specific goals.

- Another example: deepsense.ai took part in the "Learning to run" project, which aimed to train a virtual runner from scratch. The runner is an advanced and precise musculoskeletal model designed by the Stanford Neuromuscular Biomechanics Laboratory. Learning the agent how to run is a first step in building a new generation of prosthetic legs, ones that automatically recognize people's walking patterns and tweak themselves to make moving easier and more effective. While it is possible and has been done in Stanford's labs, hard-wiring all the commands and predicting all possible patterns of walking requires a lot of work from highly skilled programmers.

Challenges with Reinforcement Learning

The main challenge in reinforcement learning lays in preparing the simulation environment, which is highly dependent on the task to be performed. When the model has to go superhuman in Chess, Go or Atari games, preparing the simulation environment is relatively simple. When it comes to building a model capable of driving an autonomous car, building a realistic simulator is crucial before letting the car ride on the street. The model has to figure out how to brake or avoid a collision in a safe environment, where sacrificing even a thousand cars comes at a minimal cost. Transferring the model out of the training environment and into to the real world is where things get tricky. Scaling and tweaking the neural network controlling the agent is another challenge. There is no way to communicate with the network other than through the system of rewards and penalties. This in particular may lead to catastrophic forgetting, where acquiring new knowledge causes some of the old to be erased from the network.

Yet another challenge is reaching a local optimum – that is the agent performs the task as it is, but not in the optimal or required way. A "jumper" jumping like a kangaroo instead of doing the thing that was expected of it-walking-is a great example. Finally, there are agents that will optimize the prize without performing the task it was designed for.

Distinguishing Reinforcement Learning from Deep Learning and Machine Learning

In fact, there should be no clear divide between machine learning, deep learning and reinforcement learning. It is like a parallelogram – rectangle – square relation, where machine learning is the broadest category and the deep reinforcement learning the narrowest one.

In the same way, reinforcement learning is a specialized application of machine and deep learning techniques, designed to solve problems in a particular way.

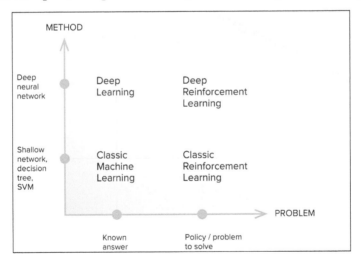

Although the ideas seem to differ, there is no sharp divide between these subtypes. Moreover, they merge within projects, as the models are designed not to stick to a "pure type" but to perform the task in the most effective way possible. So "what precisely distinguishes machine learning, deep learning and reinforcement learning" is actually a tricky question to answer.

Machine Learning

It is a form of AI in which computers are given the ability to progressively improve the performance of a specific task with data, without being directly programmed (this is Arthur Lee Samuel's definition. He coined the term "machine learning", of which there are two types, supervised and unsupervised machine learning.

Supervised Machine Learning

This happens when a programmer can provide a label for every training input into the machine learning system.

- Example – By analyzing the historical data taken from coal mines, deepsense. ai prepared an automated system for predicting dangerous seismic events up to 8 hours before they occur. The records of seismic events were taken from 24 coal mines that had collected data for several months. The model was able to recognize the likelihood of an explosion by analyzing the readings from the previous 24 hours.

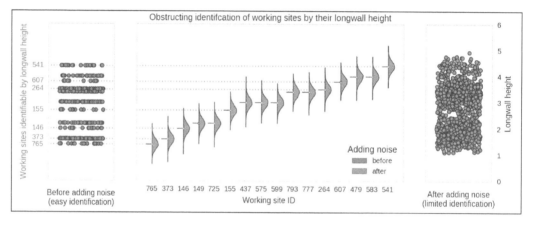

Some of the mines can be exactly identified by their main working height values. To obstruct the identification, we added some Gaussian noise. From the AI point of view, a single model was performing a single task on a clarified and normalized dataset.

Unsupervised Learning

This takes place when the model is provided only with the input data, but no explicit labels. It has to dig through the data and find the hidden structure or relationships within. The designer might not know what the structure is or what the machine learning model is going to find.

- An example we employed was for churn prediction. We analyzed customer data and designed an algorithm to group similar customers. However, we didn't choose the groups ourselves. Later on, we could identify high-risk groups (those with a high churn rate) and our client knew which customers they should approach first.

- Another example of unsupervised learning is anomaly detection, where the algorithm has to spot the element that doesn't fit in with the group. It may be a flawed product, potentially fraudulent transaction or any other event associated with breaking the norm.

Deep Learning

It consists of several layers of neural networks, designed to perform more sophisticated tasks. The construction of deep learning models was inspired by the design of the human brain, but simplified. Deep learning models consist of a few neural network layers which are in principle responsible for gradually learning more abstract features about particular data.

Although deep learning solutions are able to provide marvelous results, in terms of scale they are no match for the human brain. Each layer uses the outcome of a previous one as an input and the whole network is trained as a single whole. The core concept of creating an artificial neural network is not new, but only recently has modern hardware provided enough computational power to effectively train such networks by exposing a sufficient number of examples. Extended adoption has brought about frameworks like TensorFlow, Keras and PyTorch, all of which have made building machine learning models much more convenient.

- Example: deepsense.ai designed a deep learning-based model for the National Oceanic and Atmospheric Administration (NOAA). It was designed to recognize Right whales from aerial photos taken by researchers. From a technical point of view, recognizing a particular specimen of whales from aerial photos is pure deep learning. The solution consists of a few machine learning models performing separate tasks. The first one was in charge of finding the head of the whale in the photograph while the second normalized the photo by cutting and turning it, which ultimately provided a unified view (a passport photo) of a single whale.

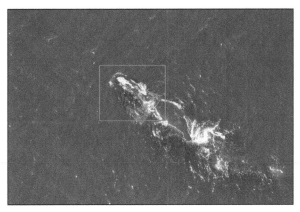

The third model was responsible for recognizing particular whales from photos that had been prepared and processed earlier. A network composed of 5 million neurons located the blowhead bonnet-tip. Over 941,000 neurons looked for the head and more than 3 million neurons were used to classify the particular whale. That's over 9 million neurons performing the task, which may seem like a lot, but pales in comparison to the more than 100 billion neurons at work in the human brain. We later used a similar deep learning-based solution to diagnose diabetic retinopathy using images of patients' retinas.

Understanding Clustering

Clustering is a type of unsupervised learning method where the machine learns to draw up conclusions from datasets on the basis of similarities and dissimilarities. This chapter delves into the subject of clustering, the various types of clustering, and their analysis and validity for a thorough understanding of the subject.

Clustering is the most important unsupervised learning approach associated with machine learning. It can be viewed as a method for data exploration which essentially means looking for patterns or structures in the data space that may be of interest in a collection of unlabeled data. Essentially no classes are associated with data instances a priori as in the case of supervised learning.

Now let us look at simplistic definition of clustering. Clustering can be defined as the method of organizing data instances into groups based on their similarity. In other words a cluster is a collection or group of data instances that are similar to each other and dissimilar to data instances belonging to other clusters.

Natural Grouping: Clustering is Subjective

A set of data instances or samples can be grouped differently based on different criteria or features, in other words clustering are subjective. The Figure below shows a set of seven people. They have been grouped into three clusters based on whether they are school employees; they belong to a family or based on the gender. Therefore choosing the attributes or features based on which clustering is to be carried out is an important aspect of clustering just as it was for classification.

Clusters: Distance Viewpoint

When we are given a set of instances or examples represented as a set of points, we need to define the notion of distance between these points. We then group the points into some number of clusters, such that members of a cluster are close or similar to each other while members of different clusters are dissimilar or farther apart than members belonging to the same cluster. The figure shows a data set that has three natural clusters where the data points group together based on the distance. An outlier is a data point that is isolated from all other data points.

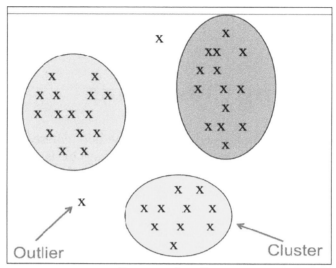

Clusters and Outlier.

Applications of Clustering

In the context of machine learning, clustering is one of the functions that have many interesting applications. One of the applications of clustering is for understanding. Understanding is achieved through appropriate grouping. Grouping related documents for browsing, grouping genes and proteins that have similar functionality, or grouping stocks with similar price fluctuations are some examples that help in understanding the commonalities and differences between groups. Another use of clustering is in summarization, in other words we reduce the size of large data sets. Some examples of clustering are shown in. The example in (a) shows how Google news uses clustering of news articles to help in better presentation of news. In fact by using appropriate features for clustering we can also bring out a personalized presentation (b) shows the use of clustering to show areas clustered based on the amount of precipitation.

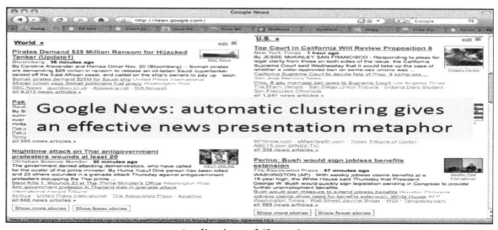

Applications of Clustering.

Let us see some real-life examples of clustering. When designing T-shirts making them to fit each person is too expensive while one-size-fits-all is not a satisfactory policy. We could group people with similar sizes to design "small", "medium" and "large" T-shirts. Example 1: groups people of similar sizes together to make "small", "medium" and "large" T-Shirts.

In today's world of online marketing, segmenting customers according to their similarities would help in targeted marketing. Features such as previous products bought, effect of discounts etc., could be used for such marketing.

Another example of clustering is in document clustering where given a collection of text documents, we can cluster them according to their content similarities in order to create a topic hierarchy.

As we can see from the varied applications clustering is one of the most utilized data mining techniques. In image processing it is used to cluster images based on their visual content. In the web scenario it is used to cluster groups of users based on their access patterns on webpages or cluster searchers based on their search behavior or to cluster webpages based on their content and links. In bioinformatics clustering can be used to group similar proteins based on similarity of their chemical structure and/or functionality. It has been used in almost every field, e. g., medicine, psychology, botany, sociology, biology, archeology, marketing, insurance, libraries, etc. Due to the large increase of online documents text clustering is now becoming very important.

Aspects of Clustering

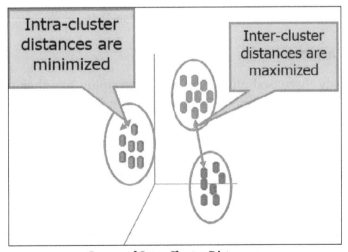

Intra and Inter Cluster Distances.

In general clustering deals with high dimensional data. Example of such data includes text documents and images. Dealing with such high dimensional data is an important aspect of clustering. Another important aspect that influences the effectiveness of clustering is the choice of distance function or the similarity or dissimilarity measure used. The basic clustering algorithms can be divided into two types namely hierarchical clustering and partitional clustering. The choice of which type and which algorithm is another important aspect of clustering. We also need to decide on the parameters to evaluate clustering quality. In general the algorithms strive to maximize inter-cluster distance and minimize intracluster distance. In other words the quality of clustering depends on the algorithm used, the distance function selected, and the application for which it is to be used.

High Dimensional Data

Often as we discussed clustering needs to deal with high dimensional data where given a cloud of data points we want to understand its structure. Clustering needs to capture the structure using some dimensionality techniques and then performing clustering.

 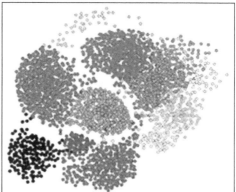

Patterns in High Dimensional Data.

Similarity Measures

As we have already discussed clustering is the grouping together of "similar" data. Choosing an appropriate (dis)similarity measure is a critical step in clustering. Similarity measure is often described as the inverse of the distance function that is less the distance more is the similarity. There are many distance functions for the different types of data such as numeric data, nominal data etc. Distance measures can also be defined specifically for different applications.

Distance Functions for Numeric Attributes

In general in the case of numeric attributes distance is denoted as dist(x_i, x_j), where x_i and x_j are data points. Please note that these data points can be vectors. The most commonly used distance functions in this context are Euclidean distance and Manhattan (city block) distance. These two distance functions are special cases of Minkowski distance.

Minkowski Distance

Given below is the Minkowski distance, where h is any positive integer. In other words the distance between two data points' x_i and x_j is defined as the hth root of the sum of the difference between them in each dimension taken to the power of h.

$$dist\left(X_i, X_j\right) = \left(\left|x_{i1} - x_{j1}\right|^h + \left|x_{i2} - x_{j2}\right|^h + ... + \left|x_{ir} - x_{jr}\right|^h\right)^{\frac{1}{h}}$$

Euclidean Distance

In the case of Euclidean distance h=2.

$$dist\left(X_i, X_j\right) = \sqrt{\left(x_{i1} - x_{j1}\right)^2 + \left(x_{i2} - x_{j2}\right)^2 + ... + \left(x_{ir} - x_{jr}\right)^2}$$

In other words Euclidean distance between two data points' x_i and x_j is the square root of the sum of the squares of the difference between them in each dimension. This is one of the most commonly used distance function for clustering data points with numerical attributes.

Manhattan Distance

In the case of Manhattan distance h=1.

$$dist\left(X_i, X_j\right) = \left|x_{i1} - x_{j1}\right| + \left|x_{i2} - x_{j2}\right| + ... + \left|x_{ir} - x_{jr}\right|$$

This distance is sometimes used because of the reduced computational cost as in this case there is no need for calculation of power and power root functions. We need to note this is not a trivial issue since we need to calculate the distance between each and every data point and the number of data points is usually large. Moreover each data point in turn may be represented by a high dimensional vector which further affects the computational cost.

Weighted Euclidean Distance

$$dist\left(X_i, X_j\right) = \sqrt{w_1\left(x_{i1} - x_{j1}\right)^2 + w_2\left(x_{i2} - x_{j2}\right)^2 + ... + w_r\left(x_{ir} - x_{jr}\right)^2}$$

Here the sum of the weights w1,w2,...wr =1 In the case of weighted Euclidean distance the difference between the data points in each dimension is weighted. Each dimension in the vector representing the points corresponds to different attributes or features so this essentially means that we can weight each feature according to its importance in defining the cluster.

Chebychev Distance

This distance is equal to the maximum difference between the values of any one of the attributes and the distance measure is given as:

$$dist\left(X_i, X_j\right) = \max\left(\left|x_{i1} - x_{j1}\right|, \left|x_{i2} - x_{j2}\right|, ..., \left|x_{ir} - x_{jr}\right|\right)$$

Distance Functions for Binary Attributes

Binary attributes have two values or states but no ordering relationships, e. g.; attribute gender has two values male and female. In the case of binary attributes normally a confusion matrix is used where the ith and jth data points are represented as vectors x_i and x_j. We use a confusion matrix to introduce the distance functions/measures.

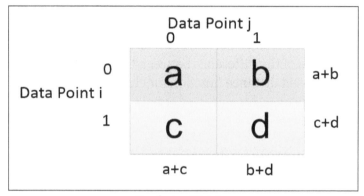

Confusion Matrix.

The figure above shows "a" corresponds to the number of attributes with the value of 0 for both data points x_i and x_j, "b" corresponds to 0 for x_i and 1 for x_j, "c" corresponds to 1 for x_i and 0 for x_j, while "d" corresponds to the number of attributes with the value of 1 for both data points x_i and x_j.

The confusion matrix can be used when the binary attribute is symmetric that is if both states (0 and 1) have equal importance, and carry the same weights. Then the distance function is the proportion of mismatches of their values:

dist(x_i,x_j) = (b+c)/(a+b+c+d)

However sometimes the binary attributes are asymmetric that is one of the states is more important than the other. We assume that state 1 represents the important state in which case the Jaccard measure using the confusion matrix can be defined as:

JDist(x_i,x_j) = (b+c)/(a+b+c)

For text documents normally we use cosine similarity which is a similarity measure not a distance measure. Cosine similarity is a measure of similarity between two vectors obtained by measuring the cosine of the angle between them. The similarity between any two given documents d_j and d_k, represented as vectors is given as:

$$sim(d_j, d_k) = \frac{\vec{d}_j \cdot \vec{d}_k}{\left|\vec{d}_j\right|\left|\vec{d}_k\right|} = \frac{\sum_{i=1}^{n} w_{i,j} w_{i,k}}{\sqrt{\sum_{i=1}^{n} w^2{}_{i,j}} \sqrt{\sum_{i=1}^{n} w^2{}_{i,k}}}$$

In this case w_i is a weight probably based on the frequency of words in the documents.

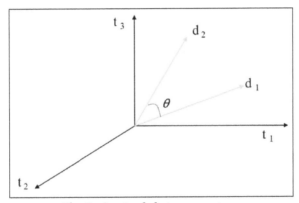

The Cosine Angle between vectors.

The result of the Cosine function is equal to 1 when the angle is 0, and it is less than 1 when the angle is of any other value. As the angle between the vectors decreases, the cosine value approaches 1, that is the two vectors are closer, and the similarity between the documents increases.

Methods of Clustering

The basic method of clustering is the hierarchical method which is of two types agglomerative and divisive. Agglomerative clustering is a bottom up method where initially we assume that each data point is by itself a cluster. Then we repeatedly combine the two "nearest" clusters into one. On the other hand divisive clustering is a top down procedure where we start with one cluster and recursively split the clusters until no more division is possible. We normally carry out point assignment where we maintain a set of clusters and allocate points to nearest cluster.

Hierarchical Clustering

Hierarchical clustering, also known as hierarchical cluster analysis, is an algorithm that groups similar objects into groups called clusters. The endpoint is a set of clusters, where each cluster is distinct from each other cluster, and the objects within each cluster are broadly similar to each other.

Why Hierarchical Clustering?

We should first know how K-means works before we dive into hierarchical clustering. Trust me; it will make the concept of hierarchical clustering all the more easier. Here's a brief overview of how K-means works:

1. Decide the number of clusters (k).

2. Select k random points from the data as centroids.

3. Assign all the points to the nearest cluster centroid.

4. Calculate the centroid of newly formed clusters.

5. Repeat steps 3 and 4.

It is an iterative process. It will keep on running until the centroids of newly formed clusters do not change or the maximum number of iterations is reached.

But there are certain challenges with K-means. It always tries to make clusters of the same size. Also, we have to decide the number of clusters at the beginning of the algorithm. Ideally, we would not know how many clusters should we have, in the beginning of the algorithm and hence it a challenge with K-means.

This is a gap hierarchical clustering bridges with aplomb. It takes away the problem of having to pre-define the number of clusters. Sounds like a dream! So, let's see what hierarchical clustering is and how it improves on K-means.

Let's say we have the below points and we want to cluster them into groups:

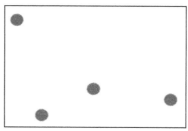

Initial points.

We can assign each of these points to a separate cluster:

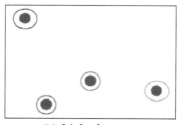

Multiple clusters.

Now, based on the similarity of these clusters, we can combine the most similar clusters together and repeat this process until only a single cluster is left:

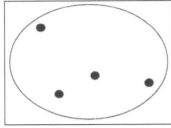

Single cluster.

We are essentially building a hierarchy of clusters. That's why this algorithm is called hierarchical clustering. For now, let's look at the different types of hierarchical clustering.

Types of Hierarchical Clustering

There are mainly two types of hierarchical clustering:

- Agglomerative hierarchical clustering.

- Divisive Hierarchical clustering.

Agglomerative Hierarchical Clustering

We assign each point to an individual cluster in this technique. Suppose there are 4 data points. We will assign each of these points to a cluster and hence will have 4 clusters in the beginning:

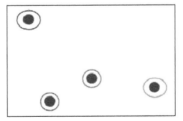

Then, at each iteration, we merge the closest pair of clusters and repeat this step until only a single cluster is left:

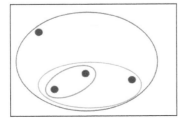

We are merging (or adding) the clusters at each step, right? Hence, this type of clustering is also known as additive hierarchical clustering.

Divisive Hierarchical Clustering

Divisive hierarchical clustering works in the opposite way. Instead of starting with n clusters (in case of n observations), we start with a single cluster and assign all the points to that cluster.

So, it doesn't matter if we have 10 or 1000 data points. All these points will belong to the same cluster at the beginning:

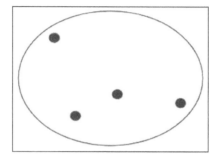

Now, at each iteration, we split the farthest point in the cluster and repeat this process until each cluster only contains a single point:

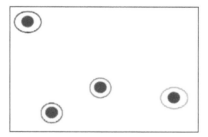

We are splitting (or dividing) the clusters at each step, hence the name divisive hierarchical clustering. Divisive hierarchical clustering will be a piece of cake once we have a handle on the agglomerative type.

Steps to Perform Hierarchical Clustering

We merge the most similar points or clusters in hierarchical clustering we know this. Now the question is how do we decide which points are similar and which are not? It's one of the most important questions in clustering.

Here's one way to calculate similarity Take the distance between the centroids of these clusters. The points having the least distance are referred to as similar points and we can merge them. We can refer to this as a distance-based algorithm as well (since we are calculating the distances between the clusters).

In hierarchical clustering, we have a concept called a proximity matrix. This store the distances between each point. Let's take an example to understand this matrix as well as the steps to perform hierarchical clustering.

Setting up the Example

Suppose a teacher wants to divide her students into different groups. She has the marks scored by each student in an assignment and based on these marks; she wants to segment them into groups. There's no fixed target here as to how many groups to have. Since the teacher does not know what type of students should be assigned to which group, it cannot be solved as a supervised learning problem. So, we will try to apply hierarchical clustering here and segment the students into different groups.

Let's take a sample of 5 students:

Student_ID	Marks
1	10
2	7
3	28
4	20
5	35

Creating a Proximity Matrix

First, we will create a proximity matrix which will tell us the distance between each of these points. Since we are calculating the distance of each point from each of the other points, we will get a square matrix of shape n X n (where n is the number of observations).

Let's make the 5 x 5 proximity matrix for our example:

ID	1	2	3	4	5
1	0	3	18	10	25
2	3	0	21	13	28
3	18	21	0	8	7
4	10	13	8	0	15
5	25	28	7	15	0

The diagonal elements of this matrix will always be 0 as the distance of a point with itself is always 0. We will use the Euclidean distance formula to calculate the rest of the distances. So, let's say we want to calculate the distance between point 1 and 2:

$\sqrt{(10-7)^2} = \sqrt{9} = 3$

Similarly, we can calculate all the distances and fill the proximity matrix.

Steps to Perform Hierarchical Clustering

Step 1: First, we assign all the points to an individual cluster:

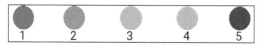

Proximity matrix.

Different colors here represent different clusters. You can see that we have 5 different clusters for the 5 points in our data.

Step 2: Next, we will look at the smallest distance in the proximity matrix and merge the points with the smallest distance. We then update the proximity matrix:

ID	1	2	3	4	5
1	0	③	18	10	25
2	③	0	21	13	28
3	18	21	0	8	7
4	10	13	8	0	15
5	25	28	7	15	0

Here, the smallest distance is 3 and hence we will merge point 1 and 2:

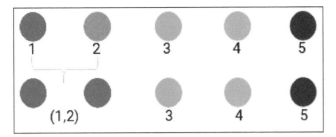

Let's look at the updated clusters and accordingly update the proximity matrix:

Student_ID	Marks
(1,2)	10
3	28
4	20
5	35

Here, we have taken the maximum of the two marks (7, 10) to replace the marks for this cluster. Instead of the maximum, we can also take the minimum value or the average values as well. Now, we will again calculate the proximity matrix for these clusters:

ID	(1,2)	3	4	5
(1,2)	0	18	10	25
3	18	0	8	7
4	10	8	0	15
5	25	7	15	0

Step 3: We will repeat step 2 until only a single cluster is left.

So, we will first look at the minimum distance in the proximity matrix and then merge the closest pair of clusters. We will get the merged clusters as shown below after repeating these steps:

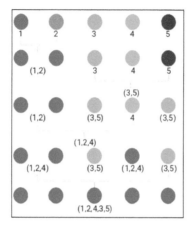

We started with 5 clusters and finally have a single cluster. This is how agglomerative hierarchical clustering works. But the burning question still remains how do we decide the number of clusters?

How should we Choose the Number of Clusters in Hierarchical Clustering?

Ready to finally answer this question that's been hanging around since we started learning? To get the number of clusters for hierarchical clustering, we make use of an awesome concept called a Dendrogram.

"A dendrogram is a tree-like diagram that records the sequences of merges or splits".

Let's get back to our teacher-student example. Whenever we merge two clusters, a dendrogram will record the distance between these clusters and represent it in graph form. Let's see how a dendrogram looks like:

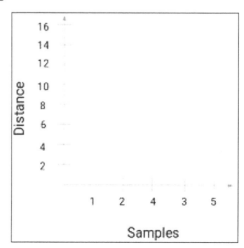

We have the samples of the dataset on the x-axis and the distance on the y-axis. Whenever two clusters are merged, we will join them in this dendrogram and the height of the join will be the distance between these points. Let's build the dendrogram for our example:

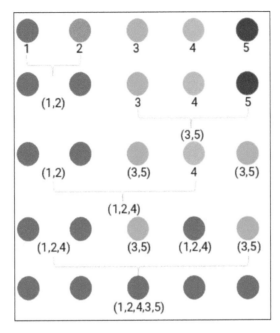

Take a moment to process the above image. We started by merging sample 1 and 2 and the distance between these two samples was 3. Let's plot this in the dendrogram:

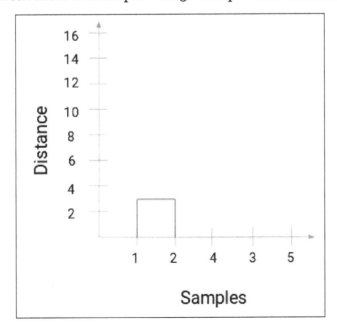

Here, we can see that we have merged sample 1 and 2. The vertical line represents the distance between these samples. Similarly, we plot all the steps where we merged the clusters and finally, we get a dendrogram like this:

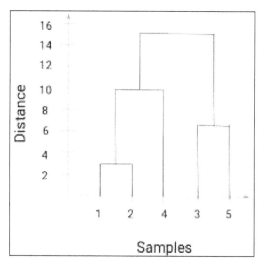

We can clearly visualize the steps of hierarchical clustering. More the distance of the vertical lines in the dendrogram, more the distance between those clusters.

Now, we can set a threshold distance and draw a horizontal line (Generally, we try to set the threshold in such a way that it cuts the tallest vertical line). Let's set this threshold as 12 and draw a horizontal line:

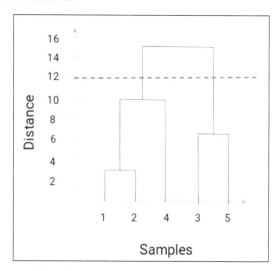

The number of clusters will be the number of vertical lines which are being intersected by the line drawn using the threshold. In the above example, since the red line intersects 2 vertical lines, we will have 2 clusters. One cluster will have a sample (1,2,4) and the other will have a sample (3,5). Pretty straightforward, right?

This is how we can decide the number of clusters using a dendrogram in Hierarchical Clustering.

Solving the Wholesale Customer Segmentation Problem using Hierarchical Clustering

The data is hosted on the UCI Machine Learning repository. The aim of this problem is to segment the clients of a wholesale distributor based on their annual spending on diverse product categories, like milk, grocery, region, etc.

Let's explore the data first and then apply Hierarchical Clustering to segment the clients. We will first import the required libraries:

```
1. import pandas as pd

2. import numpy as np

3. import matplotlib.pyplot as plt

4. %matplotlib inline
```

Load the data and look at the first few rows:

```
1. data = pd.read_csv('Wholesale customers data.csv')

2. data.head()
```

S.NO.	Channel	Region	Fresh	Milk	Grocery	Frozen	Detergents_Paper	Delicassen
0	2	3	12669	9656	7561	214	2674	1338
1	2	3	7057	9810	9568	1762	3293	1776
2	2	3	6353	8808	7684	2405	3516	7844
3	1	3	13265	1196	4221	6404	507	1788
4	2	3	22615	5410	7198	3915	1777	5185

There are multiple product categories Fresh, Milk, Grocery, etc. The values represent the number of units purchased by each client for each product. Our aim is to make clusters from this data that can segment similar clients together. We will, of course, use Hierarchical Clustering for this problem.

But before applying Hierarchical Clustering, we have to normalize the data so that the scale of each variable is the same. Why is this important? Well, if the scale of the variables is not the same, the model might become biased towards the variables with a higher magnitude like Fresh or Milk.

So, let's first normalize the data and bring all the variables to the same scale:

```
1. from sklearn.preprocessing import normalize

2. data_scaled = normalize(data)
```

64

3. ```
data_scaled = pd.DataFrame(data_scaled, columns=data.columns)
```

4. ```
data_scaled.head()
```

S.NO.	Channel	Region	Fresh	Milk	Grocery	Frozen	Deter-gents_Pa-per	Delicassen
0	0.000112	0.708333	0.708333	0.539874	0.422741	0.011965	0.149505	0.074809
1	0.000188	0.442198	0.442198	0.614704	0.599540	0.110409	0.206342	0.111286
2	0.000187	0.396552	0.396552	0.549792	0.479632	0.150119	0.219467	0.489619
3	0.000194	0.856837	0.856837	0.077254	0.272650	0.413659	0.032749	0.115494
4	0.000119	0.895416	0.895416	0.214203	0.284997	0.155010	0.070358	0.205294

Here, we can see that the scale of all the variables is almost similar. Now, we are good to go. Let's first draw the dendrogram to help us decide the number of clusters for this particular problem:

1. ```
import scipy.cluster.hierarchy as shc
```

2. ```
plt.figure(figsize=(10, 7))
```

3. ```
plt.title("Dendrograms")
```

4. ```
dend = shc.dendrogram(shc.linkage(data_scaled, method='ward'))
```

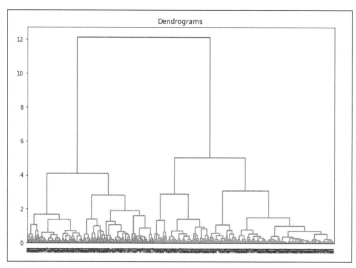

The x-axis contains the samples and y-axis represents the distance between these samples. The vertical line with maximum distance is the blue line and hence we can decide a threshold of 6 and cut the dendrogram:

1. ```
plt.figure(figsize=(10, 7))
```

2. ```
plt.title("Dendrograms")
```

3. `dend = shc.dendrogram(shc.linkage(data_scaled, method='ward'))`

4. `plt.axhline(y=6, color='r', linestyle='--')`

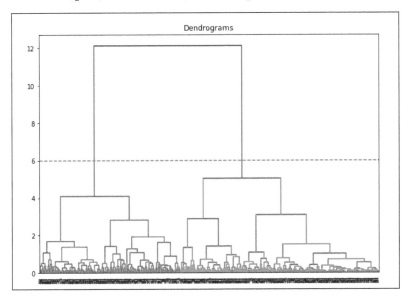

We have two clusters as this line cuts the dendrogram at two points. Let's now apply hierarchical clustering for 2 clusters:

1. `from sklearn.cluster import AgglomerativeClustering`

2. `cluster = AgglomerativeClustering(n_clusters=2, affinity='euclid-ean', linkage='ward')`

3. `cluster.fit_predict(data_scaled)`

```
array([1, 1, 1, 0, 0, 1, 0, 1, 1, 1, 0, 0, 0, 0, 0, 1, 1, 0, 0, 0, 0,
       0, 1, 0, 0, 0, 0, 1, 0, 0, 1, 0, 0, 1, 1, 0, 1, 1, 0, 0, 0, 1, 1,
       1, 1, 1, 1, 1, 1, 0, 1, 0, 1, 0, 1, 1, 1, 0, 1, 0, 1, 1, 1, 0, 1,
       1, 0, 1, 0, 0, 0, 0, 0, 1, 0, 0, 1, 0, 1, 0, 1, 1, 0, 1, 1, 0,
       0, 0, 0, 0, 1, 0, 1, 1, 1, 0, 0, 0, 1, 1, 1, 0, 0, 0, 1, 1, 1, 1,
       0, 1, 0, 0, 0, 0, 0, 1, 0, 0, 0, 0, 0, 1, 0, 0, 0, 0, 1, 0, 0, 0,
       0, 0, 0, 0, 1, 1, 0, 1, 0, 0, 0, 0, 0, 1, 0, 0, 0, 0, 0, 1, 0, 1,
       0, 1, 1, 0, 1, 1, 1, 0, 0, 1, 1, 1, 1, 1, 0, 0, 1, 1, 1, 1, 1, 1,
       0, 0, 0, 1, 0, 0, 1, 1, 1, 0, 0, 1, 1, 1, 0, 0, 0, 1, 0, 0, 0, 1,
       0, 0, 1, 1, 0, 1, 1, 1, 0, 1, 1, 1, 0, 1, 0, 1, 1, 1, 1, 0, 1, 0,
       0, 1, 0, 0, 0, 0, 0, 0, 1, 0, 0, 1, 0, 1, 0, 1, 0, 0, 0, 0, 0, 0,
       0, 0, 1, 1, 0, 0, 0, 0, 0, 1, 0, 0, 1, 0, 0, 0, 0, 0, 0, 0, 0, 1,
       1, 1, 1, 0, 1, 0, 0, 1, 1, 0, 1, 1, 0, 1, 0, 0, 0, 0, 0, 0, 0, 0,
       0, 0, 0, 0, 1, 0, 1, 1, 0, 0, 0, 0, 1, 1, 0, 1, 1, 1, 1, 1, 1, 0,
       0, 1, 0, 0, 1, 0, 0, 1, 0, 1, 0, 1, 1, 0, 0, 0, 0, 0, 0, 1, 0, 0,
       0, 1, 0, 1, 0, 0, 0, 0, 0, 0, 1, 1, 1, 1, 0, 1, 1, 0, 1, 1, 0, 1,
       1, 1, 0, 1, 0, 1, 1, 1, 0, 0, 1, 0, 0, 1, 0, 0, 0, 0, 0, 0, 1, 0,
       0, 0, 1, 0, 1, 1, 0, 0, 0, 0, 1, 0, 1, 0, 0, 0, 0, 1, 1, 0, 0, 0,
       1, 0, 0, 0, 0, 0, 0, 0, 0, 0, 0, 1, 0, 0, 0, 1, 1, 0, 0, 1, 1, 1,
       1, 0, 1, 0, 0, 0, 0, 0, 1, 0, 1, 0, 1, 0, 0, 1, 0, 0, 0, 1, 0, 1])
```

We can see the values of 0s and 1s in the output since we defined 2 clusters. 0 represents the points that belong to the first cluster and 1 represents points in the second cluster. Let's now visualize the two clusters:

1. `plt.figure(figsize=(10, 7))`

2. `plt.scatter(data_scaled['Milk'], data_scaled['Grocery'], c=cluster.labels_)`

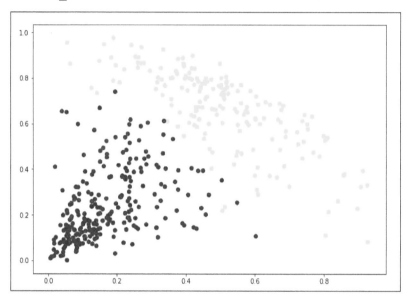

K-means Clustering

The K-means algorithm is an iterative algorithm which divides the given data set into K disjoint groups. As already discussed K-means is the most widely used clustering techniques. This partitional method uses prototypes for representing the cluster. For a given K we need to find a partition of K clusters that optimizes the chosen partitioning criterion or cost function.

The K-means algorithm is a heuristic method where each cluster is represented by the center of the cluster and the algorithm converges when the centroids of the clusters do not change. The K-means algorithm is the simplest partitioning method for clustering and widely used in data mining applications.

Steps of K-means

Initialize k values of centroids. The following two steps are repeated until the data points do not change partitions and there is no change in the centroid.

- Partition the data points according to the current centroids. The similarity between each data point and each centroid is determined and the data points are moved to the partition to which it is most similar.

- The new centroids of the data points in each partition is then calculated.

These steps are given in the flow diagram shown below.

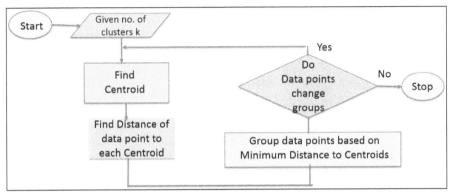

Flow Diagram of K-means algorithm.

Algorithm for K-means Clustering

Now let us discuss in detail the K-means algorithm. Let X = {$x_1,x_2,x_3,\ldots\ldots,x_n$} be the set of n data points and V = {$v_1,v_2,\ldots\ldots,v_c$} be the set of centroids.

- We first randomly select 'k' cluster centroids.

- We then calculate the distance between each data point and the cluster centroids.

- We then find the cluster whose centroid is nearest to the data point. We then assign the data point to this cluster.

- We then recalculate the new cluster centroid using:

$$J(V) = \sum_{i=1}^{k}\sum_{j=1}^{k_i} (\|\,\mathbf{x}_i - \mathbf{v}_j\,\|)^2$$

where, 'k_i' represents the number of data points in ith cluster.

- We then recalculate the distance between each data point and the newly obtained cluster centroids.

- If no data point has been reassigned then we stop, otherwise we repeat from step 3.

In the example shown in figure below, we see that initially the cluster centroids are chosen at random as we are talking about an unsupervised learning technique where we are not provided with the labelled samples. Even after the first round using these randomly chosen centroids the complete set of data points are partitioned all at once. As you can see after round 2 the centroids have moved since the data points have been used to calculate the new centroids. The process is repeated and the centroids are relocated until convergence occurs when no data point changes partitions.

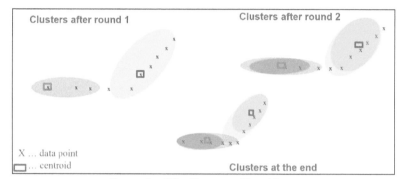

Example of the K-means Algorithm.

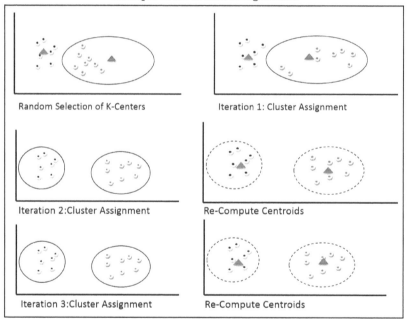

Steps of Cluster Assignment and Centroid Computation.

Issues Associated with the K-means Algorithm

Getting the K-right

The first question we need address is to choose the correct value of K that is how many partitions we should have. One way of selecting K is to first try different values of K and studying the change in the average distance to centroid as K increases. As we can see from Figure the average changes rapidly until the right value of K when the changes are slow.

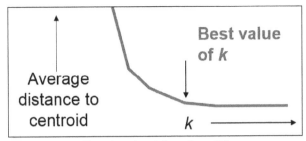

Choosing the right value of K.

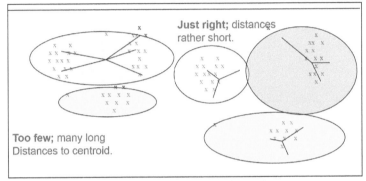

Illustration of Different Values of K.

The figure above shows the case of 2 clusters which is too few since the distances to the centroids is too long while when there are 3 clusters the distances are shortand just right.

Problems with Selecting Initial Points

One of the issues associated with K-means clustering is the initial choice of the the K-centroids. Though we have explained that these initial centroids can be chosen at random this may not lead to fast convergence. If there are K clusters then the chance of selecting one centroid from each cluster is small and the chance becomes even lower when K is large. If we assume that clusters are of same size, n that is each cluster has n data points then the number of ways of selecting K centroids is large and the probability that we choose the K across clusters is small.

$$p = \frac{number\ of\ ways\ to\ select\ one\ centroid\ from\ each\ cluster}{number\ of\ ways\ to\ select\ k centroids} = \frac{K!n^K}{(Kn)^K} = \frac{K!}{K^K}$$

For example, if K = 10, then probability = $10!/10^{10}$ = 0. 00036.

Sometimes the randomly chosen initial centroids will readjust themselves in the right direction but there are chances that they do not as shown in figure. Therefore this initial cluster problem needs to be addressed. One way to do this is to conduct multiple runs but even then due to the low probability, this approach may not work. Another method we sample and use hierarchical clustering to determine the initial centroids. Another approach is first select more than K initial centroids and then select among these initial centroids which are the most widely separated. Another method is carrying out pre-processing where we can normalize the data and eliminate outliers. On the other hand in post-processing we can eliminate small clusters that may represent outliers and split or merge clusters.

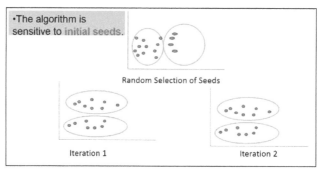

Effect of selection of Initial Seeds.

According to the error in the clustering measured using in Mean Squared Error (MSE). Bisecting K-means is a variant of K-means where the clusters are bisected using basic K-means and one of the clusters with the lowest MSE is selected from the bi-section.

Stopping/Convergence Criterion

The stopping criteria can be defined in any one of the following ways. We can stop the iteration when there are no or a minimum number of re-assignments of data points to different clusters. We can also define the stopping criteria to be when there is no (or minimum) change of centroids, or in terms of error as minimum decrease in the sum of squared error (SSE). We will discuss this error later on in this module in the section on evaluation.

The numerical example given below can be used to understand the K-means algorithm. Suppose we have 4 types of medicines and each has two attributes pH and weight index. Our goal is to group these objects into K=2 group of medicines.

Medicine	Weight	pH-Index
A	1	1
B	2	1
C	4	3
D	5	4

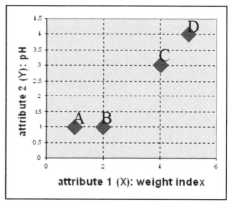

Mapping of the Data points into the Data Space.

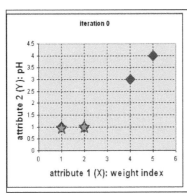

$$c_1 = A, c_2 = B$$

$$\mathbf{D}^0 = \begin{bmatrix} 0 & 1 & 3.61 & 5 \\ 1 & 0 & 2.83 & 4.24 \end{bmatrix} \begin{matrix} c_1 = (1,1) & group-1 \\ c_2 = (2,1) & group-2 \end{matrix}$$

$$\begin{matrix} A & B & C & D \\ \begin{bmatrix} 1 & 2 & 4 & 5 \\ 1 & 1 & 3 & 4 \end{bmatrix} & & & \begin{matrix} X \\ Y \end{matrix} \end{matrix}$$

$$d(D, c_1) = \sqrt{(5-1)^2 + (4-1)^2} = 5$$

$$d(D, c_2) = \sqrt{(5-2)^2 + (4-1)^2} = 4.24$$

Assign each object to the cluster with the nearest seed point

(a)

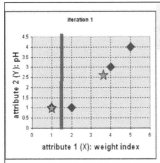

Knowing the members of each cluster, now we compute the new centroid of each group based on these new memberships.

$$c_1 = (1, \ 1)$$

$$c_2 = \left(\frac{2+4+5}{3}, \ \frac{1+3+4}{3} \right)$$

$$= \left(\frac{11}{3}, \ \frac{8}{3} \right)$$

(b)

Step 2: Renew membership based on new centroids

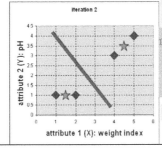

Compute the distance of all objects to the new centroids

$$\mathbf{D}^1 = \begin{bmatrix} 0.5 & 0.5 & 3.20 & 4.61 \\ 4.30 & 3.54 & 0.71 & 0.71 \end{bmatrix} \begin{matrix} c_1 = (1\frac{1}{2},1) & group-1 \\ c_2 = (4\frac{1}{2},3\frac{1}{2}) & group-2 \end{matrix}$$

$$\begin{matrix} A & B & C & D \\ \begin{bmatrix} 1 & 2 & 4 & 5 \\ 1 & 1 & 3 & 4 \end{bmatrix} & & & \begin{matrix} X \\ Y \end{matrix} \end{matrix}$$

Assign the membership to objects

(C)

Step 3: Repeat the first two steps until its convergence

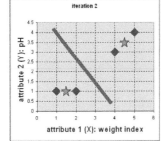

Knowing the members of each cluster, now we compute the new centroid of each group based on these new memberships.

$$c_1 = \left(\frac{1+2}{2}, \ \frac{1+1}{2} \right) = (1\frac{1}{2}, \ 1)$$

$$c_2 = \left(\frac{4+5}{2}, \ \frac{3+4}{2} \right) = (4\frac{1}{2}, \ 3\frac{1}{2})$$

(d)

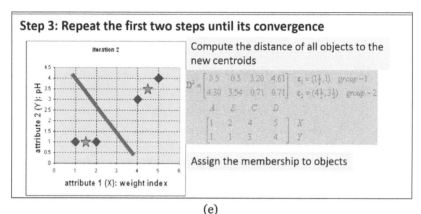

(e)

The Iterations for the example on Effect of selection of Initial Seeds.

The Figure (a) shows the random selection of the initial centroids as $c_1 = (1,1)$ for cluster A and $c_2 = (2,1)$ for cluster B. We illustrate with data point D and calculate the distance of D with each of the randomly selected centroids (also sometimes called as seed points). We find that D is closer to c1and we assign D to that cluster. Figure (b) shows the assignment of each data point to one of the clusters. In our example only one data point D is assigned to A so its centroid does not change. But however cluster B has three data points associated with it and the new centroid c_2 now becomes (11/3, 8/3). Now we compute the new assignments as shown in Figure(c) and (d) shows the new values of c_1 and c_2. Figure (e) shows the results after convergence.

Evaluating K-means Clusters

The most common measure is Sum of Squared Error (SSE). This is defined as follows:

For each point, the error is the distance to the nearest cluster,

$$SSE = \sum_{j=1}^{k} \sum_{X \in Cj} dist(X, \mathbf{m}_j)^2$$

where C_j is the jth cluster, m_j is the centroid of cluster C_j (the mean vector of all the data points in C_j), and $dist(x, m_j)$ is the distance between data point x and centroid m_j.

Given two clusterings (clustering is the set of clusters formed), we can choose the one with the smallest error. One straight forward way to reduce SSE is to increase K, the number of clusters. A good clustering with smaller K can have a lower SSE than a poor clustering with higher K.

Strengths and Weaknesses of K-means

Strengths of K-means

K-means is the most popular clustering algorithm. The major strengths of K-means is that it is easy to understand and implement. It generally has a time complexity of the O(tkn), where n is the number of data points, K is the number of clusters, and t is the number of iterations. Since both K and t are small, K- means is considered a linear time algorithm. It terminates at a local optimum if SSE is used. However the global optimum is hard to find due to complexity, which is its weakness.

Weaknesses of K-means

- The algorithm is only applicable for data where the concept of mean can be defined. For categorical data, where K-means is called as K-mode the centroid is represented by most frequent values. The user needs to specify the value of K.

- A different initialization (selection of centroids) may sometimes produce a different clustering. The algorithm itself requires the labeling and interpretation of the clusters to be carried out in subsequent phase.

- The algorithm is sensitive to outliers, where outliers are data points that are very far away from other data points. These outliers could be errors in the data recording or some special data points with very different values. Including these outliers in the calculation of the centroid may affect the whole clustering process. One method to deal with outliers is to remove some data points in the clustering process that are much further away from the centroids than other data points.

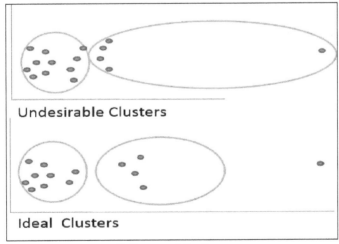

Influence of Outliers.

We may prefer to monitor these possible outliers over a few iterations and then decide to remove them. Another method is to perform random sampling. Since in sampling we only choose a small subset of the data points, the chance of selecting an outlier is very small. Then we assign the rest of the data points to the clusters by distance or similarity comparison, or classification.

Applications

Some of the common applications are optical character recognition, biometrics, diagnostic systems, military applications, document clustering, etc.

Why K-means?

Despite many of its weaknesses, K-means is still the most popular algorithm due to its simplicity, efficiency and because other clustering algorithms have their own lists of weaknesses. In general there is no clear evidence that any other clustering algorithm performs better in general although some algorithms may be more suitable for some specific types of data or applications. Comparing different clustering algorithms is a difficult task since no knowledge of the correct clusters is available.

K-means Variations

Clustering typically assumes that each instance is given a definite or hard assignment to exactly one cluster. This means no uncertainty is allowed in class membership or for an instance to belong to more than one cluster. A variation called soft clustering gives probabilities that an instance belongs to each of the set of clusters. In this case each data point is assigned a probability distribution across a set of discovered categories (probabilities of all categories must sum to 1).

Cluster Analysis

Clustering analysis is a form of exploratory data analysis in which observations are divided into different groups that share common characteristics.

The purpose of cluster analysis (also known as classification) is to construct groups (or classes or clusters) while ensuring the following property: within a group the observations must be as similar as possible, while observations belonging to different groups must be as different as possible.

There are two main types of classification:

- K-means clustering.

- Hierarchical clustering.

The first is generally used when the number of classes is fixed in advance, while the second is generally used for an unknown number of classes and helps to determine this optimal number. Both methods are illustrated below through applications by hand and in R.

Clustering algorithms use the distance in order to separate observations into different groups. Therefore, before diving into the presentation of the two classification methods, a reminder exercise on how to compute distances between points is presented.

Application 1: Computing Distances

Let a data set containing the points a = (0,0)' b = (1,0)' and c = (5,5)'. Compute the matrix of Euclidean distances between the points by hand and in R.

The points are as follows:

```
# We create the points in R
a <- c(0, 0)
b <- c(1, 0)
c <- c(5, 5)X <- rbind(a, b, c) # a, b and c are combined per row
colnames(X) <- c("x", "y") # rename columnsX # display the points##
x y
## a 0 0
## b 1 0
## c 5 5
```

By the Pythagorean Theorem, we will remember that the distance between 2 points:

$$\left(x_a, y_b\right) \text{and} \left(x_b, y_b\right) \text{in } \mathbb{R}^2$$

is given by,

$$\sqrt{\left(x_a - x_b\right)^2 + \left(y_a - y_b\right)^2}.$$

So for instance, for the distance between the points b = (1,0)' and c = (5,5)' presented in the statement above, we have:

$$\sqrt{\left(x_b - x_c\right)^2 + \left(y_b - y_c\right)^2} = \sqrt{\left(1-5\right)^2 + \left(0-5\right)^2} = 6.403124$$

We can proceed similarly for all pairs of points to find the distance matrix by handIn R, the dist() function allows you to find the distance of points in a matrix or data frame in a very simple way:

```
# The distance is found using the dist() function:
distance <- dist(X, method = "euclidean")
distance # display the distance matrix##      a      b
## b 1. 000000
## c 7. 071068 6. 403124
```

Note that the argument method = "euclidean" is not mandatory because the Euclidean method is the default one.

The distance matrix resulting from the dist() function gives the distance between the different points. The Euclidean distance between the points b and c is 6. 403124, which corresponds to what we found above via the Pythagorean formula.

Note: If two variables do not have the same units, one may have more weight in the calculation of the Euclidean distance than the otherIn that case, it is preferable to scale the dataScaling data allows to obtain variables independent of their unit, and this can be done with the `scale()` function.

Now that the distance has been presented, let's see how to perform clustering analysis with the k-means algorithm.

k-means Clustering

The first form of classification is the method called k-means clustering or the mobile center algorithm. As a reminder, this method aims at partitioning n observations into k clusters in which each observation belongs to the cluster with the closest average, serving as a prototype of the cluster.

It is presented below via an application in R and by hand.

Application 2: k-means Clustering

Data

For this exercise, the `Eurojobs.csv` database is used. This database contains the percentage of the population employed in different industries in 26 European countries in 1979. It contains 10 variables:

- `Country`: The name of the country (identifier).

- `Agr` % of workforce employed in agriculture.

- `Min` % in mining.

- `Man` % in manufacturing.

- `PS` % in power supplies industries.

- `Con` % in construction.

- `SI` % in service industries.

- `Fin` % in finance.

- `SPS` % in social and personal services.

- `TC` % in transportation and communications.

```
# Import data
```

```
Eurojobs <- read. csv(
file = "data/Eurojobs. csv",
sep = dec = header = TRUE
)
head(Eurojobs) # head() is used to display only the first 6 observa-
tions##    Country Agr Min Man PS Con  SI Fin SPS TC
## 1   Belgium 3. 3 0. 9 27. 6 0. 9 8. 2 19. 1 6. 2 26. 6 7. 2
## 2   Denmark 9. 2 0. 1 21. 8 0. 6 8. 3 14. 6 6. 5 32. 2 7. 1
## 3    France 10. 8 0. 8 27. 5 0. 9 8. 9 16. 8 6. 0 22. 6 5. 7
## 4 W. Germany 6. 7 1. 3 35. 8 0. 9 7. 3 14. 4 5. 0 22. 3 6. 1
## 5   Ireland 23. 2 1. 0 20. 7 1. 3 7. 5 16. 8 2. 8 20. 8 6. 1
## 6    Italy 15. 9 0. 6 27. 6 0. 5 10. 0 18. 1 1. 6 20. 1 5. 7
```

Note that there is a numbering before the first variable `Country`. For more clarity, we will replace this numbering by the country. To do this, we add the argument `row.names = 1` in the import function `read.csv()` to specify that the first column corresponds to the row names:

```
Eurojobs <- read. csv(
 file = "data/Eurojobs. csv",
 sep = dec = header = TRUE, row. names = 1
)
Eurojobs # displays dataset##              Agr Min Man PS Con  SI Fin SPS TC
## Belgium      3. 3 0. 9 27. 6 0. 9 8. 2 19. 1 6. 2 26. 6 7. 2
## Denmark      9. 2 0. 1 21. 8 0. 6 8. 3 14. 6 6. 5 32. 2 7. 1
## France      10. 8 0. 8 27. 5 0. 9 8. 9 16. 8 6. 0 22. 6 5. 7
## W. Germany   6. 7 1. 3 35. 8 0. 9 7. 3 14. 4 5. 0 22. 3 6. 1
## Ireland     23. 2 1. 0 20. 7 1. 3 7. 5 16. 8 2. 8 20. 8 6. 1
## Italy       15. 9 0. 6 27. 6 0. 5 10. 0 18. 1 1. 6 20. 1 5. 7
## Luxembourg   7. 7 3. 1 30. 8 0. 8 9. 2 18. 5 4. 6 19. 2 6. 2
## Netherlands  6. 3 0. 1 22. 5 1. 0 9. 9 18. 0 6. 8 28. 5 6. 8
## United Kingdom 2. 7 1. 4 30. 2 1. 4 6. 9 16. 9 5. 7 28. 3 6. 4
## Austria     12. 7 1. 1 30. 2 1. 4 9. 0 16. 8 4. 9 16. 8 7. 0
## Finland     13. 0 0. 4 25. 9 1. 3 7. 4 14. 7 5. 5 24. 3 7. 6
## Greece      41. 4 0. 6 17. 6 0. 6 8. 1 11. 5 2. 4 11. 0 6. 7
## Norway       9. 0 0. 5 22. 4 0. 8 8. 6 16. 9 4. 7 27. 6 9. 4
## Portugal    27. 8 0. 3 24. 5 0. 6 8. 4 13. 3 2. 7 16. 7 5. 7
## Spain       22. 9 0. 8 28. 5 0. 7 11. 5 9. 7 8. 5 11. 8 5. 5
## Sweden       6. 1 0. 4 25. 9 0. 8 7. 2 14. 4 6. 0 32. 4 6. 8
## Switzerland  7. 7 0. 2 37. 8 0. 8 9. 5 17. 5 5. 3 15. 4 5. 7
## Turkey      66. 8 0. 7 7. 9 0. 1 2. 8 5. 2 1. 1 11. 9 3. 2
## Bulgaria    23. 6 1. 9 32. 3 0. 6 7. 9 8. 0 0. 7 18. 2 6. 7
## Czechoslovakia 16. 5 2. 9 35. 5 1. 2 8. 7 9. 2 0. 9 17. 9 7. 0
## E. Germany   4. 2 2. 9 41. 2 1. 3 7. 6 11. 2 1. 2 22. 1 8. 4
## Hungary     21. 7 3. 1 29. 6 1. 9 8. 2 9. 4 0. 9 17. 2 8. 0
## Poland      31. 1 2. 5 25. 7 0. 9 8. 4 7. 5 0. 9 16. 1 6. 9
## Rumania     34. 7 2. 1 30. 1 0. 6 8. 7 5. 9 1. 3 11. 7 5. 0
## USSR        23. 7 1. 4 25. 8 0. 6 9. 2 6. 1 0. 5 23. 6 9. 3
```

```
## Yugoslavia    48. 7 1. 5 16. 8 1. 1 4. 9 6. 4 11. 3 5. 3 4. 0
```

```
dim(Eurojobs) # displays the number of rows and columns
```

```
## [1] 26 9
```

We now have a "clean" dataset of 26 observations and 9 quantitative continuous variables on which we can base the classification. Note that in this case it is not necessary to standardize the data because they are all expressed in the same unit (in percentage). If this was not the case, we would have had to standardize the data via the `scale()` function (do not forget it otherwise your results may be completely different).

The so-called k-means clustering is done via the `kmeans()` function, with the argument centers that corresponds to the number of desired clusters. In the following we apply the classification with 2 classes and then 3 classes as examples.

Kmeans **with 2 Groups**

```
model <- kmeans(Eurojobs, centers = 2)# displays the class determined by
# the model for all observations:
print(model$cluster)##    Belgium    Denmark    France    W. Germany
Ireland
##        1          1          1         1          2
##     Italy   Luxembourg Netherlands United Kingdom     Austria
##        1          1          1         1          1
##     Finland     Greece     Norway    Portugal     Spain
##        1          2          1         2          2
##     Sweden   Switzerland    Turkey    Bulgaria Czechoslovakia
##        1          1         2         2          1
##  E. Germany    Hungary    Poland     Rumania      USSR
##        1          2         2         2          2
##  Yugoslavia
##        2
```

Note that the argument `centers = 2` is used to set the number of clusters, determined in advance. In this exercise the number of clusters has been determined arbitrarily. This number of clusters should be determined according to the context and goal of your analysis, or based on methods. Calling `print (model$cluster)` or `model$cluster` is the same. This output specifies the group (i. e. , 1 or 2) to which each country belongs to.

The cluster for each observation can be stored directly in the dataset as a column:

```
Eurojobs_cluster <- data. frame(Eurojobs,
                cluster = as. factor(model$cluster))
```

```
head(Eurojobs_cluster)##        Agr Min Man PS Con  SI Fin SPS TC cluster
## Belgium   3. 3 0. 9 27. 6 0. 9 8. 2 19. 1 6. 2 26. 6 7. 2    1
## Denmark   9. 2 0. 1 21. 8 0. 6 8. 3 14. 6 6. 5 32. 2 7. 1    1
## France   10. 8 0. 8 27. 5 0. 9 8. 9 16. 8 6. 0 22. 6 5. 7    1
## W. Germany 6. 7 1. 3 35. 8 0. 9 7. 3 14. 4 5. 0 22. 3 6. 1    1
## Ireland  23. 2 1. 0 20. 7 1. 3 7. 5 16. 8 2. 8 20. 8 6. 1    2
## Italy    15. 9 0. 6 27. 6 0. 5 10. 0 18. 1 1. 6 20. 1 5. 7   1
```

Quality of a k-means Partition

The quality of a k-means partition is found by calculating the percentage of the TSS "explained" by the partition using the following formula:

$$\frac{BSS}{TSS} \times 100\%$$

where BSS and TSS stand for Between Sum of Squares and Total Sum of Squares, respectively. The higher the percentage, the better the score (and thus the quality) because it means that BSS is large and/or WSS is small.

Here is how you can check the quality of the partition in R:

```
# BSS and TSS are extracted from the model and stored
(BSS <- model$betweenss)## [1] 4823. 535(TSS <- model$totss)## [1] 9299.
59# We calculate the quality of the partition
BSS TSS * 100## [1] 51. 86826
```

The quality of the partition is 51. 87%. This value has no real interpretation in absolute terms except that a higher quality means a higher explained percentage. However, it is more insightful when it is compared to the quality of other partitions (with the same number of clusters!) in order to determine the best partition among the ones considered.

nstart for Several Initial Centers and Better Stability

The k-means algorithm uses a random set of initial points to arrive at the final classification. Due to the fact that the initial centers are randomly chosen, the same command kmeans(Eurojobs, centers = 2) may give different results every time it is run, and thus slight differences in the quality of the partitions. The nstart argument in the kmeans() function allows to run the algorithm several times with different initial centers, in order to obtain a potentially better partition:

```
model2 <- kmeans(Eurojobs, centers = 2, nstart = 10)
```

```
100 * model2$betweenss model2$totss
```

```
## [1] 54. 2503
```

Depending on the initial random choices, this new partition will be better or not compared to the first one. In our example, the partition is better as the quality increased to 54. 25%.

One of the main limitation often cited regarding k-means is the stability of the results. As the initial centers are randomly chosen, running the same command may yield different results. Adding the `nstart` argument in the `kmeans()` function limits this issue as it will generate several different initializations and take the most optimal one, leading to a better stability of the classification.

`kmeans()` with 3 Groups

We now perform the k-means classification with 3 clusters and compute its quality:

```
model3 <- kmeans(Eurojobs, centers = 3)
BSS3 <- model3$betweenss
TSS3 <- model3$totss
BSS3 TSS3 * 100## [1] 74. 59455
```

It can be seen that the classification into three groups allows for a higher explained percentage and a higher quality. This will always be the case: with more classes, the partition will be finer, and the BSS contribution will be higher. On the other hand, the "model" will be more complex, requiring more classes. In the extreme case where k = n (each observation is a singleton class), we have BSS = TSS, but the partition has lost all interest.

Optimal Number of Clusters

In order to find the optimal number of clusters for a k-means, it is recommended to choose it based on:

- The context of the problem at hand, for instance if you know that there is a specific number of groups in your data (this is option is however subjective).

- The following four approaches:

  - Elbow method (which uses the within cluster sums of squares).

  - Average silhouette method.

  - Gap statistic method.

  - `NbClust()` function.

Elbow Method

The Elbow method looks at the total within-cluster sum of square (WSS) as a function of the number of clusters.

```
# load required packages
library(factoextra)
library(NbClust)# Elbow method
fviz_nbclust(Eurojobs, kmeans, method = "wss") +
  geom_vline(xintercept = 4, linetype = 2) + # add line for better visu-
alisation
  labs(subtitle = "Elbow method") # add subtitle
```

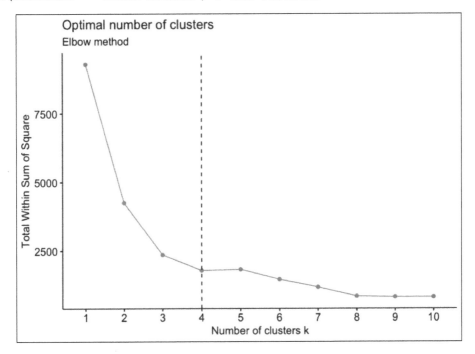

The location of a knee in the plot is usually considered as an indicator of the appropriate number of clusters because it means that adding another cluster does not improve much better the partition. This method seems to suggest 4 clusters. The Elbow method is sometimes ambiguous and an alternative is the average silhouette method.

Silhouette Method

The Silhouette method measures the quality of a clustering and determines how well each point lies within its cluster.

```
#Silhouette method
fviz_nbclust(Eurojobs, kmeans, method = "silhouette") +
  labs(subtitle = "Silhouette method"
```

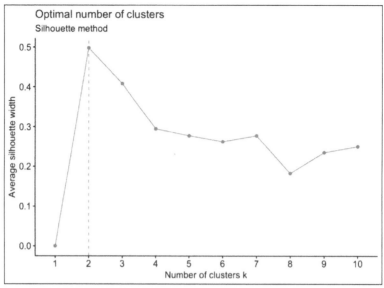

The Silhouette method suggests 2 clusters.

Gap Statistic Method

```
# Gap statistic
set. seed(42)
fviz_nbclust(Eurojobs, kmeans,
nstart = 25,
method = "gap_stat",
nboot = 500
) + # reduce it for lower computation time (but less precise results)
labs(subtitle = "Gap statistic method")
```

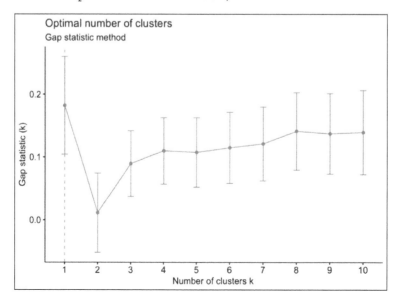

The optimal number of clusters is the one that maximizes the gap statistic. This method suggests only 1 cluster (which is therefore a useless clustering). As you can see these three methods do not necessarily lead to the same result. Here, all 3 approaches suggest a different number of clusters.

```
NbClust()
```

A fourth alternative is to use the NbClust() function, which provides 30 indices for choosing the best number of clusters.

```
nbclust_out <- NbClust(
  data = Eurojobs,
  distance = "euclidean",
  min. nc = 2, # minimum number of clusters
  max. nc = 5, # maximum number of clusters
  method = "kmeans"
) # one of: "ward. D", "ward. D2", "single", "complete", "average",
"mcquitty", "median", "centroid", "kmeans"
```

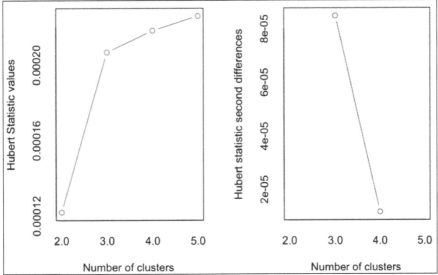

```
## *** The Hubert index is a graphical method of determining the number
of clusters.
##          In the plot of Hubert index, we seek a significant knee that
corresponds to a
##          significant increase of the value of the measure i. e the
significant peak in Hubert
##          index second differences plot.
##
```

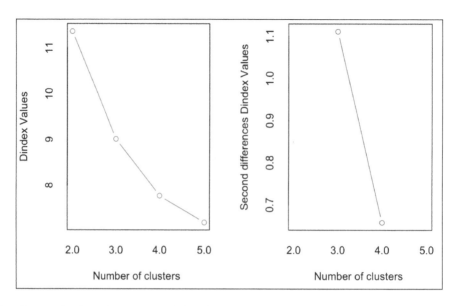

```
## *** The D index is a graphical method of determining the number of
clusters.
##          In the plot of D index, we seek a significant knee (the
significant peak in Dindex
##          second differences plot) that corresponds to a significant
increase of the value of
##          the measure.
##
## ***************************************************************
*
## * Among all indices:
## * 5 proposed 2 as the best number of clusters
## * 16 proposed 3 as the best number of clusters
## * 2 proposed 5 as the best number of clusters
##
##          ***** Conclusion *****
##
## * According to the majority rule, the best number of clusters is 3
##
##
## ***************************************************************
*# create a dataframe of the optimal number of clusters
nbclust_plot <- data. frame(clusters = nbclust_out$Best. nc[1, ])
# select only indices which select between 2 and 5 clusters
nbclust_plot <- subset(nbclust_plot, clusters >= 2 & clusters <= 5)#
create plot
ggplot(nbclust_plot) +
 aes(x = clusters) +
 geom_histogram(bins = 30L, fill = "#0c4c8a") +
 labs(x = "Number of clusters", y = "Frequency among all indices",
title = "Optimal number of clusters") +
 theme_minimal()
```

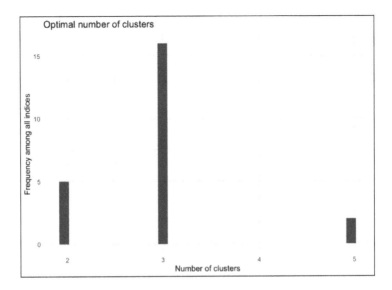

Based on all 30 indices, the best number of clusters is 3 clusters.

Visualizations

It is also possible to plot clusters by using the fviz_cluster() function. Note that a principal component analysis is performed to represent the variables in a 2 dimensions plane.

We visualize the data in 2 clusters, as suggested by the average silhouette method.

```
library(factoextra)

km_res <- kmeans(Eurojobs, centers = 2, nstart = 20)
fviz_cluster(km_res, Eurojobs, ellipse. type = "norm")
```

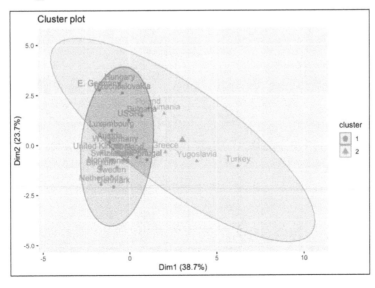

Now that the k-means clustering has been detailed in R, see how to do the algorithm by hand in the following sections.

Manual Application and Verification in R

Perform by hand the k-means algorithm for the points shown in the graph below, with $k = 2$ and with the points $i = 5$ and $i = 6$ as initial centers. Compute the quality of the partition you just found and then check your answers in R.

Assume that the variables have the same units so there is no need to scale the data.

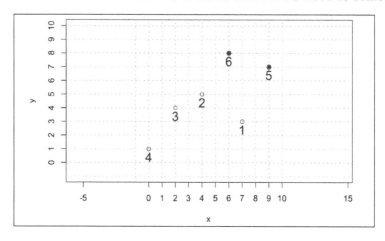

Solution by Hand

Step 1. Here are the coordinates of the 6 points:

point	x	y
1	7	3
2	4	5
3	2	4
4	0	1
5	9	7
6	6	8

And the initial centers:

- Group 1: point 5 with center $(9, 7)$.

- Group 2: point 6 with center $(6, 8)$.

Step 2. Compute the distance matrix point by point with the Pythagorean Theorem. Remind that the distance between point a and point b is found with:

$$\sqrt{(x_a - x_b)^2 + (y_a - y_b)^2}$$

We apply this theorem to each pair of points, to finally have the following distance matrix (rounded to two decimals):

```
round(dist(X), 2) ##       1    2    3    4    5
## 2 3. 61
## 3 5. 10 2. 24
## 4 7. 28 5. 66 3. 61
## 5 4. 47 5. 39 7. 62 10. 82
## 6 5. 10 3. 61 5. 66 9. 22 3. 16
```

Step 3. Based on the distance matrix computed in step 2, we can put each point to its closest group and compute the coordinates of the center.

We first put each point in its closest group:

- Point 1 is closer to point 5 than to point 6 because the distance between points 1 and 5 is 4. 47 while the distance between points 1 and 6 is 5. 10.

- Point 2 is closer to point 6 than to point 5 because the distance between points 2 and 5 is 5. 39 while the distance between points 2 and 6 is 3. 61.

- Point 3 is closer to point 6 than to point 5 because the distance between points 3 and 5 is 7. 62 while the distance between points 3 and 6 is 5. 66.

- Point 4 is closer to point 6 than to point 5 because the distance between points 4 and 5 is 10. 82 while the distance between points 4 and 6 is 9. 22.

Note that computing the distances between each point and the points 5 and 6 is sufficient. There is no need to compute the distance between the points 1 and 2 for example, as we compare each point to the initial centers (which are points 5 and 6).

We then compute the coordinates of the centers of the two groups by taking the mean of the coordinates x and y:

- Group 1 includes the points 5 and 1 with $(8, 5)$ as center: $8 = (9 + 7) 2$ and $5 = (7 + 3)/2$.

- Group 2 includes the points 6, 2, 3 and 4 with $(3, 4. 5)$ as center: $3 = (6 + 4 + 2 + 0) 4$ and $4. 5 = (8 + 5 + 4 + 1) 4$.

We thus have:

	points	center
cluster 1	5 & 1	(8, 5)
cluster 2	6, 2, 3 & 4	(3, 4.5)

Step 4. We make sure that the allocation is optimal by checking that each point is in the nearest cluster. The distance between a point and the center of a cluster is again computed thanks to the Pythagorean theorem. Thus, we have:

points	Distance to cluster 1	Distance to cluster 2
1	2.24	4.27
2	4	1.12
3	6.08	1.12
4	8.94	4.61
5	2.24	6.5
6	3.61	4.61

The minimum distance between the points and the two clusters is colored in green.

We check that each point is in the correct group (i. e. , the closest cluster). According to the distance in the table above, point 6 seems to be closer to the cluster 1 than to the cluster 2. Therefore, the allocation is not optimal and point 6 should be reallocated to cluster 1.

Step 5. We compute again the centers of the clusters after this reallocation. The centers are found by taking the mean of the coordinates x and y of the points belonging to the cluster. We thus have:

	points	center
cluster 1	1, 5 & 6	(7.33, 6)
cluster 2	2, 3 & 4	(2, 3.33)

where, for instance, 3. 33 is simply (5 + 4 + 1) 3.

Step 6. Repeat step 4 until the allocation is optimal. If the allocation is optimal, the algorithm stops. In our example we have:

points	Distance to cluster 1	Distance to cluster 2
1	3.02	5.01
2	3.48	2.61
3	5.69	0.67
4	8.87	3.07
5	1.95	7.9
6	2.4	5.08

All points are correctly allocated to its nearest cluster, so the allocation is optimal and the algorithm stops.

Step 7. State the final partition and the centers. In our example:

	points	center
cluster 1	1, 5 & 6	(7.33, 6)
cluster 2	2, 3 & 4	(2, 3.33)

Now that we have the clusters and the final centers, we compute the quality of the partition we just found. Remember that we need to compute the BSS and TSS to find the quality. Below the steps to compute the quality of this partition by k-means, based on this summary table:

cluster 1			cluster 2		
point	x	y	point	x	y
1	7	3	2	4	5
5	9	7	3	2	4
6	6	8	4	0	1
mean	7.33	6		2	3.33

Step 1. Compute the overall mean of the x and y coordinates:

$$\bar{x} = \frac{7+4+2+0+9+6+3+5+4+1+7+8}{12} = 4.67$$

Step 2. Compute TSS and WSS:

$$TSS = (7-4.67)^2 + (4-4.67)^2 + (2-4.67)^2 + (0-4.67)^2$$

$$+(9-4.67)^2 + (6-4.67)^2 + (3-4.67)^2 + (5-4.67)^2$$

$$+(4-4.67)^2 + (1-4.67)^2 + (7-4.67)^2 + (8-4.67)^2 = 88.67$$

Regarding WSS, it is splitted between cluster 1 and cluster 2.

For cluster 1:

$$WSS[1] = (7-7.33)^2 + (9-7.33)^2 + (6-7.33)^2 + (6-7.33)^2$$

$$+(3-6)^2 + (7-6)^2 + (8-6)^2 = 18.67$$

For cluster 2:

$$WSS[2] = (4-2)^2 + (2-2)^2 + (0-2)^2 + (5-3.33)^2 + (4-3.33)^2 + (1-3.33)^2 = 16.67$$

And the total WSS is:

WSS = WSS[1] + WSS[2] = 18. 67 + 16. 67 = 35. 34

To find the BSS:

BSS = TSS − WSS = 88. 67 − 35. 34 = 53. 33

Finally, the quality of the partition is:

$$Quality = \frac{BSS}{TSS} = \frac{53.33}{88.67} = 0.6014$$

So the quality of the partition is 60. 14%. We are now going to verify all these solutions (the partition, the final centers and the quality) in R.

Solution in R

As you can imagine, the solution in R us much shorter and requires much less computation on the user side. We first need to enter the data as a matrix or dataframe:

```
X <- matrix(c(7, 3, 4, 5, 2, 4, 0, 1, 9, 7, 6, 8),
 nrow = 6, byrow = TRUE
```

```
)
X # display the coordinates of the points##    [,1] [,2]
## [1,]   7   3
## [2,]   4   5
## [3,]   2   4
## [4,]   0   1
## [5,]   9   7
## [6,]   6   8
```

We now perform the k-means via the `kmeans()` function with the point 5 and 6 as initial centers:

```
# take rows 5 and 6 of the X matrix as initial centers
res. k <- kmeans(X, centers = X[c(5, 6), ],
algorithm = "Lloyd")
```

Unlike in the previous application with the dataset `Eurojobs. csv` where the initial centers are randomly chosen by R, in this second application we want to specify which points are going to be the two initial centers. For this, we need to set `centers = X[c(5,6), ]` to indicate that that there are 2 centers, and that they are going to be the points 5 and 6.

The reason for adding the argument `algorithm = "Lloyd"` can be found in the usage of the R function `kmeans()`. In fact, there are several variants of the k-means algorithm. The default choice is the Hartigan and Wong version, which is more sophisticated than the basic version detailed in the solution by hand. By using the original version of Lloyd, we find the same solution in R and by hand. For more information, you can consult the documentation of the `kmeans()` function.

The solution in R is then found by extracting

- The partition with `$cluster`:

```
res. k$cluster
```

```
## [1] 1 2 2 2 1 1
```

Points 1, 5 and 6 belong to cluster 1, points 2, 3 and 4 belong to cluster 2.

- The coordinates of the final centers with `$centers`:

```
# We extract the coordinates of the 2 final centers, rounded to 2
decimals
round(res. k$centers, digits = 2)##   [,1] [,2]
## 1 7. 33 6. 00
## 2 2. 00 3. 33
```

- And then the quality of the partition by dividing the BSS to the TSS:

```
res. k$betweenss res. k$totss
```

```
## [1] 0. 6015038
```

The 3 results are equal to what we found by hand (except the quality which is slightly different due to rounding).

Cluster Validation

The term cluster validation is used to design the procedure of evaluating the goodness of clustering algorithm results. This is important to avoid finding patterns in a random data, as well as, in the situation where you want to compare two clustering algorithms.

Generally, clustering validation statistics can be categorized into 3 classes:

- Internal cluster validation, which uses the internal information of the clustering process to evaluate the goodness of a clustering structure without reference to external information. It can be also used for estimating the number of clusters and the appropriate clustering algorithm without any external data.

- External cluster validation, which consists in comparing the results of a cluster analysis to an externally known result, such as externally provided class labels. It measures the extent to which cluster labels match externally supplied class labels. Since we know the "true" cluster number in advance, this approach is mainly used for selecting the right clustering algorithm for a specific data set.

- Relative cluster validation, which evaluates the clustering structure by varying different parameter values for the same algorithm (e. g: varying the number of clusters k). It's generally used for determining the optimal number of clusters.

Internal Measures for Cluster Validation

Recall that the goal of partitioning clustering algorithms is to split the data set into clusters of objects, such that:

- The objects in the same cluster are similar as much as possible.

- The objects in different clusters are highly distinct.

That is, we want the average distance within cluster to be as small as possible; and the average distance between clusters to be as large as possible. Internal validation measures reflect often the compactness, the connectedness and the separation of the cluster partitions.

- Compactness or cluster cohesion: Measures how close are the objects within the same cluster. A lower within-cluster variation is an indicator of a good compactness (i. e., a good clustering). The different indices for evaluating the compactness of clusters are base on distance measures such as the cluster-wise within average/median distances between observations.

- Separation: Measures how well-separated a cluster is from other clusters. The indices used as separation measures include:

  ◦ Distances between cluster centers.

  ◦ The pairwise minimum distances between objects in different clusters.

- Connectivity: corresponds to what extent items are placed in the same cluster as their nearest neighbors in the data space. The connectivity has a value between 0 and infinity and should be minimized.

Generally most of the indices used for internal clustering validation combine compactness and separation measures as follow:

$$\text{Index} = \frac{(\alpha \times \text{Separation})}{(\beta \times \text{Compactness})}$$

Where α and β are weights.

Silhouette Coefficient

The silhouette analysis measures how well an observation is clustered and it estimates the average distance between clusters. The silhouette plot displays a measure of how close each point in one cluster is to points in the neighboring clusters.

For each observation i, the silhouette width s_i is calculated as follows:

- For each observation i, calculate the average dissimilarity a_i between i and all other points of the cluster to which i belongs.

- For all other clusters C, to which i does not belong, calculate the average dissimilarity d(i,C) of i to all observations of C. The smallest of these d(i,C) is defined as $b_i = \min_C d(i,C)$. The value of b_i can be seen as the dissimilarity between i and its "neighbor" cluster, i. e. , the nearest one to which it does not belong.

- Finally the silhouette width of the observation i is defined by the formula: $S_i = (b_i - a_i)/\max(a_i, b_i)$.

Silhouette width can be interpreted as follow:

- Observations with a large S_i (almost 1) are very well clustered.

- A small S_i (around 0) means that the observation lies between two clusters.

- Observations with a negative S_i are probably placed in the wrong cluster.

Dunn Index

The Dunn index is another internal clustering validation measure which can be computed as follow:

- For each cluster, compute the distance between each of the objects in the cluster and the objects in the other clusters.

- Use the minimum of this pairwise distance as the inter-cluster separation (min. separation).

- For each cluster, compute the distance between the objects in the same cluster.

- Use the maximal intra-cluster distance (i. e maximum diameter) as the intra-cluster compactness.

- Calculate the Dunn index (D) as follow:

$$D = \frac{\text{min.separation}}{\text{max.diameter}}$$

If the data set contains compact and well-separated clusters, the diameter of the clusters is expected to be small and the distance between the clusters is expected to be large. Thus, Dunn index should be maximized.

External Measures for Clustering Validation

The aim is to compare the identified clusters (by k-means, pam or hierarchical clustering) to an external reference.

It's possible to quantify the agreement between partitioning clusters and external reference using either the corrected Rand index or Meila's variation index VI, which are implemented in the R function cluster. stats()[fpc package]. The corrected Rand index varies from -1 (no agreement) to 1 (perfect agreement). External clustering validation, can be used to select suitable clustering algorithm for a given data set.

Dimensional Reductions for Machine Learning

Dimensionality reduction is the process through which the number of input variables in a dataset is reduced while still retaining the meaningful properties of the original data. Feature selection, feature reduction, principal component analysis, Fisher linear discriminant analysis, generalized discriminant analysis, singular value decomposition, etc. are a few concepts which are elaborated in this chapter for a better understanding.

Dimensional Reduction

In any machine learning problem, if the number of observables or features is increased then it takes more time to compute, more memory to store inputs and intermediate results and more importantly much more data samples are needed for the learning. From a theoretical point of view, increasing the number of features should lead to better performance. However in practice, the inclusion of more features leads to a decrease in performance. This aspect is called the curse of dimensionality and is basically because the number of training examples required increases exponentially as dimensionality increases. A lot of machine learning methods have at least $O(nd^2)$ complexity where n is the number of samples and d is the dimensionality. A typical example is the need to estimate covariance matrix for which as d becomes large the number of samples is of the $O(nd^2)$ which involves huge computations. In other words if the number of features that is dimension d is large, the number of samples n, may be too small for accurate parameter estimation.

For example, the covariance matrix has d^2 parameters.

$$\Sigma = \begin{bmatrix} \sigma_1^2 & \cdots & \sigma_{1d} \\ \vdots & \ddots & \vdots \\ \sigma_{d1} & \cdots & \sigma_d^2 \end{bmatrix}$$

Covariance Matrix.

If the model parameters are high then there will be over fitting. An interesting paradox is that if n < d^2 we are better off assuming that features are uncorrelated, even if we know this assumption is wrong. We are likely to avoid over fitting because we fit a model with less parameters.

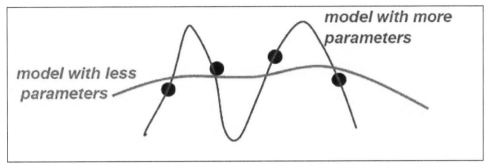

Model with More and Less Number of Parameters.

Suppose we want to use the nearest neighbor approach with k = 1 (1NN). Suppose we start with only one feature, this feature is not discriminative, i.e. it does not separate the classes well.

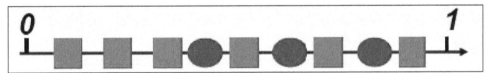

NN with only One Feature.

Now we decide to use 2 features. For the 1NN method to work well we need a lot of samples, i.e. samples have to be dense. To maintain the same density as in 1D (9 samples per unit length), how many samples do we need? As we discussed we need 9^2 samples to maintain the same density as in 1D. Of course, when we go from 1 feature to 2, no one gives us more samples, we still have 9. This is way too sparse for 1NN to work well.

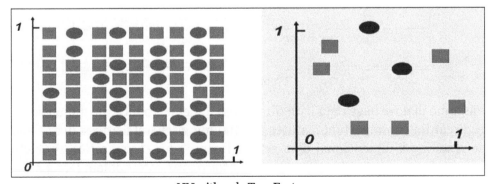

NN with only Two Features.

Things are even more of a problem when we decide to use 3 features. If 9 were dense enough in 1D, in 3D we need 9^3=729 samples. In general, if n samples are dense enough in 1D - Then in d dimensions we need n^d samples.

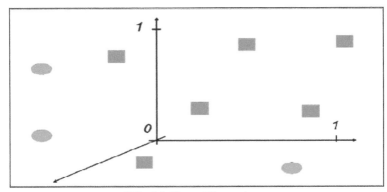

NN with Three Dimensions.

Dimensionality Reduction

Some features (dimensions) bear little useful information, which essentially means that we can drop some features. In dimensionality reduction high-dimensional points are projected to a low dimensional space while preserving the "essence" of the data. In projecting from a higher dimensional space to a lower dimensional space the distances are preserved as well as possible. After this projection the learning problems are solved in low dimensions.

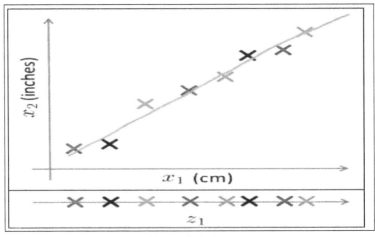

From 2D to 1D.

Let us assume that we have data with dimension d. Let us reduce the dimensionality to k<d by discarding unimportant features or combining several features in one and then use the resulting k-dimensional data set for learning for classification problem (e.g. parameters of probabilities P(x|C) or learning for regression problem (e.g. parameters for model y=g(x|Thetha)).

For a fixed number of samples, as we add features, the graph of classification error is shown in Figure below. We see that there exist an optimal number of features which results in minimum classification error.

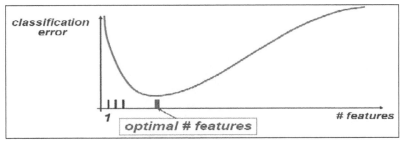

Optimal Number of Features for Classification.

Thus for each fixed sample size **n**, there is an optimal number of features that we should use. In dimensionality reduction we strive to find that set of features that are effective.

Why Dimensionality Reduction?

Why do we need to carry out dimensionality reduction? Essentially it reduces time complexity since there will be less computation and therefore more efficient learning. It also reduces space complexity since there is less number of parameters resulting in more efficient storage. Moreover simpler models are more robust on small datasets since complex models may result in over fitting especially in the case of smaller datasets. The dimensionality reduction helps in data visualization (structure, groups, outliers, etc. specifically when reduction is to 2 or 3 dimensions. Most machine learning and data mining techniques may not be effective for high dimensional data since the intrinsic dimension (that is the actual features that decide the classification) may be small, for example the number of genes actually responsible for a disease may be small but the dataset may contain a large number of other genes as features. The dimension-reduced data can be used for visualizing, exploring and understanding the data. In addition cleaning the data will allow simpler models to be built later.

The Process of Dimensionality Reduction

The process of reducing the number of random variables (features) used to represent the samples under consideration can be carried out by combining, transforming or selecting features. We have to estimate which features can be removed from the data. Several features can be combined together without loss or even with gain of information (e.g. income of all family members for loan application), however we need to estimate which features to combine from the data.

The simplest way to carry out dimensionality reduction is to keep just one variable and discard all others. However this is too simplistic and not reasonable. Another simple way is to weigh all variables equally but again this is not reasonable unless all variables have the same variance. Another method is to weigh the features based on some criteria and find the weighted average. However the issue is the choice of the criterion. The basic issues for dimensionality reduction are two fold namely how do we represent the data, whether we use vector space and what is the criteria to be used in carrying out the reduction process. Dimensionality can be reduced basically using two methods: feature reduction and feature selection.

Criterion for Reduction

There are many criteria that can be used for dimensionality reduction. These include criteria that are mainly geometric based and information theory based. These criteria need to capture the variation in data since these variations are "signals" or information contained in the data. We need to normalize each variable first and then discover variables or dimensions that are highly correlated or dependent. When variables are highly related they can be combined to form a simpler representation.

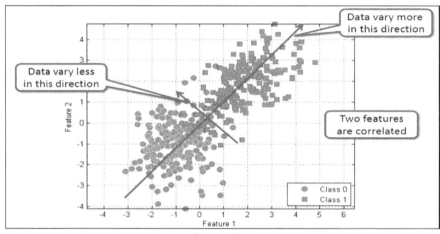

Dependency of Features.

Feature Selection

Feature selection is the process of reducing the number of input variables when developing a predictive model. It is desirable to reduce the number of input variables to both reduce the computational cost of modeling and, in some cases, to improve the performance of the model.

When building a machine learning model in real-life, it's almost rare that all the variables in the dataset are useful to build a model. Adding redundant variables reduces the generalization capability of the model and may also reduce the overall accuracy of a classifier. Furthermore adding more and more variables to a model increases the overall complexity of the model.

As per the Law of Parsimony of 'Occam's Razor', the best explanation to a problem is that which involves the fewest possible assumptions. Thus, feature selection becomes an indispensable part of building machine learning models.

Goal

The goal of feature selection in machine learning is to find the best set of features that allows one to build useful models of studied phenomena. The techniques for feature selection in machine learning can be broadly classified into the following categories:

- Supervised Techniques: These techniques can be used for labeled data, and are used to identify the relevant features for increasing the efficiency of supervised models like classification and regression.

- Unsupervised Techniques: These techniques can be used for unlabeled data.

From a taxonomic point of view, these techniques are classified as under:

- Filter methods,

- Wrapper methods,

- Embedded methods,

- Hybrid methods.

Filter Methods

Filter methods pick up the intrinsic properties of the features measured via univariate statistics instead of cross-validation performance. These methods are faster and less computationally expensive than wrapper methods. When dealing with high-dimensional data, it is computationally cheaper to use filter methods. Let's, discuss some of these techniques:

Information Gain

```
1  from sklearn.feature_selection import mutual_info_classif
2  import matplotlib.pyplot as plt
3  %matplotlib inline
4
5  importances = mutual_info_classif(X, Y)
6  feat_importances = pd.Series(importances, dataframe.columns[0:len(dataframe.columns)-1])
7  feat_importances.plot(kind='barh', color = 'teal')
8  plt.show()
```

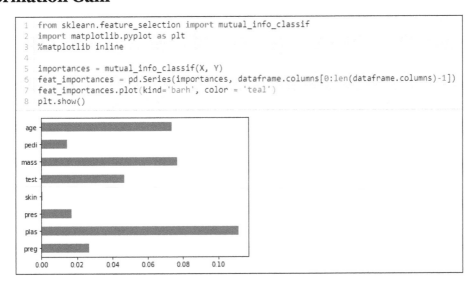

Information gain calculates the reduction in entropy from the transformation of a dataset. It can be used for feature selection by evaluating the Information gain of each variable in the context of the target variable.

Chi-square Test

The Chi-square test is used for categorical features in a dataset. We calculate Chi-square between each feature and the target and select the desired number of features with the best Chi-square scores. In order to correctly apply the chi-squared in order to test the relation between various features in the dataset and the target variable, the following conditions have to be met: the variables have to be categorical, sampled independently and values should have an expected frequency greater than 5.

```
1   from sklearn.feature_selection import SelectKBest
2   from sklearn.feature_selection import chi2
3
4   # Convert to categorical data by converting data to integers
5   X_cat = X.astype(int)
6
7   # Three features with highest chi-squared statistics are selected
8   chi2_features = SelectKBest(chi2, k = 3)
9   X_kbest_features = chi2_features.fit_transform(X_cat, Y)
10
11  # Reduced features
12  print('Original feature number:', X_cat.shape[1])
13  print('Reduced feature number:', X_kbest_features.shape[1])

Original feature number: 8
Reduced feature number: 3
```

Fisher's Score

Fisher score is one of the most widely used supervised feature selection methods. The algorithm which we will use returns the ranks of the variables based on the fisher's score in descending order. We can then select the variables as per the case.

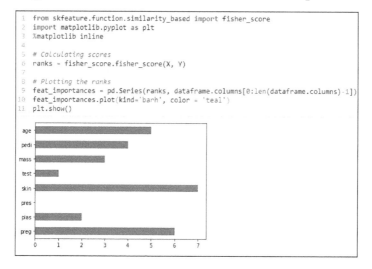

Correlation Coefficient

Correlation is a measure of the linear relationship of 2 or more variables. Through correlation, we can predict one variable from the other. The logic behind using correlation for feature selection is that the good variables are highly correlated with the target. Furthermore, variables should be correlated with the target but should be uncorrelated among them.

If two variables are correlated, we can predict one from the other. Therefore, if two features are correlated, the model only really needs one of them, as the second one does not add additional information. We will use the Pearson Correlation here.

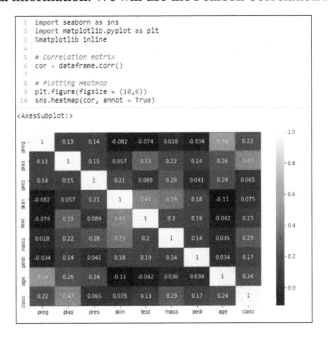

```
 1   import seaborn as sns
 2   import matplotlib.pyplot as plt
 3   %matplotlib inline
 4
 5   # Correlation matrix
 6   cor = dataframe.corr()
 7
 8   # Plotting Heatmap
 9   plt.figure(figsize = (10,6))
10   sns.heatmap(cor, annot = True)
```

We need to set an absolute value, say 0.5 as the threshold for selecting the variables. If we find that the predictor variables are correlated among themselves, we can drop the variable which has a lower correlation coefficient value with the target variable. We can also compute multiple correlation coefficients to check whether more than two variables are correlated to each other. This phenomenon is known as multicollinearity.

Variance Threshold

The variance threshold is a simple baseline approach to feature selection. It removes all features which variance doesn't meet some threshold. By default, it removes all zero-variance features, i.e., features that have the same value in all samples. We assume that features with a higher variance may contain more useful information, but note that we are not taking the relationship between feature variables or feature and target variables into account, which is one of the drawbacks of filter methods.

```
1  from sklearn.feature_selection import VarianceThreshold
2
3  # Resetting the value of X to make it non-categorical
4  X = array[:,0:8]
5
6  v_threshold = VarianceThreshold(threshold=0)
7  v_threshold.fit(X)  # fit finds the features with zero variance
8  v_threshold.get_support()

array([ True,   True,   True,   True,   True,   True,   True,   True])
```

The get_support returns a Boolean vector where True means that the variable does not have zero variance.

Mean Absolute Difference (MAD)

'The mean absolute difference (MAD) computes the absolute difference from the mean value. The main difference between the variance and MAD measures is the absence of the square in the latter. The MAD, like the variance, is also a scale variant.' This means that higher the MAD, higher the discriminatory power.

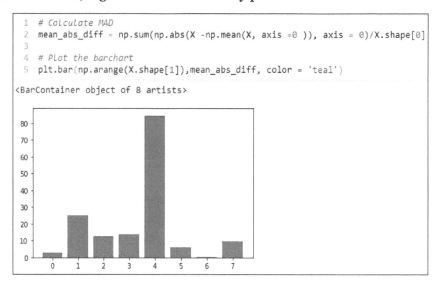

```
1  # Calculate MAD
2  mean_abs_diff = np.sum(np.abs(X -np.mean(X, axis =0 )), axis = 0)/X.shape[0]
3
4  # Plot the barchart
5  plt.bar(np.arange(X.shape[1]),mean_abs_diff, color = 'teal')

<BarContainer object of 8 artists>
```

Dispersion Ratio

'Another measure of dispersion applies the arithmetic mean (AM) and the geometric mean (GM). For a given (positive) feature X_i on n patterns, the AM and GM are given by,

$$\mathbf{AM_i} = \overline{\mathbf{X_i}} = \frac{1}{n}\sum\nolimits_{j=1}^{n} \mathbf{X_{ij}}, \qquad \mathbf{GM_i} = \left(\prod\nolimits_{j=1}^{n} \mathbf{X_{ij}} \right)^{\frac{1}{n}},$$

respectively; since $\mathbf{AM}_i \geq \mathbf{GM}_i$, with equality holding if and only if $\mathbf{X}_{i1} = \mathbf{X}_{i2} = ... = \mathbf{X}_{in}$, then the ratio,

$$\mathbf{RM}_i = \frac{\mathbf{AM}_i}{\mathbf{GM}_i} \in [1, +\infty),$$

can be used as a dispersion measure. Higher dispersion implies a higher value of Ri, thus a more relevant feature. Conversely, when all the feature samples have (roughly) the same value, Ri is close to 1, indicating a low relevance feature.'

```
1  X = X+1 # To avoid 0 for denominator
2  # Arithmetic Mean
3  am = np.mean(X, axis =0 )
4  #Geometric Mean
5  gm = np.power(np.prod(X, axis =0 ),1/X.shape[0])
6  # Ratio of Arithmetic Mean and Geometric Mean
7  disp_ratio = am/gm
8  # Plotting the bar chart
9  plt.bar(np.arange(X.shape[1]),disp_ratio, color = 'teal')
```

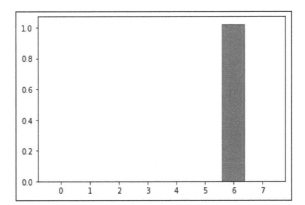

Wrapper Methods

Wrappers require some method to search the space of all possible subsets of features, assessing their quality by learning and evaluating a classifier with that feature subset. The feature selection process is based on a specific machine learning algorithm that we are trying to fit on a given dataset. It follows a greedy search approach by evaluating all the possible combinations of features against the evaluation criterion. The wrapper methods usually result in better predictive accuracy than filter methods. Let's, discuss some of these techniques:

Forward Feature Selection

This is an iterative method wherein we start with the best performing variable against the target. Next, we select another variable that gives the best performance in combination with the first selected variable. This process continues until the preset criterion is achieved.

```
1  # Forward Feature Selection
2  from mlxtend.feature_selection import SequentialFeatureSelector
3  ffs = SequentialFeatureSelector(lr, k_features='best', forward = True, n_jobs=-1)
4  ffs.fit(X, Y)
5  features = list(ffs.k_feature_names_)
6  features = list(map(int, features))
7  lr.fit(x_train[features], y_train)
8  y_pred = lr.predict(x_train[features])
```

Backward Feature Elimination

This method works exactly opposite to the Forward Feature Selection method. Here, we start with all the features available and build a model. Next, we the variable from the model which gives the best evaluation measure value. This process is continued until the preset criterion is achieved.

```
1  # Backward Feature Selection
2  from sklearn.linear_model import LogisticRegression
3  from mlxtend.feature_selection import SequentialFeatureSelector
4  lr = LogisticRegression(class_weight = 'balanced', solver = 'lbfgs', random_state=42, n_jobs=-1, max_iter=500)
5  lr.fit(X, Y)
6  bfs = SequentialFeatureSelector(lr, k_features='best', forward = False, n_jobs=-1)
7  bfs.fit(X, Y)
8  features = list(bfs.k_feature_names_)
9  features = list(map(int, features))
10 lr.fit(x_train[features], y_train)
11 y_pred = lr.predict(x_train[features])
```

This method is also known as the Sequential Feature Selection method.

Exhaustive Feature Selection

```
1  # Exhaustive Feature Selection
2  from mlxtend.feature_selection import ExhaustiveFeatureSelector
3
4  # import the algorithm you want to evaluate on your features.
5  from sklearn.ensemble import RandomForestClassifier
6
7  # create the ExhaustiveFeatureSelector object.
8  efs = ExhaustiveFeatureSelector(RandomForestClassifier(),
9              min_features=4,
10             max_features=8,
11             scoring='roc_auc',
12             cv=2)
13
14 # fit the object to the training data.
15 efs = efs.fit(X, Y)
16
17 # print the selected features.
18 selected_features = x_train.columns[list(efs.best_idx_)]
19 print(selected_features)
20
21 # print the final prediction score.
22 print(efs.best_score_)

Features: 163/163

Int64Index([0, 1, 2, 3, 4, 5, 6, 7], dtype='int64')
0.8252014925373135
```

This is the most robust feature selection method covered so far. This is a brute-force evaluation of each feature subset. This means that it tries every possible combination of the variables and returns the best performing subset.

Recursive Feature Elimination

'Given an external estimator that assigns weights to features (e.g., the coefficients of a linear model), the goal of recursive feature elimination (RFE) is to select features by recursively considering smaller and smaller sets of features. First, the estimator is trained on the initial set of features and the importance of each feature is obtained either through a coef_ attribute or through a feature_importances_ attribute.

Then, the least important features are pruned from the current set of features. That procedure is recursively repeated on the pruned set until the desired number of features to select is eventually reached.'

```
1  # Recursive Feature Selection
2  from sklearn.feature_selection import RFE
3  rfe = RFE(lr, n_features_to_select=7)
4  rfe.fit(x_train, y_train)
5  y_pred = rfe.predict(x_train)
```

Embedded Methods

These methods encompass the benefits of both the wrapper and filter methods, by including interactions of features but also maintaining reasonable computational cost. Embedded methods are iterative in the sense that takes care of each iteration of the model training process and carefully extracts those features which contribute the most to the training for a particular iteration.

LASSO Regularization (L1)

```
1   from sklearn.linear_model import LogisticRegression
2   from sklearn.feature_selection import SelectFromModel
3
4   # Set the regularization parameter C=1
5   logistic = LogisticRegression(C=1, penalty="l1", solver='liblinear', random_state=7).fit(X, Y)
6   model = SelectFromModel(logistic, prefit=True)
7
8   X_new = model.transform(X)
9
10  # Dropped columns have values of all 0s, keep other columns
11  selected_columns = selected_features.columns[selected_features.var() != 0]
12  selected_columns

Int64Index([0, 1, 2, 3, 4, 5, 6, 7], dtype='int64')
```

Regularization consists of adding a penalty to the different parameters of the machine learning model to reduce the freedom of the model, i.e. to avoid over-fitting. In linear model regularization, the penalty is applied over the coefficients that multiply each of the predictors. From the different types of regularization, Lasso or L1 has the property that is able to shrink some of the coefficients to zero. Therefore, that feature can be removed from the model.

Random Forest Importance

Random Forests is a kind of a Bagging Algorithm that aggregates a specified number of decision trees. The tree-based strategies used by random forests naturally rank by how well they improve the purity of the node, or in other words a decrease in the impurity (Gini impurity) over all trees. Nodes with the greatest decrease in impurity happen at the start of the trees, while notes with the least decrease in impurity occur at the end of trees. Thus, by pruning trees below a particular node, we can create a subset of the most important features.

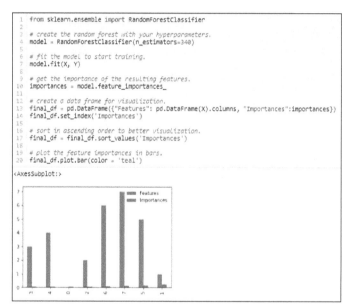

```python
from sklearn.ensemble import RandomForestClassifier

# create the random forest with your hyperparameters.
model = RandomForestClassifier(n_estimators=340)

# fit the model to start training.
model.fit(X, Y)

# get the importance of the resulting features.
importances = model.feature_importances_

# create a data frame for visualization.
final_df = pd.DataFrame({"Features": pd.DataFrame(X).columns, "Importances":importances})
final_df.set_index('Importances')

# sort in ascending order to better visualization.
final_df = final_df.sort_values('Importances')

# plot the feature importances in bars.
final_df.plot.bar(color = 'teal')
```

Principal Component Analysis

Large datasets are increasingly widespread in many disciplines. In order to interpret such datasets, methods are required to drastically reduce their dimensionality in an interpretable way, such that most of the information in the data is preserved. Many techniques have been developed for this purpose, but principal component analysis (PCA) is one of the oldest and most widely used. Its idea is simple—reduce the dimensionality of a dataset, while preserving as much 'variability' (i.e. statistical information) as possible.

Although it is used, and has sometimes been reinvented, in many different disciplines it is, at heart, a statistical technique and hence much of its development has been by statisticians.

This means that 'preserving as much variability as possible' translates into finding new variables that are linear functions of those in the original dataset, that successively maximize variance and that are uncorrelated with each other. Finding such new variables, the principal components (PCs), reduces to solving an eigenvalue/eigenvector problem. The earliest literature on PCA dates from Pearson and Hotelling, but it was not until electronic computers became widely available decades later that it was computationally feasible to use it on datasets that were not trivially small. Since then its use has burgeoned and a large number of variants have been developed in many different disciplines. Substantial books have been written on the subject and there are even whole books on variants of PCA for special types of data. The formal definition of PCA will be given, in a standard context, together with a derivation showing that it can be obtained as the solution to an eigenproblem or, alternatively, from the singular value decomposition (SVD) of the (centred) data matrix. PCA can be based on either the covariance matrix or the correlation matrix. In either case, the new variables (the PCs) depend on the dataset, rather than being pre-defined basis functions, and so are adaptive in the broad sense. The main uses of PCA are descriptive, rather than inferential; an example will illustrate this.

Principal Component Analysis as an Exploratory Tool for Data Analysis

The standard context for PCA as an exploratory data analysis tool involves a dataset with observations on pnumerical variables, for each of n entities or individuals. These data values define pn-dimensional vectors $x_1,...,x_p$ or, equivalently, an n×p data matrix X, whose jth column is the vector x_j of observations on the jth variable. We seek a linear combination of the columns of matrix X with maximum variance. Such linear combinations are given by $\sum_{j=1}^{p} a_j x_j = X_a$, where a is a vector of constants $a_1, a_2,...,a_p$. The variance of any such linear combination is given by var(Xa)=a'Sa, where S is the sample covariance matrix associated with the dataset and ' denotes transpose. Hence, identifying the linear combination with maximum variance is equivalent to obtaining a p-dimensional vector a which maximizes the quadratic form a'Sa. For this problem to have a well-defined solution, an additional restriction must be imposed and the most common restriction involves working with unit-norm vectors, i.e. requiring a'a=1. The problem is equivalent to maximizing a'Sa−λ(a'a−1), where λ is a Lagrange multiplier. Differentiating with respect to the vector a, and equating to the null vector, produces the equation,

$$S_a - \lambda a = 0 \Leftrightarrow S_a = \lambda a.$$

Thus, a must be a (unit-norm) eigenvector, and λ the corresponding eigenvalue, of the covariance matrix S. In particular, we are interested in the largest eigenvalue, λ_1

(and corresponding eigenvector a_1), since the eigenvalues are the variances of the linear combinations defined by the corresponding eigenvector a: var(Xa)=a'Sa=λa'a=λ. Equation above remains valid if the eigenvectors are multiplied by −1, and so the signs of all loadings (and scores) are arbitrary and only their relative magnitudes and sign patterns are meaningful.

Any p×p real symmetric matrix, such as a covariance matrix S, has exactly p real eigenvalues, λ_k (k=1,...,p), and their corresponding eigenvectors can be defined to form an orthonormal set of vectors, i.e. $a'_k a_k'$=1 if k=k' and zero otherwise. A Lagrange multipliers approach, with the added restrictions of orthogonality of different coefficient vectors, can also be used to show that the full set of eigenvectors of S are the solutions to the problem of obtaining up to p new linear combinations $Xa_k = \sum_{j=1}^{p} a_{jk} x_j$, which successively maximize variance, subject to uncorrelatedness with previous linear combinations. Uncorrelatedness results from the fact that the covariance between two such linear combinations, Xa_k and $Xa_{k'}$, is given by $a'_k Sa_k = \lambda_k a'_{k'} a_k$=0 if k'≠k.

It is these linear combinations Xa_k that are called the principal components of the dataset, although some authors confusingly also use the term 'principal components' when referring to the eigenvectors a_k. In standard PCA terminology, the elements of the eigenvectors a_k are commonly called the PC loadings, whereas the elements of the linear combinations Xa_k are called the PC scores, as they are the values that each individual would score on a given PC.

It is common, in the standard approach, to define PCs as the linear combinations of the centred variables x*j, with generic element $x_{ij}^* = x_{ij} - \bar{x}_j$, where $\bar{x}_j$ denotes the mean value of the observations on variable j. This convention does not change the solution (other than centring), since the covariance matrix of a set of centred or uncentred variables is the same, but it has the advantage of providing a direct connection to an alternative, more geometric approach to PCA.

Denoting by X* the n×p matrix whose columns are the centred variables x*$_j$, we have

$$(n-1)S = X^{*'}X^*.$$

Equation above links up the eigen decomposition of the covariance matrix S with the singular value decomposition of the column-centred data matrix X*. Any arbitrary matrix Y of dimension n×p and rank r (necessarily, $r \leq \min\{n, p\}$) can be written as,

$$Y = ULA',$$

where U, A are n×r and p×r matrices with orthonormal columns (U'U=Ir=A'A, with I_r the r×r identity matrix) and L is an r×r diagonal matrix. The columns of A are called the right singular vectors of Y and are the eigenvectors of the p×p matrix Y'Y associated with its non-zero eigenvalues. The columns of U are called the left singular vectors of Y and are the eigenvectors of the $n \times n$ matrix YY' that correspond to its non-zero eigenvalues. The diagonal elements of matrix L are called the singular values of Y and are the non-negative square roots of the (common) non-zero eigenvalues of both matrix Y'Y and matrix YY'. We assume that the diagonal elements of L are in decreasing order, and this uniquely defines the order of the columns of U and A (except for the case of equal singular values). Hence, taking Y=X*, the right singular vectors of the column-centred data matrix X* are the vectors ak of PC loadings. Due to the orthogonality of the columns of A, the columns of the matrix product X*A=ULA'A=UL are the PCs of X*. The variances of these PCs are given by the squares of the singular values of X*, divided by n^{-1}. Equivalently, and given equation $(n-1)S = X^{*'}X^{*}$ and the above properties,

$$(n-1)S = X^{*'}X^{*} = (ULA')(ULA') = ALU'ULA' = AL^{2}A'.$$

where L^{2} is the diagonal matrix with the squared singular values (i.e. the eigenvalues of (n−1)S). Equation above gives the spectral decomposition, or eigendecomposition, of matrix (n−1)S. Hence, PCA is equivalent to an SVD of the column-centred data matrix X*.

The properties of an SVD imply interesting geometric interpretations of a PCA. Given any rank r matrix Y of size $n \times p$, the matrix Yq of the same size, but of rank q<r, whose elements minimize the sum of squared differences with corresponding elements of Y is given by,

$$Y_{q} = U_{q}L_{q}A_{q}'$$

where L_{q} is the q×q diagonal matrix with the first (largest) q diagonal elements of L and U_{q}, A_{q} are the n×q and p×q matrices obtained by retaining the q corresponding columns in U and A.

In our context, the n rows of a rank r column centred data matrix X* define a scatterplot of n points in an r-dimensional subspace- $\mathbb{R}^{p}$, with the origin as the centre of gravity of the scatterplot. The above result implies that the 'best' n-point approximation to this scatterplot, in a q-dimensional subspace, is given by the rows of X*q, defined as in equation above, where 'best' means that the sum of squared distances between corresponding points in each scatterplot is minimized, as in the original approach by Pearson. The system of q axes in this representation is given by the first q PCs and defines a principal subspace. Hence, PCA is at heart a dimensionality-reduction method, whereby a set of p original variables can be replaced by an optimal set of q derived variables, the PCs. When q=2 or q=3, a graphical approximation of the n-point scatterplot is possible and is frequently used for an initial visual representation of the full dataset. It is important to note that this result is incremental (hence adaptive) in its dimensions, in the sense that the best subspace of dimension q+1 is obtained by adding a further column of coordinates to those that defined the best q-dimensional solution.

The quality of any q-dimensional approximation can be measured by the variability associated with the set of retained PCs. In fact, the sum of variances of the p original variables is the trace (sum of diagonal elements) of the covariance matrix $\mathbf{S}$. Using simple matrix theory results it is straightforward to show that this value is also the sum of the variances of all p PCs. Hence, the standard measure of quality of a given PC is the proportion of total variance that it accounts for,

$$\pi_j = \frac{\lambda_j}{\sum_{j=1}^{p} \lambda_j} = \frac{\lambda_j}{tr(\mathbf{S})},$$

where tr($\mathbf{S}$) denotes the trace of $\mathbf{S}$. The incremental nature of PCs also means that we can speak of a proportion of total variance explained by a set S of PCs (usually, but not necessarily, the first q PCs), which is often expressed as a percentage of total variance accounted for:

$$\sum_{j \in S} \pi_j \times 100\%.$$

It is common practice to use some predefined percentage of total variance explained to decide how many PCs should be retained (70% of total variability is a common, if subjective, cut-off point), although the requirements of graphical representation often lead to the use of just the first two or three PCs. Even in such situations, the percentage of total variance accounted for is a fundamental tool to assess the quality of these low-dimensional graphical representations of the dataset. The emphasis in PCA is almost always on the first few PCs, but there are circumstances in which the last few may be of interest, such as in outlier detection or some applications of image analysis.

Example: Fossil teeth data.

Kuehneotherium is one of the earliest mammals and remains have been found during quarrying of limestone in South Wales, UK. The bones and teeth were washed into fissures in the rock, about 200 million years ago, and all the lower molar teeth used in this analysis are from a single fissure. However, it looked possible that there were teeth from more than one species of Kuehneotherium in the sample.

Of the nine variables, three measure aspects of the length of a tooth, while the other six are measurements related to height and width. A PCA was performed using the prcomp command of the R statistical software. The first two PCs account for 78.8% and 16.7%, respectively, of the total variation in the dataset, so the two-dimensional scatter-plot of the 88 teeth given by figure below is a very good approximation to the original scatter-plot in nine-dimensional space. It is, by definition, the best variance-preserving two-dimensional plot of the data, representing over 95% of total variation. All of the loadings in the first PC have the same sign, so it is a weighted average of all variables, representing 'overall size'. In figure below, large teeth are on the left and small teeth on the right. The second PC has negative loadings for the three length variables and positive loadings for the other six variables, representing an aspect of the 'shape' of teeth. Fossils near the top of figure below have smaller lengths, relative to their heights and widths, than those towards the bottom. The relatively compact cluster of points in the bottom half of figure is thought to correspond to a species of Kuehneotherium, while the broader group at the top cannot be assigned to Kuehneotherium, but to some related, but as yet unidentified, animal.

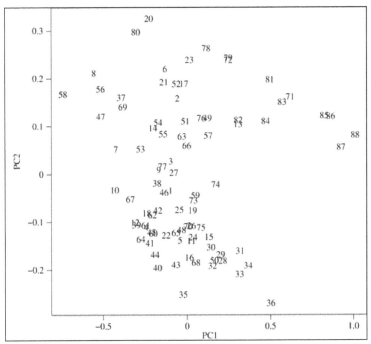

The two-dimensional principal subspace for the fossil teeth data. The coordinates in either or both PCs may switch signs when different software is used.

Covariance and Correlation Matrix Principal Component Analysis

So far, PCs have been presented as linear combinations of the (centred) original variables. However, the properties of PCA have some undesirable features when these variables have different units of measurement. While there is nothing inherently wrong, from a strictly mathematical point of view, with linear combinations of variables with different units of measurement (their use is widespread in, for instance, linear regression), the fact that PCA is defined by a criterion (variance) that depends on units of measurement implies that PCs based on the covariance matrix $\mathbf{S}$ will change if the units of measurement on one or more of the variables change (unless allp variables undergo a common change of scale, in which case the new covariance matrix is merely a scalar multiple of the old one, hence with the same eigenvectors and the same proportion of total variance explained by each PC). To overcome this undesirable feature, it is common practice to begin by standardizing the variables.

Each data value x_{ij} is both centred and divided by the standard deviation s_j of the n observations of variable j,

$$z_{ij} = \frac{x_{ij} - \overline{x}_j}{s_j}.$$

Thus, the initial data matrix X is replaced with the standardized data matrix Z, whose jth column is vector z_j with the n standardized observations of variable j. Standardization, is useful because most changes of scale are linear transformations of the data, which share the same set of standardized data values.

Since the covariance matrix of a standardized dataset is merely the correlation matrix R of the original dataset, a PCA on the standardized data is also known as a correlation matrix PCA. The eigenvectors a_k of the correlation matrix R define the uncorrelated maximum-variance linear combinations $Za_k = \sum_{j=1}^{p} a_{jk} z_j$ of the standardized variables $z_1, \ldots, z_p$. Such correlation matrix PCs are not the same as, nor are they directly related to, the covariance matrix PCs defined previously. Also, the percentage variance accounted for by each PC will differ and, quite frequently, more correlation matrix PCs than covariance matrix PCs is needed to account for the same percentage of total variance. The trace of a correlation matrix R is merely the number p of variables used in the analysis, hence the proportion of total variance accounted for by any correlation matrix PC is just the variance of that PC divided by p. The SVD approach is also valid in this context. Since $(n-1)R = Z'Z$, an SVD of the standardized data matrix Z amounts to a correlation matrix PCA of the dataset, along the lines described after equation $(n-1)S = X^* X^*$.

Correlation matrix PCs are invariant to linear changes in units of measurement and are therefore the appropriate choice for datasets where different changes of scale are conceivable for each variable. Some statistical software assumes by default that a PCA means a correlation matrix PCA and, in some cases, the normalization used for the vectors of loadings a_k of correlation matrix PCs is not the standard $a'_k a_k = 1$. In a correlation matrix PCA, the coefficient of correlation between the jth variable and the kth PC is given by,

$$r_{\text{var}_j, PC_k} = \sqrt{\lambda_k} \, a_{jk}.$$

Thus, if the normalization $\tilde{a}'_k \tilde{a}_k = \lambda_k$ is used instead of $a'_k a = 1$, the coefficients of the new loading vectors $\tilde{a}_k$ are the correlations between each original variable and the kth PC.

In the fossil teeth data, all nine measurements are in the same units, so a covariance matrix PCA makes sense. A correlation matrix PCA produces similar results, since the variances of the original variable do not differ very much. The first two correlation matrix PCs account for 93.7% of total variance. For other datasets, differences can be more substantial.

Biplots

One of the most informative graphical representations of a multivariate dataset is via a biplot, which is fundamentally connected to the SVD of a relevant data matrix, and therefore to PCA. A rank q approximation X^*_q of the full column-centred data matrix X^*, defined by equation $Y_q = U_q L_q A'_q$ is written as $X^*q=GH'$, where $G=U_q$ and $H=A_q L_q$ (although other options are possible). The n rows g_i of matrix G define graphical markers for each individual, which are usually represented by points. The p rows h_j of matrix H define markers for each variable and are usually represented by vectors. The properties of the biplot are best discussed assuming that q=p, although the biplot is defined on a low-rank approximation (usually q=2), enabling a graphical representation of the markers. When q=p the biplot has the following properties:

- The cosine of the angle between any two vectors representing variables is the coefficient of correlation between those variables; this is a direct result of the fact that the matrix of inner products between those markers is $HH'=AL^2A'=(n-1)$ S, so that inner products between vectors are proportional to covariances (variances for a common vector).

- Similarly, the cosine of the angle between any vector representing a variable and the axis representing a given PC is the coefficient of correlation between those two variables.

- The inner product between the markers for individual i and variable j gives the (centred) value of individual i on variable j. This is a direct result of the fact that $GH'=X^*$. The practical implication of this result is that orthogonally projecting the point representing individual i onto the vector representing variable j recovers the (centred) value $x_{ij} - \overline{x}_j$.

- The Euclidean distance between the markers for individuals i and i' is proportional to the Mahalanobis distance between them.

These results are only exact if all q=p dimensions are used. For q<p, the results are merely approximate and the overall quality of such approximations can be measured by the percentage of variance explained by the q largest variance PCs, which were used to build the marker matrices G and H.

Figure gives the biplot for the correlation matrix PCA of the fossil teeth data. The variable markers are displayed as arrows and the tooth markers as numbers. The group of three nearly horizontal and very tightly knit variable markers for two width variables and one height variable, WIDTH, HTMDT and TRIWIDTH, suggests a group of highly correlated variables, which are also strongly correlated with the first PC (represented by the horizontal axis). The very high proportion of variability explained by the two-dimensional principal subspace provides solid grounds for these conclusions. In fact, the smallest of the three true coefficients of correlation between these three variables is

0.944 (HTMDT and TRIWIDTH), and the smallest magnitude correlation between PC1 and any of these variables is 0.960 (TRIWIDTH). The sign difference in PC2 loadings between the three length variables (towards the bottom left of the plot) and the other variables is clearly visible. Projecting the marker for individual 58 onto the positive directions of all variable markers suggests that fossil tooth 58 (on the left of the biplot) is a large tooth. Inspection of the data matrix confirms that it is the largest individual on six of the nine variables, and close to largest on the remaining three. Likewise, individuals 85–88 (on the right) are small-sized teeth. Individuals whose markers are close to the origin have values close to the mean for all variables.

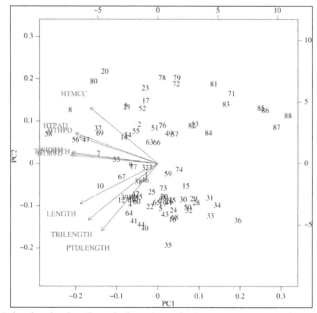

Biplot for the fossil teeth data (correlation matrix PCA), obtained using R's biplot command.

Centrings

PCA amounts to an SVD of a column-centred data matrix. In some applications, centring the columns of the data matrix may be considered inappropriate. In such situations, it may be preferred to avoid any pre-processing of the data and to subject the uncentred data matrix to an SVD or, equivalently, to carry out the eigendecomposition of the matrix of non-centred second moments, T, whose eigenvectors define linear combinations of the uncentred variables. This is often referred to as an uncentred PCA and there has been an unfortunate tendency in some fields to equate the name SVD only with this uncentred version of PCA.

Uncentred PCs are linear combinations of the uncentred variables which successively maximize non-central second moments, subject to having their crossed non-central second moments equal to zero. Except when the vector of column means $\bar{x}$ (i.e. the centre of gravity of the original n-point scatterplot in p-dimensional space) is near zero (in which case centred and uncentred moments are similar), it is not immediately intuitive that there should be similarities between both variants of PCA. Cadima & Jolliffe have explored the relations between the standard (column-centred) PCA and uncentred PCA and found them to be closer than might be expected, in particular when the size of vector $\bar{x}$ is large. It is often the case that there are great similarities between many eigenvectors and (absolute) eigenvalues of the covariance matrix $\mathbf{S}$ and the corresponding matrix of non-centred second moments, T.

In some applications, row centrings, or both row- and column-centring (known as double-centring) of the data matrix, have been considered appropriate. The SVDs of such matrices give rise to row-centred and doubly centred PCA, respectively.

When n<p

Datasets where there are fewer observed entities than variables (n<p) are becoming increasingly frequent, thanks to the growing ease of observing variables, together with the high costs of repeating observations in some contexts (such as microarrays). For example, has an example in genomics in which n=59 and p=21 225.

In general, the rank of an n×p data matrix is $r \le \min\{n-1, p\}$. If the data matrix has been column-centred, it is $r \le \min\{n-1, p\}$. When n<p, it is the number of observed individuals, rather than the number of variables, that usually determines the matrix rank. The rank of the column-centred data matrix $\mathbf{X}^*$ (or its standardized counterpart $\mathbf{Z}$) must equal the rank of the covariance (or correlation) matrix. The practical implication of this is that there are only r non-zero eigenvalues; hence r PCs explain all the variability in the dataset. Nothing prevents the use of PCA in such contexts, although some software, as is the case with R's princomp (but not the prcomp) command, may balk at such datasets. PCs can be determined as usual, by either an SVD of the (centred) data matrix or the eigenvectors/values of the covariance (or correlation) matrix.

Recent research has examined how well underlying 'population' PCs are estimated by the sample PCs in the case where n≪p, and it is shown that in some circumstances there is little resemblance between sample and population PCs. However, the results are typically based on a model for the data which has a very small number of structured PCs, and very many noise dimensions, and which has some links with recent work in RPCA.

Adaptations of Principal Component Analysis

The basic idea of PCA, leading to low-dimensional representations of large datasets in an adaptive and insightful way, is simple. There are many ways to adapt PCA to achieve modified goals or to analyses data of different types. Because PCA is used in a large number of areas, research into modifications and adaptations is spread over literatures from many disciplines. Four such adaptations, chosen fairly arbitrarily from the many that exist, namely functional PCA, modifications of PCA to simplify interpretations, RPCA and symbolic data PCA.

Functional Principal Component Analysis

In some applications, such as chemical spectroscopy, observations are functional in nature, changing with some continuous variable which, for simplicity, we assume is time. The dataset is then a collection of n functions $x_i(t)$.

How to incorporate such functional features in the analysis is the goal of functional data analysis. Early work on functional PCA performed a standard PCA on an n×p data matrix obtained by sampling n curves $x_i(t)$ at each of p points in time (t_j, with j=1,...,p), so that the element in row i, column j, of the data matrix is $x_i(t_j)$. The resulting p-dimensional vectors of loadings from a PCA of this data matrix are then viewed as sampled principal functions, which can be smoothed to recover functional form and can be interpreted as principal sources of variability in the observed curves. The above approach does not make explicit use of the functional nature of the n observations $x_i(t)$. To do so requires adapting concepts. In the standard setting, we consider linear combinations of p vectors, which produce new vectors. Each element of the new vectors is the result of an inner product of row i of the data matrix, $(x_{i1}, x_{i2}, ..., x_{ip})$, with a p-dimensional vector of weights, $a = (a_1, ..., a_p): \sum_{j=1}^{p} a_j x_{ij}$. If rows of the data matrix become functions, a functional inner product must be used instead, between a 'loadings function', a(t), and the ith functional observation, $x_i(t)$. The standard functional inner product is an integral of the form $\int a(t) x_i(t) dt$, on some appropriate compact interval. Likewise, the analogue of the p×p covariance matrix S is a bivariate function S(s,t) which, for any two given time instants s and t, returns the respective covariance, defined as,

$$S(s,t) = \frac{1}{n-1} \sum_{i=1}^{\pi} \left[x_i(s) - \overline{x}(s) \middle\| x_i(t) = \overline{x}(t) \right] = \frac{1}{n-1} \sum_{i=1}^{\pi} x_j^*(s) x_i^*(t).$$

where $\overline{x}(t) = (1/n) \sum_{i=1}^{n} x_i(t)$ is the mean function and $x_i^*(t) = x_i(t) - \overline{x}(t)$ is the ith centred function.

The analogue of the eigen-equation $S_a - \lambda a = 0 \Leftrightarrow S_a = \lambda a$. involves an integral transform, which reflects the functional nature of S(s,t) and of inner products,

$$\int S(s,t) a(t) dt = \lambda a(s).$$

The *eigenfunctions* a(t) which are the analytic solutions of equation above cannot, in general, be determined. Ramsay and Silverman discuss approximate solutions based on numerical integration. An alternative approach, which they explore in greater detail, involves the assumption that the curves $x_i(t)$ can be written as linear combinations of a set of *Gbasis functions* $\phi_1(t),...,\phi_G(t), \phi1(t),...,\phi G(t)$, so that, for any data function i,

$$x_i(t) = \sum_{j=1}^{G} c_{ij}\phi_j(t).$$

These basis functions can be chosen to reflect characteristics that are considered relevant in describing the observed functions. Thus, Fourier series functions may be chosen to describe periodic traits and splines for more general trends (B-splines are recommended). Other basis functions that have been used and can be considered are wavelets, exponential, power or polynomial bases. In theory, other bases, adapted to specific properties of a given set of observed functions, may be considered, although the computational problems that arise from any such choice must be kept in mind. The advantage of the basis function approach lies in the simplification of the expressions given previously. Denoting the n-dimensional vector of functions $x_i(t)$ as x(t), the G-dimensional vector of basis functions as $\Phi(t)$ and the n×G matrix of coefficients c_{ij} as **C**, the n data functions in equation above can be written as a single equation $x(t)=C\Phi(t)$. The eigenfunction a(t) can also be written in terms of the basis functions, with $a(t)=\Phi(t)'\mathbf{b}$ for some G-dimensional vector of coefficients $b=(b_1,...,b_G)$. Assuming furthermore that x(t) and $\Phi(t)$ are centred, the covariance function at time (s,t) becomes,

$$S(s,t) = \frac{1}{n-1}x(t)'x(t) = \frac{1}{n-1}\phi(s)'\mathbf{C'C}\phi(t)$$

and eigen-equation $\int S(s,t)a(t)dt = \lambda a(s)$ becomes, after some algebraic manipulation,

$$\frac{1}{n-1}\phi(s)'\mathbf{C'CWb} = \lambda\phi(s)'\mathbf{b},$$

where W is the G×G matrix of inner products $\int \phi_j(t)\phi_{j'}(t)dt$ between the basis functions. Since this equation must hold for all values of s, it reduces to,

$$\frac{1}{n-1}\mathbf{C'CWb} = \lambda\mathbf{b}.$$

If the basis functions are orthonormal, **W** is the G×G identity matrix and we end up with a standard eigenvalue problem which provides the solutions $a(t)=\Phi(t)'\mathbf{b}$ to equation $\int S(s,t)a(t)dt = \lambda a(s)$.

Ramsay & Silverman further explore methods in which data functions $x_i(t)$ are viewed as solutions to differential equations, an approach which they call principal differential analysis, in order to highlight its close connections with PCA.

Research on functional PCA has continued apace since the publication of Ramsay and Silverman's comprehensive text. Often this research is parallel to, or extends, similar ideas for data of non-functional form. For example, deciding how many PCs to retain is an important topic. A large number of suggestions have been made for doing so and many selection criteria are based on intuitive or descriptive ideas, such as the obvious 'proportion of total variance'. Other approaches are based on models for PCs.

As with other statistical techniques, it is possible that a few outlying observations may have a disproportionate effect on the results of a PCA. Numerous suggestions have been made for making PCA more robust to the presence of outliers for the usual data structure. One suggestion, using so-called S-estimators, is extended to functional PCA.

Simplified Principal Components

PCA gives the best possible representation of a p-dimensional dataset in q dimensions (q<p) in the sense of maximizing variance in q dimensions. A disadvantage is, however, that the new variables that it defines are usually linear functions of all p original variables. Although it was possible to interpret the first two PCs in the fossil teeth example, it is often the case for larger p that many variables have non-trivial coefficients in the first few components, making the components difficult to interpret. A number of adaptations of PCA have been suggested that try to make interpretation of the q dimensions simpler, while minimizing the loss of variance due to not using the PCs themselves. There is a trade-off between interpretability and variance. Two such classes of adaptations are briefly described here.

Rotation

The idea of rotating PCs is borrowed from factor analysis. Suppose, as before, that A_q is the p×q matrix, whose columns are the loadings of the first q PCs. Then XA_q is the n×q matrix whose columns are the scores on the first q PCs for the n observations. Now let T be an orthogonal (q×q) matrix. Multiplication of A_q by T performs an orthogonal rotation of the axes within the space spanned by the first q PCs, so that $B_q = A_q T$ is a p×q matrix whose columns are loadings of q rotated PCs. The matrix XBq is an n×q matrix containing the corresponding rotated PC scores. Any orthogonal matrix T could be used to rotate the components, but if it is desirable to make the rotated components easy to interpret, then T is chosen to optimize some simplicity criterion. A number of such criteria have been suggested, including some that include non-orthogonal (oblique) rotation. The most popular is perhaps the varimax criterion in which an orthogonal matrix

T is chosen to maximize $Q = \sum_{k=1}^{q} \left[\sum_{j=1}^{p} b_{jk}^4 - (1/p)\left(\sum_{j=1}^{p} b_{jk}^2\right)^2 \right]$, Inline Formula, where b_{jk} is the (j,k)th element of B_q.

Rotation can considerably simplify interpretation and, when viewed with respect to the q-dimensional space that is rotated, no variance is lost, as the sum of variances of the q rotated components is the same as for the unrotated components. What is lost is the successive maximization of the unrotated PCs, so that the total variance of the q components is more evenly distributed between components after rotation.

Drawbacks of rotation include the need to choose from the plethora of possible rotation criteria, though this choice often makes less difference than the choice of how many components to rotate. The rotated components can look quite different if q is increased by 1, whereas the successively defined nature of unrotated PCs means that this does not happen.

Adding a Constraint

Another approach to simplification of PCs is to impose a constraint on the loadings of the new variables. Again, there are a number of variants of this approach, one of which adapts the LASSO (least absolute shrinkage and selection operator) approach from linear regression. In this approach, called SCoTLASS (simplified component technique–LASSO), components are found which successively solve the same optimization problem as PCA, but with the additional constraint $\sum_{j=1}^{p} |a_{jk}| \leq \tau$, where T is a tuning parameter. For $\tau > \sqrt{P}$, the constraint has no effect and PCs are obtained, but as T decreases more and more loadings are driven to zero, thus simplifying interpretion. These simplified components necessarily account for less variance than the corresponding number of PCs, and usually several values of T are tried to determine a good trade-off between added simplicity and loss of variance.

A difference between the rotation and constraint approaches is that the latter has the advantage for interpretation of driving some loadings in the linear functions exactly to zero, whereas rotation usually does not. Adaptations of PCA in which many coefficients are exactly zero are generally known as sparse versions of PCA, and there has been a substantial amount of research on such PCs in recent years.

A related technique to SCoTLASS adds a penalty function to the variance criterion maximized, so that the optimization problem becomes to successively find a_k, k=1,2,...,p, that maximize $a'_k Sa_k + \psi \sum_{j=1}^{p} |a_{jk}|$, subject to $a'_k a_k = 1$, where ψ is a tuning parameter.

The original SCoTLASS optimization problem is non-convex and is also not solvable by simple iterative algorithms, although it is possible to re-express SCoTLASS as an equivalent, though still non-convex, optimization problem for which simple algorithms can be used. Another approach, due to d'Aspremont et al, reformulates SCoTLASS in a more complex manner, but then drops one of the constraints in this new formulation in order to make the problem convex.

Achieving sparsity is important for large p and particularly when n≪p. A number of authors have investigated versions of sparse PCA for this situation using models for the data in which the vast majority of the variables are completely unstructured noise.

Example: Sea-level pressure data. One discipline in which PCA has been widely used is atmospheric science. It was first suggested in that field by Obukhov and Lorenz and, uniquely to that discipline, it is usually known as empirical orthogonal function (EOF) analysis.

The format of the data in atmospheric science is different from that of most other disciplines. This example is taken from. The data consist of measurements of winter (December, January and February) monthly mean sea-level pressure (SLP) over the Northern Hemisphere north of 20°N. The dataset is available on a 2.5°×2.5° regular grid and spans the period from January 1948 to December 2000. Some preprocessing is done to adjust for the annual cycle and the different areas covered by grid squares at different latitudes. In many atmospheric science examples, the variables are measurements at grid points, and the loadings, known as EOFs, are displayed as smooth spatial patterns, as in figure 3 for the first two correlation-based EOFs for the SLP data. There are 1008 variables (grid-points) in this dataset, and the first two PCs account for 21% and 13% of the variation in these 1008 variables. Figure below gives a pattern which is commonly known as the Arctic Oscillation (AO). It is a measure of the north–south pressure gradient in the Atlantic Ocean and, to a lesser extent, in the Pacific Ocean and is a major source of variation in weather patterns. The second EOF is dominated by variation in the Pacific Ocean. The PCs for examples of this type are time series so the first PC, for example, will display which years have high values of the AO and which have low values.

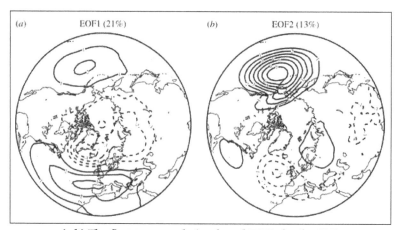

(a,b) The first two correlation-based EOFs for the SLP
data account for 21% and 13% of total variation.

Figure shows simplified EOFs based on SCoTLASS. The main difference from the EOFs in figure 3 is for the first EOF, which is now completely dominated by the north–south pressure gradient in the Atlantic (the North Atlantic Oscillation) with exactly zero loadings for many grid-points. The simplification is paid for by a reduction in percentage of variation explained for the corresponding simplified PC (17% compared with 21%). The second simplified PC is very similar to the original second EOF, also explaining 13% of variation.

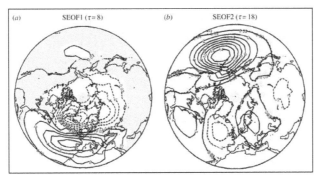

(a,b) LASSO-based simplified EOFs for the SLP data. Grey areas are grid-points with exactly zero loadings.

Robust Principal Component Analysis

By its very nature, PCA is sensitive to the presence of outliers and therefore also to the presence of gross errors in the datasets. This has led to attempts to define robust variants of PCA and the expression RPCA has been used for different approaches to this problem. Early work by Huber discussed robust alternatives to covariance or correlation matrices and ways in which they can be used to define robust PCs.

The need for methods to deal with very large datasets in areas such as image processing, machine learning, bioinformatics or Web data analysis has generated a recent renewed interest in robust variants of PCA and has led to one of the most vigorous lines of research in PCA-related methods. Wright et al. defined RPCA as a decomposition of an n×p data matrix X into a sum of two n×p components: a low-rank component L and a sparse component S. More precisely, a convex optimization problem was defined as identifying the matrix components of X=L+S that minimize a linear combination of two different norms of the components:

$$\min_{L,S} \|L\|_* + \lambda \|S\|_1 ,$$

where $\|L\|_* = \sum_r \sigma_r(L)$, the sum of the singular values of L, is the nuclear norm of L, and $\lambda \|S\|_1 = \sum_i \sum_j |s_{ij}|$ is the ℓ_1-norm of matrix S. The motivation for such a decomposition is the fact that, in many applications, low-rank matrices are associated with a general pattern (e.g. the 'correct' data in a corrupted dataset, a face in facial recognition, or a background image in video surveillance data), whereas a sparse matrix is associated with disturbances (e.g. corrupted data values, effects of light or shading in facial recognition, a moving object or person in the foreground of data surveillance images). Sparse components are also called 'noise', in what can be confusing terminology since in some applications it is precisely the 'noise' component that is of interest. Candès et al. return to this problem, also called principal component pursuit, and give theoretical results proving that, under not very stringent conditions, it is possible to exactly recover the low-rank and sparse components with high probability and that the choice of $\lambda = 1/\sqrt{\max(n,m)}$ works well in a general setting, avoiding the need to choose a tuning parameter. Results are extended to the case of data matrices with missing values. Further variations consider more complex structures for the 'noise' component. The results of alternative algorithms in the presence of different types of 'noise' are compared in the context of image-processing and facial recognition problems. Their results show that classical PCA performs fairly well, when compared with these new methods, in terms of both time and the quality of low-rank solutions that are produced.

Symbolic Data Principal Component Analysis

There is a recent body of work with so-called symbolic data, which is a general designation for more complex data structures, such as intervals or histograms.

Interval data arise when one wishes to retain a measure of underlying variability in the observations. This may occur if we wish to reflect the lack of precision of a measuring instrument or, more fundamentally, because the data are summary observations for which associated variability is considered inherent to the measurement. This is often the case when each observation corresponds to a group, rather than an individual, as would be the case with measurements on species, for which a range of values is considered part of the group value. If all p observed variables are of this type, each observation is represented by a hyper-rectangle, rather than a point, in p-dimensional space. Extensions of PCA for such data seek PCs that are also of interval type, and which therefore also reflect ranges of values.

Another common type of symbolic data is given by histograms, which can be considered a generalization of interval-valued data where for each observation there are several intervals (the histogram bins) and associated frequencies. A recent review covers several proposed definitions of PCA-type analyses for histogram data. Most of them require the definition of concepts such as distances between histograms (the Wasserstein distance being a common choice) or the sum and mean of histograms.

Fisher Linear Discriminant Analysis

The main idea of Fisher linear discriminant approach is finding the projection to a line such that samples from different classes projected on the line are well separated.

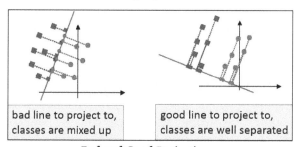

Bad and Good Projections.

The Basis of Fisher Discriminant

Suppose we have 2 classes and d-dimensional samples $X_1, ... X_n$, where n1 samples come from the first class and n2 samples come from the second class. Consider projection on a line, and let the line direction be given by unit vector V. Scalar $V^t X_i$ is the distance of projection of X_i from the origin. Thus $V^t X_i$ is the projection of X_i into a one dimensional subspace.

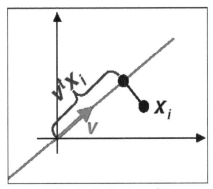

$V^t X_i -$ the Projection of X_i.

Thus the projection of sample X_i onto a line in direction V is given by $V^t X_i$. How do we measure separation between projections of different classes? Let $\tilde{\mu}_1$ and $\tilde{\mu}_2$ be the means of projections of classes 1 and 2 and let μ_1 and μ_2 be the means of classes 1 and 2 and $|\tilde{\mu}_1 - \tilde{\mu}_2|$ seems like a good measure.

Means of Projections:

$$\tilde{\mu}_1 = \frac{1}{n_1} \sum_{x_i \in C1}^{n_1} v^t x_i = v^t \left(\frac{1}{n_1} \sum_{x_i \in C_1}^{n_1} x_i \right) = v^t \tilde{\mu}_1$$

similarly, $\tilde{\mu}_2 = v^t \mu_2$

Now let us discuss the goodness of $|\tilde{\mu}_1 - \tilde{\mu}_2|$ as a measure of separation. The larger $|\tilde{\mu}_1 - \tilde{\mu}_2|$ the better is the expected separation. The vertical axes is a better line than the horizontal axes to project to for class separability. However $\hat{\mu}_1 - \hat{\mu}_1 |\tilde{\mu}_1 - \tilde{\mu}_2|$.

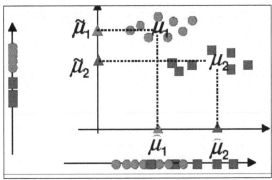

The $|\tilde{\mu}_1 - \tilde{\mu}_2|$ Measure of Separation.

The problem with $\left|\tilde{\mu}_1 - \tilde{\mu}_2\right|$ is that it does not consider the variance of the classes. We need to normalize $\left|\tilde{\mu}_1 - \tilde{\mu}_2\right|$ by a factor which is proportional to variance.

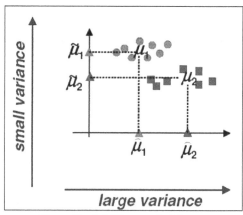

Normalized Difference in Means.

Let us consider some samples $Z_1,...Z_n,$. Sample mean is as given below,

$$\mu_z = \frac{1}{n}\sum_{i=1}^{n}Z_i$$

Now let us define their scatter as,

$$s = \sum_{i=1}^{n}\left(Z_i - \mu_z\right)^2$$

Thus scatter is just sample variance multiplied by n. In other words, scatter measures the same concept as variance, the spread of data around the mean, only that scatter is just on a different scale than variance.

Fisher Linear Discriminant

Fisher Solution to finding the projection to a line such that samples from different classes projected on the line are well separated is to normalize $\left|\tilde{\mu}_1 \quad \tilde{\mu}_2\right|$ by scatter.

Let $\mathbf{y}_i = V^t X_i$, i.e. $\mathbf{y}_i$'s are the projected samples and the scatter for projected samples of class 1 is as given below,

$$\tilde{s}_1^2 = \sum_{yi\in Class\ 1}\left(y_1 - \tilde{\mu}_2\right)^2$$

Similarly the scatter for projected samples of class 2 is,

$$\tilde{s}_2^2 = \sum_{yi\in Class\ 2}\left(y_1 - \tilde{\mu}_2\right)^2$$

We need to normalize by both scatter of class 1 and scatter of class 2. Thus Fisher linear discriminant needs to project on line in the direction v which maximizes J(v).

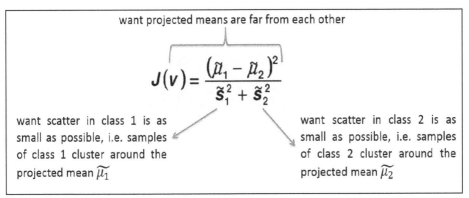

$$J(v) = \frac{(\tilde{\mu}_1 - \tilde{\mu}_2)^2}{\tilde{s}_1^2 + \tilde{s}_2^2}$$

want projected means are far from each other

want scatter in class 1 is as small as possible, i.e. samples of class 1 cluster around the projected mean $\widetilde{\mu_1}$

want scatter in class 2 is as small as possible, i.e. samples of class 2 cluster around the projected mean $\widetilde{\mu_2}$

Definition of J(V).

Here J(v) is defined such that we want the projected means to be far from each other and the scatter of each class to be as small as possible that is we want the samples of the respective classes to cluster around the projected means. If we find v which makes J(v) large, we are guaranteed that the classes are well separated.

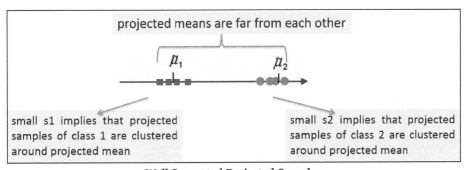

projected means are far from each other

μ_1 μ_2

small s1 implies that projected samples of class 1 are clustered around projected mean

small s2 implies that projected samples of class 2 are clustered around projected mean

Well Separated Projected Samples.

All we need to do now is to express J explicitly as a function of v and maximize it. This is fairly straightforward but needs application of linear algebra and calculus. We define the separate class scatter matrices S1 and S2 for classes 1 and 2. These measure the scatter of original samples x_i (before projection) as follows:

$$S_1 = \sum_{xi \in Class\ 1} (X_i - \mu_1)(X_i - \mu_1)^t$$

$$S_2 = \sum_{xi \in Class\ 2} (X_i - \mu_2)(X_i - \mu_2)^t$$

Now let us consider the samples belonging to two classes as given below:

- Class 1 has 5 samples c1=[(1,2),(2,3),(3,3),(4,5),(5,5)].

- Class 2 has 6 samples c2=[(1,0),(2,1),(3,1),(5,3),(6,5)].

Now let us arrange data in 2 separate matrices as follows:

$$C_1 = \begin{bmatrix} 1 & 2 \\ \vdots & \vdots \\ 5 & 5 \end{bmatrix} \qquad C_2 = \begin{bmatrix} 1 & 0 \\ \vdots & \vdots \\ 6 & 5 \end{bmatrix}$$

It is to be noted that PCA performs very poorly on this data because the direction of largest variance is not helpful for classification.

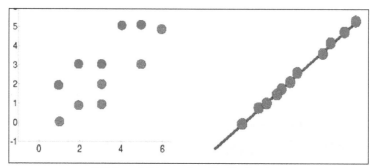

PCA based Dimensionality Reduction.

Now let us first compute the mean for each class.

M1= mean(c1)=[3 3.6] M2= mean (c2) = [3.3 2]

Now based on these means let us compute the scatter matrices S1 and S2 for each class as follows:

$$S_1 = 4 * \mathrm{cov}(c_1) = \begin{bmatrix} 10 & 8.0 \\ 8.0 & 7.2 \end{bmatrix} \qquad S_2 = 5 * \mathrm{cov}(c_2) = \begin{bmatrix} 17.3 & 16 \\ 16 & 16 \end{bmatrix}$$

Now the within the class scatter is a follows:

$$S_W = S_1 + S_2 = \begin{bmatrix} 27.3 & 24 \\ 24 & 23.2 \end{bmatrix}$$

This matrix has full rank, and we do not have to solve for Eigen values. The inverse of $S_{w,}$:

$$S_W \text{ is } S_w^{-1} = inv(S_w) = \begin{bmatrix} 0.39 & -0.41 \\ -0.41 & 0.47 \end{bmatrix}$$

Finally, the optimal line direction **v** is as given below:

$$v = S_w^{-1}(\mu_1 - \mu_2) = \begin{bmatrix} -0.79 \\ 0.89 \end{bmatrix}$$

Notice, that as long as the line has the right direction, its exact position does not matter. Finally the last step is to compute the actual 1D vector y. Let's do it separately for each class:

$$Y_1 = v^t c_1^t = \begin{bmatrix} -0.65 & 0.73 \end{bmatrix} \begin{bmatrix} 1...5 \\ 2...5 \end{bmatrix} = \begin{bmatrix} 0.81...0.4 \end{bmatrix}$$

$$Y_2 = v^t c_2^t = \begin{bmatrix} -0.65 & 0.73 \end{bmatrix} \begin{bmatrix} 1...6 \\ 0...5 \end{bmatrix} = \begin{bmatrix} -0.65... -0.25 \end{bmatrix}$$

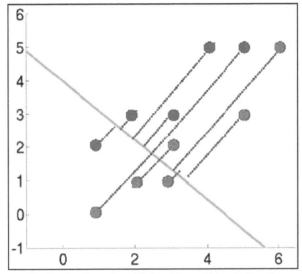

Projection based on Fisher Linear Discriminant.

Generalized Discriminant Analysis

Generalized discriminant analysis (GDA) is a commonly used method for dimensionality reduction. In its general form, it seeks a nonlinear projection that simultaneously maximizes the between-class dissimilarity and minimizes the with in class dissimilarity to increase class separability. In real-world applications where labeled data are scarce, GDA may not work very well. However, unlabeled data are often available in large quantities at very low cost.

The optimization procedure leads to estimation of the class labels for the unlabeled data. We propose a novel confidence measure and a method for selecting those unlabeled data points whose labels are estimated with high confidence. The selected unlabeled data can then be used to augment the original labeled data set for performing GDA. We also propose a variant of SSGDA, called M-SSGDA, which adopts the manifold assumption to utilize the unlabeled data. Extensive experiments on many benchmark data sets demonstrate the effectiveness of our proposed methods.

Linear discriminant analysis (LDA) is a commonly used method for dimensionality reduction. It seeks a linear projection that simultaneously maximizes the between class dissimilarity and minimizes the within-class dissimilarity to increase class separability, typically for classification applications. Despite its simplicity, the effectiveness and computational efficiency of LDA make it a popular choice for many applications. Nevertheless, LDA does have some limitations. One of these arises in situations when the sample size is much smaller than the dimensionality of the feature space, leading to the so-called small sample size (SSS) problem due to severe under-sampling of the underlying data distribution. As a result, the within-class scatter matrix that characterizes the within-class variability is not of full rank and hence it is not invertible. A number of methods have been proposed to overcome this problem, e.g., PseudoLDA, RLDA PCA+LDA, LDA/QR, NullLDA, and DualLDA. PseudoLDA overcomes the singularity problem by substituting the inverse of the within-class scatter matrix with its pseudo-inverse. RLDA adds a positive constant value to each eigenvalue of the within-class scatter matrix to overcome this problem. PCA+LDA first applies PCA to project the data into a lower-dimensional space so that the within-class scatter matrix computed there is nonsingular, and then applies LDA in the lower-dimensional space. LDA/QR is also a two-stage method which can be divided into two steps: first project the data to the range space of the between-class scatter matrix and then apply LDA in this space. NullLDA first projects the data to the null space of the within-class scatter matrix and then maximizes the between-class scatter in this space. It is similar to the discriminative common vectors (DCV) method.

DualLDA, which combines the ideas from PCA+LDA and NullLDA, maximizes the between class scatter matrix in the range space and the null space of the within-class scatter matrix separately and then integrates the two parts together to get the final transformation proposes a unified framework for RLDA, NullLDA and other variants of LDA. There is also another approach to address the SSS problem, with 2DLDA being the representative of this approach. The major difference between 2DLDA and the algorithms above lies in their data representation. Specifically, 2DLDA operates on data represented as (2D) matrices, instead of (1D) vectors, so that the dimensionality of the data representation can be kept small as a way to alleviate the SSS problem.

Another limitation of LDA is that it only gives a linear projection of the data points. Fortunately, the kernel approach can be applied easily via the so-called kernel trick to extend LDA to its kernel version, called generalized discriminant analysis (GDA) (or referred to as kernel discriminant analysis in some papers), that can project the data points nonlinearly. Similar to the linear case, there are many variants of GDA corresponding to those of LDA, such as, KPCA+LDA, KDA/QR, kernel-DCV, Kernel Uncorrelated Discriminant Analysis and 2D-GDA. Unlike in LDA, using GDA requires one to select the kernel and set the kernel parameters. Inspired by previous research in multi-kernel learning address this problem by learning the optimal kernel matrix as a convex combination of some pre-defined kernel matrices using semi definite programming (SDP).

Besides addressing these two limitations of LDA, some interesting recent works also address other issues, e.g., to study the relationships between two variants of LDA, to reformulate multi-class LDA as a multivariate linear regression problem.

In many real-world applications, it is impractical to expect the availability of large quantities of labeled data because labeling data is a costly process. On the other hand, unlabeled data are available in large quantities at very low cost. Over the past decade or so, one form of semi-supervised learning, which attempts to utilize unlabeled data to aid classification or regression tasks under situations with limited labeled data, has emerged as a hot and promising research topic within the machine learning community. A good survey of semi-supervised learning methods can be found in. Some early semi-supervised learning methods include Co-Training and transductive SVM (TSVM). Recently, graph-based semi-supervised learning methods, have aroused the interest of many researchers. Unlike earlier methods, these methods model the geometric relationships between all data points in the form of a graph and then propagate the label information from the labeled data points through the graph to the unlabeled data points.

There are some works on semi-supervised extension of LDA, to utilize unlabeled data to alleviate the SSS problem. Assume that the low-dimensional representations of similar data points are also similar and formulate this notion by means of a regularization term in the objective function utilizing some similarity measure. Inspired by TSVM, utilizes unlabeled data to maximize the optimality criterion of LDA. However, these works mainly focus on the linear case, i.e., LDA, but not GDA which is the more general case.

We are given a training set of n data points, $\mathcal{D} = \{x_1, \ldots, x_n\}$, where $x_i \in R^N$, $i = 1, \ldots, n$. Let $\mathcal{D}$ be partitioned into $C \geq 2$ disjoint classes Π_i, $i = 1, \ldots,$, where class Π_i contains n_i examples. The total scatter matrix S_t and the between-class scatter matrix $\mathbf{S}_b$ are defined as,

$$S_t = \sum_{i=1}^{n} \left(\phi(x_i) - \bar{m} \right) \left(\phi(x_i) - \bar{m} \right)^T$$

$$S_b = \sum_{k=1}^{C} n_k \left(\bar{m}_k - \bar{m} \right) \left(\bar{m}_k - \bar{m} \right)^T,$$

where $\phi(\cdot)$ denotes the feature mapping corresponding to a kernel function $k(\cdot, \cdot)$, $\bar{m} = (\sum_{i=1}^{n} \phi(x_i)) / n$ is the sample mean of the whole data set $\mathcal{D}$ and $\bar{m}_k = (\sum_{x_i \in \Pi_k} \phi(x_i)) / n_k$ is the class mean of Π_k.

Let $X = (\phi(x_1), \ldots, \phi(x_n))$, $M = (\bar{m}_1, \ldots \bar{m}_C)$, $\pi = (n_1, \ldots, n_C)T$, $\mathbf{H}_n = \mathbf{I}_n - \frac{1}{n} 1_n 1_n^T$ be the $n \times n$ centering matrix where $\mathbf{I}_n$ is an $n \times n$ identity matrix and 1_n is an $n \times 1$ vector of all ones, $D = \text{diag}(n_1, \ldots, n_C)$ be a diagonal matrix whose (i, i)th element is n_i, E be an $n \times C$ class indicator matrix whose (i, j)th element is equal to 1 if x_i is from the jth class and 0 otherwise. It is easy to see that $1_n^T \mathbf{E} = 1_C^T = 1_c^T \mathbf{D} = \pi^T$ and $M = XED^{-1}$ where A^{-1} denotes the inverse of matrix A if A is nonsingular and the pseudo-inverse if A is singular. From the definitions of S_t and S_b in Equations,

$$S_t = \sum_{i=1}^{n} \left(\phi(x_i) - \bar{m} \right) \left(\phi(x_i) - \bar{m} \right)^T$$

$$S_b = \sum_{k=1}^{C} n_k \left(\bar{m}_k - \bar{m} \right) \left(\bar{m}_k - \bar{m} \right)^T ,$$

We can rewrite them in matrix form as,

$$S_t = XH_n H_n X^T = XH_n X^T$$

and

$$S_b = \left(M - \frac{1}{n} X 1_n 1_C^T \right) D \left(M - \frac{1}{n} X 1_n 1_C^T \right)^T$$

$$= \left(XED^{-1} - \frac{1}{n} X 1_n 1_C^T \right) D \left(XED^{-1} - \frac{1}{n} X 1_n 1_C^T \right)^T$$

$$= X \left(ED^{-1} - \frac{1}{n} 1_n 1_C^T \right) D \left(D^{-1} E^T - \frac{1}{n} 1_C 1_n^T \right) X^T$$

$$= X \left(E - \frac{1}{n} 1_n 1_C^T D \right) D^{-1} \left(E^T - \frac{1}{n} D 1_C 1_n^T \right) X^T$$

$$= X \left(E - \frac{1}{n} 1_n 1_n^T E \right) D^{-1} \left(E^T - \frac{1}{n} E^T 1_n 1_n^T \right) X^T$$

$$= XH_n ED^{-1} E^T H_n X^T .$$

The second last equation holds because $1_n^T \mathbf{E} = 1_C^T \mathbf{D}$.

GDA seeks to find a projection matrix W* that maximizes the trace function of S_b and S_t:

$$W^* = \arg\max_w trace\left(\left(W^T S_t W \right)^{-1} W^T S_b W \right),$$

where trace(·) denotes the trace of a square matrix. Since we do not know the explicit form of (·) for most kernel functions, we cannot solve Equation above directly. From the represented theorem, we have W= XP. So problem above becomes,

$$P^* = \arg\max_P trace\left(\left(P^T KH_n KP \right)^{-1} P^T KH_n ED^{-1} E^T H_n KP \right).$$

According to, the optimal solution P* for the problem above can be computed from the eigenvectors of $(KH_nK)^{-1} KH_nED^{-1}E^TH_nK$. Because the rank of $KH_nED^{-1}E^TH_nK$ is at most $C - 1$, P^* contains $C - 1$ columns in most situations.

Semi-supervised Generalized Discriminant Analysis

Optimal Solution for GDA

The following theorem on the optimal solution to the problem above is relevant here. Theorem: Given $A \in R^{n \times n}$ and $B \in R^{n \times n}$ are positive semi-definite matrices and the rank of B is t, then for $P \in R^{n \times t}$,

$$\max_{P} trace\left(\left(P^T A P \right)^{-1} P^T B P \right) = trace\left(A^{-1} B \right).$$

From Theorem above, we can easily get the following corollary since KH_nK and $KH_nED^{-1}E^TH_nK$ are positive semi-definite matrices and the rank of $KH_nED^{-1}E^TH_nK$ is $C - 1$.

Corollary: For $P \in R^{n \times (C-1)}$,

$$\max_{P} trace\left(\left(P^T KH_nKP \right)^{-1} P^T KH_nED^{-1}E^T H_nKP \right)$$

$$= trace\left(\left(KH_nK \right)^{-1} KH_nED^{-1}E^T H_nK \right).$$

SSGDA: Exploiting Unlabeled Data to Maximize the Optimality Criterion

Suppose we have l labeled data points $x_1, \ldots, x_l \in R^N$ with class labels from C classes Π_i, $i = 1, \ldots, C$, and m unlabeled data points $x_{l+1}, \ldots, x_{l+m} \in R^N$ with unknown class labels. So we have totally $n = l+m$ examples available for training and these n data points consist of the training set D where each class Π_i is just a subset of D. Usually $l \ll m$. When l is very small compared with the input dimensionality, GDA generally does not perform very well. To remedy this problem, we want to incorporate unlabeled data to improve its performance.

Inspired by TSVM, which utilizes unlabeled data to maximize the margin, we use unlabeled data here to maximize the optimality criterion of LDA. According to Corollary above, we utilize unlabeled data to maximize trace $((KH_nK)^{-1}KH_nED^{-1}E^TH_nK)$ via estimating the class labels of the unlabeled data points.

We first rewrite the objective function as trace$(ED^{-1}E^TS)$ where $S = H_nK(KH_nK)^{-1}KH_n$.

Since $ED^{-1}E^T = \sum_{i=1}^{C} \frac{e_1 e_1^T}{n_1}$ where e_i is the ith column of E, the objective function can be formulated as,

$$trace\left(ED^{-1}E^T S \right) = trace\left(\sum_{i=1}^{C} \frac{e_i e_i^T}{n_i} S \right) = \sum_{i=1}^{C} \frac{e_i^T S e_i}{n_i}.$$

Since those entries in E for the unlabeled data points are unknown, we maximize the objective function with respect to E. Recalled that ni is the number of data points in the ith class and so $n_i = e_i^T 1_n$. By defining some new variables for the sake of notational simplicity, we formulate the optimization problem as:

$$\max_{E,\{t_k\}} \quad \sum_{k=1}^{C} \frac{e_k^T S e_k}{t_k}$$

$$s.t. \quad t_k = e_k^T 1_n, \quad k = 1,...C$$

$$e_{ij} = \begin{cases} 1 & if \ x_i \in \Pi_j \\ 0 & otherwise \end{cases} \quad i = 1,...l$$

$$e_{ij} \in \{0,1\}, \ i = l+1,...,n, \ j = 1,..,C$$

$$\sum_{j=1}^{C} e_{ij} = 1, \ i = l+1,...,n,$$

where e_{ij} is the jth element of e_i and also the (i, j)th element of E.

Unfortunately this is an integer programming problem which is known to be NP-hard and often cannot be efficiently solved. We seek to make this integer programming problem tractable by relaxing the constraint $e_{ij} \in \{0, 1\}$ in equation above to $e_{ij} \geq 0$, giving rise to a modified formulation of the optimization problem:

$$\max_{E,\{t_k\}} \quad \sum_{k=1}^{C} \frac{e_k^T S e_k}{t_k}$$

$$s.t. \quad t_k = e_k^T 1_n, \quad k = 1,...C$$

$$e_{ij} = \begin{cases} 1 & if \ x_i \in \Pi_j \\ 0 & otherwise \end{cases} \quad i = 1,...l$$

$$e_{ij} \geq 0, \ i = l+1,...,n, \ j = 1,..,C$$

$$\sum_{j=1}^{C} e_{ij} = 1, \ i = l+1,...,n.$$

With such relaxation, the matrix entries of **E** for the unlabeled data points may be interpreted as posterior class probabilities. However, even though the constraints in the optimization problem above are linear, the problem seeks to maximize a convex function which, unfortunately, does not correspond to a convex optimization problem. If we re-express the optimization problem in equation above as minimizing a concave function, we can adopt the constrained concave-convex procedure (CCCP), to solve this non-convex optimization problem. For our case, the convex part of the objective function degenerates to the special case of a constant function which always returns zero.

CCCP is an iterative algorithm. In each iteration, the concave part of the objective function for the optimization problem is replaced by its first-order Taylor series approximation at the point which corresponds to the result obtained in the previous iteration. Specifically, in the ($p+1$)th iteration, we solve the following optimization problem:

$$\max_{E,\{t_k\}} \sum_{k=1}^{C} \left(\frac{2\left(e_k^{(p)}\right)^T S}{t_k^{(p)}} e_k - \frac{\left(e_k^{(p)}\right)^T S e_k^{(p)}}{\left(t_k^{(p)}\right)^2} t_k \right)$$

$$s.t. \quad t_k = e_k^T 1_n, \ k = 1,...,C$$

$$e_{ij} = \begin{cases} 1 & if \ x_i \in \prod_j \\ 0 & otherwise \end{cases} \quad i = 1,...l$$

$$e_{ij} \geq 0, \ i = l+1,...,n, \ j = 1,..,C$$

$$\sum_{j=1}^{C} e_{ij} = 1, \ i = l+1,...,n.$$

where $e_k^{(p)}$ and $t_k^{(p)}$ ($k = 1, \ldots ,C$) were obtained in the pth iteration. The objective function in above equation is just the first-order Taylor series approximation of that in equation,

$$\max_{E,\{t_k\}} ... \sum_{j=1}^{C} e_{ij} = 1, \ i = l+1,...,n.$$

by ignoring some constant terms.

Since the optimization problem above is a linear programming (LP) problem, it can be solved efficiently and hence can handle large-scale applications. Because the optimal solution of an LP problem falls on the boundary of its feasible set (or called constraint set), the matrix entries of the optimal e_{ij} computed in each iteration must be in $\{0, 1\}$, which automatically satisfies the constraints in equation, $\max_{E,\{t_k\}} ... \sum_{j=1}^{C} e_{ij} = 1, i = l+1,...,n.$

As the optimization problem is non-convex, the final solution that CCCP obtains generally depends on its initial value. For the labeled data points, the corresponding entries in *eij* are held fixed based on their class labels. For the unlabeled data points, we initialize the corresponding entries in *eij* with equal prior probabilities for all classes:

$$e_{ij}^{(0)} = \begin{cases} 1 & if \ x_i \in \prod_j \\ 0 & otherwise \end{cases} \quad i = 1,...l, \ j = 1,....,C$$

$$e_{ij}^{(0)} = \frac{1}{C}, \ i = l+1,...,n, \ j = 1,....,C.$$

The initial values for $\{t_k^0\}$ can be computed based on the equality constraints in equation,

$$\max_{E,\{t_k\}}...\sum_{j=1}^{C}e_{ij}=1,\, i=l+1,...,n.$$

which establish the relationships between E and t_k.

M-SSGDA: Incorporating the Manifold Assumption

The manifold assumption is adopted by many graph based semi-supervised learning methods. Under this assumption, nearby points are more likely to have the same class label for classification problems and similar low-dimensional representations for dimensionality reduction problems. We adopt this assumption to extend SSGDA to M-SSGDA.

Given the data set $\mathcal{D} = \{x_1, . . ., x_n\}$, we first construct a K-nearest neighbor graph $G = (V,E)$, with the vertex set $V = \{1, . . ., n\}$ corresponding to the labeled and unlabeled data points and the edge set $E \subseteq V \times V$ representing the relationships between data points. Each edge is assigned a weight w_{ij} which reflects the similarity between points x_i and x_j:

$$w_{ij} = \begin{cases} \exp\left(-\dfrac{\|x_i - x_j\|_2^2}{\sigma_i \sigma_j}\right) & if\ x_i \in N_K\left(x_j\right) or\ x_j \in N_K\left(x_j\right) \\ 0 & otherwise \end{cases}$$

where $\|\cdot\|_2$ denotes the 2-norm of a vector, $N_K(x_i)$ denotes the neighborhood set of K-nearest neighbors of x_i, σ_i the distance between x_i and its Kth nearest neighbor, and σ_j the distance between x_j and its Kth nearest neighbor. This way of constructing the nearest neighbor graph is called local scaling, which is different from that in SDA. In SDA, a constant value of 1 is set for all neighbors. This is unsatisfactory especially when some neighbors are relatively far away.

By incorporating the manifold assumption into our problem, we expect nearby points to be more likely to have the same class label and hence the two corresponding rows in **E** are more likely to be the same. We thus modify the optimization equation,

$$\max_{E,\{t_k\}}...\sum_{j=1}^{C}e_{ij}=1,\, i=l+1,...,n.$$

by adding one more term to the objective function:

$$\max_{E,\{t_k\}} \quad \sum_{k=1}^{C} \frac{e_k^T S e_k}{t_k} - \lambda \sum_{i=1}^{n} \sum_{j=i+1}^{n} w_{ij} \left\| e^i - e^j \right\|_1$$

$$s.t. \quad t_k = e_k^T 1_n, \ k = 1,\dots C$$

$$e_{ij} = \begin{cases} 1 & if \ x_i \in \Pi_j \\ 0 & otherwise \end{cases} \quad i = 1,\dots,l$$

$$e_{ij} \geq 0, \ i = l+1,\dots,n, \ j = 1,\dots,C$$

$$\sum_{j=1}^{C} e_{ij} = 1, \ i = l+1,\dots,n.$$

where $\lambda > 0$ is a regularization parameter, e^i denotes the ith row of E, and $\| \cdot \|_1$ is the 1-norm of a vector.

Since the objective function of the optimization problem above is the difference of two convex functions, we can also adopt CCCP to solve it. Similar to SSGDA, in each iteration of CCCP, we also need to solve an LP problem:

$$\max_{E,\{t_k\}} \quad \sum_{k=1}^{C} \left(\frac{2\left(e_k^{(P)}\right)^T S}{t_k^{(P)}} e_k - \frac{2\left(e_k^{(P)}\right)^T S e_k^{(P)}}{\left(t_k^{(P)}\right)^2} t_k \right)$$

$$s.t. \quad -\lambda \sum_{i=1}^{n} \sum_{j=i+1}^{n} w_{ij} \left\| e^i - e^j \right\|_1$$

$$t_k = e_k^T 1_n, \ k = 1,\dots,C$$

$$e_{ij} = \begin{cases} 1 & if \ x_i \in \Pi_j \\ 0 & otherwise \end{cases} \quad i = 1,\dots,l$$

$$e_{ij} \geq 0, \ i = l+1,\dots,n, \ j = 1,\dots,C$$

$$\sum_{j=1}^{C} e_{ij} = 1, \ i = l+1,\dots,n.$$

One reason for choosing the 1-norm in the problem, $\max_{E,\{t_k\}}\dots\sum_{j=1}^{C} e_{ij} = 1, \ i = l+1,\dots,n$ is to

keep the problem above as an LP problem which has an efficient and effective solution.

Augmenting the Labeled Data Set with Unlabeled Data

For both SSGDA and M-SSGDA, CCCP estimates the class labels of all the unlabeled data points by solving the corresponding optimization problems with respect to E. One might then use all these unlabeled data points with estimated class labels to expand the labeled data set and then apply GDA again. However, it should be noted that not all the class labels can be estimated accurately. Thus, including those points with noisy class labels may impair the performance of GDA. Here we propose an effective method for selecting only those unlabeled data points whose labels are estimated with sufficiently high confidence.

Since all matrix entries in *eij* obtained by CCCP are either 0 or 1, they cannot serve as posterior class probabilities for defining a measure to characterize the label estimation confidence. Here we propose an alternative scheme. We first use SSGDA or M-SSGDA to estimate the class labels for the unlabeled data. Then we use all the unlabeled data points with their estimated labels as well as the original labeled data set to perform GDA. Then, in the embedding space, we consider the neighborhood of each unlabeled data point by taking into account unlabeled data points only. If an unlabeled point has a sufficiently large proportion (determined by some threshold θ, usually chosen to be larger than 0.5) of neighboring unlabeled points with the same estimated class label as its own, we consider the estimated class label of this unlabeled point to have high confidence and hence select it to augment the labeled data set. Finally we performance GDA on the augmented labeled data set to get the final transformation.

The SSGDA (or M-SSGDA) algorithm is summarized in Table below:

Input: labeled data x_i $(i = 1, \ldots, l)$, unlabeled data x_i $(i = l+1, \ldots, n)$, K, θ, ε
Initialize $\mathbf{E}^{(0)}$ using Eq. (8);   Initialize $t_k^{(0)}$ based on $\mathbf{E}^{(0)}$ for $k = 1, \ldots, C$;   Construct the K-nearest neighbor graph; $p = 0$;   Repeat $\qquad p = p + 1$; $\qquad$ Solve the optimization problem (7) or (10); $\qquad$ Update $\mathbf{E}^{(p)}$ and $t_k^{(p)}$ using the result of the optimization problem for $k = 1, \ldots, C$;   Until $\|\mathbf{E}^{(p)} - \mathbf{E}^{(p-1)}\|_F \leq \varepsilon$ Select the unlabeled data points with high confidence based on the threshold θ;   Add the selected unlabeled data points with their estimated labels into the labeled data set   and perform GDA on the augmented labeled data set to get the transformation $\mathbf{P}$.
Output: the transformation $\mathbf{P}$

In order to gain some insight into our method, we investigate the dual form of the optimization problem $\max\limits_{E,\{t_k\}} \ldots \sum\limits_{j=1}^{C} \mathbf{e}_{ij} = 1, i = l+1, \ldots, n.$

We denote $r_k^{(p)} \dfrac{\left(e_k^{(p)}\right)^{T} S e_k^{(p)}}{\left(t_k^{(p)}\right)^2} 1_n - \dfrac{2 S e_k^{(p)}}{t_k^{(p)}}$. We plug the first equality constraint of the optimization problem above into its objective function and get the following Lagrangian:

$$L\left(E, \alpha, \beta\right) = \sum_{k=1}^{C} \left(r_k^{(p)}\right)^{T} e_k - \sum_{k=1}^{C}\sum_{i=1}^{l} \alpha_{ki}\left(e_{ik} - \delta_k^{c(i)}\right)$$

$$-\sum_{k=1}^{C}\sum_{i=l+1}^{l}\alpha_{ki}e_{ik} - \sum_{i=l+1}^{n}\beta_i\left(\sum_{k=1}^{C}e_{ik}-1\right),$$

where $c(i)$ is the class label of labeled data point i and $\delta_k^{c(i)}$ is the delta function whose value is 1 if $c(i) = k$ and 0 otherwise.

So the dual form of the optimization problem $\max\limits_{E,\{t_k\}}...\sum\limits_{j=1}^{C}e_{ij} = 1, i = l+1,...,n$ is:

$$\max_{\alpha,\beta} \quad \sum_{k=1}^{C}\sum_{i=1}^{l}\alpha_{ki}\delta_k^{c(i)} + \sum_{i=l+1}^{n}\beta_i$$

$$s.t. \quad \alpha_{ki} = r_{ki}^{(p)}, i = 1,...,l, \ k = 1,...C$$

$$\alpha_{ki} + \beta_i = r_{ki}^{(p)}, \ i = l+1,...,n, \ k = 1,...C$$

$$\alpha_{ki} \geq 0, i = l+1,...,n, k = 1,..,C$$

where $r_{ki}^{(p)}$ is the ith element of vector $r_k^{(p)}$.

The Karush-Kuhn-Tucker (KKT) condition $\max\limits_{E,\{t_k\}}...\sum\limits_{j=1}^{C}e_{ij} = 1, i = l+1,...,n$ for the optimization problem above is:

$$\alpha_{ki}e_{ik} = 0, \ \ i = l+1,...,n, \ k = 1,..,C.$$

From the first constraint of the optimization problem $\max\limits_{\alpha,\beta}...\alpha_{ki} \geq 0, i = l+1,...,n, k = 1,..,C$ we can see that each α_{ki} has a constant value for $i = 1, ..., l, k = 1, ...,C$. So we can simplify the optimization problem $\max\limits_{\alpha,\beta}...\alpha_{ki} \geq 0, i = l+1,...,n, k = 1,..,C$ by eliminating the first summation term in the objective function and the first constraint as:

$$\max_{\alpha\beta} \quad \sum_{k=1}^{n}\beta_i$$

$$s.t. \quad \alpha_{ki} + \beta_i = r_{ki}^{(p)}, \ i = l+1,...,n, \ k = 1,....,C$$

$$\alpha_{ki} \geq 0, \ i = l+1,...,n, k = 1,..,C$$

which can be further simplified as:

$$\max_{\alpha\beta} \quad \sum_{i=l+1}^{n}\beta_i$$

$$s.t. \quad \beta_i \leq r_{ki}^{(p)}, \ i = l+1,...,n, \ k = 1,....,C.$$

So the optimal solution of β_i can be obtained as $\beta_i = \min_k\left\{r_{ki}^{(p)}\right\}$ for $i = l + 1, ..., n$.

For each unlabeled data point, if we assume $e_{ik}^* > 0$, then from the KKT condition $\alpha_{ki}e_{ik} = 0, \ i = l+1,...,n, \ k = 1,..,C$ we can get $\alpha_{k*i} = 0$ and also $\beta_i = r_{k*i}^{(p)}$ according to the first constraint of the optimization problem $\max\limits_{\alpha\beta}\dots\alpha_{ki}\geq 0, i=l+1,\dots,n, k=1,\dots,C$. So,

$$r_{k*i}^{(p)}=\min_{k}\left\{r_{ki}^{(p)}\right\}$$

and

$$k^{*}=\arg\min_{k}\left\{r_{ki}^{(p)}\right\}.$$

So $r_{k*i}^{(p)}$ can be seen as the negative confidence that the ith data point belongs to the kth class and hence we can classify each data point to the class corresponding to the minimal negative confidence. If there is a unique minimum, then we can get $e_{ik^{*}}=1$ and $e_{ik'}=0$ for $k'\neq k^{*}$; otherwise, we can first find the set of unlabeled data points for which there exists a unique minimum and e_{ik} can be easily determined, and then we can solve

a smaller LP problem $\max\limits_{E,\{t_k\}}\dots\sum\limits_{j=1}^{C}e_{ij}=1, i=l+1,\dots,n$ by plugging in the known elements e_{ij}.

From our experiments, the latter situation seldom occurs and this can speed up the

optimization problem $\max\limits_{E,\{t_k\}}\dots\sum\limits_{j=1}^{C}e_{ij}=1, i=l+1,\dots,n$ which even does not need to solve an LP problem.

For problem $\max\limits_{E,\{t_k\}}\dots\sum\limits_{j=1}^{C}e_{ij}=1, i=l+1,\dots,n$, when the number of unlabeled data points is large, the computational cost to find the optimal value is still very large. Here we use an alternating method to solve problem before. That is, at one time we optimize problem

before with respect to ei with $\{e(j\neq i)\}$ fixed. Let $r_k^{(p)}\dfrac{\left(e_k^{(p)}\right)^{T}Se_k^{(p)}}{\left(t_k^{(p)}\right)^{2}}1_n-\dfrac{2Se_k^{(p)}}{t_k^{(p)}}$ .We first rewrite problem before as:

$$\min_{E}\quad\sum_{k=1}^{C}r_k^{T}e_k+\lambda\sum_{i=1}^{n}\sum_{i=l+1}^{n}w_{ij}\left\|e^{i}-e^{j}\right\|_{1}$$

$$s.t.\ e_{ij}=\begin{cases}1 & if\ x_i\in\Pi_j\\0 & otherwise\end{cases}\ i=1,\dots,l$$

$$e_{ij}\geq 0,\ i=l+1,\dots,n, j=1,\dots,C$$

$$\sum_{j=1}^{C}e_{ij}=1, i=l+1,\dots,n.$$

which can be reformulated as,

$$\min\quad\sum_{k=1}^{n}e^{k}\left(e^{k}\right)+\sum_{i=1}^{n}\sum_{j=i+1}^{n}{}_{ij}\left\|e^{i}-e^{j}\right\|$$

$$s.t. \ e_{ij} = \begin{cases} & if \quad \in \prod \\ & otherwise \end{cases} \quad i = 1, \dots, l$$

$$e_{ij} \geq 0, \ i = l+1, \dots, n, j = 1, \dots, C$$

$$\sum e_{ij} = 1, \ i = l+1, \dots, n,$$

where $R = (r_1, \dots, r_C)$ and r^k is the kth row of R. So when using an alternating method, the optimization problem with respect to e^i $(i > l)$ can be formulated as,

$$\min_{e^i} \ e^i \left(r^i \right)^T | + \lambda \sum_{j \neq i \& w_{ij} > 0} w_{ij} \left\| e^i - e^j \right\|_1$$

$$s.t. \ e_{ij} \geq 0, \ j = 1, \dots, C$$

$$\sum_{j=1}^{C} e_{ij} = 1.$$

Compared with the original problem $\max_{E, \{t_k\}} \dots \sum_{j=1}^{C} e_{ij} = 1, i = l+1, \dots, n$ there is no need to specify the constraints for labeled data in problem above which reduces the complexity of the optimization problem. The problem above has C variables and $C + 1$ constraints and so it can be solved efficiently. Since problem $\max_{E, \{t_k\}} \dots \sum_{j=1}^{C} e_{ij} = 1, i = l+1, \dots, n$ is a convex problem and each step in the alternating method decreases the objective function value, the learning procedure can converge to the global optimum.

The computational cost of SSGDA and M-SSGDA includes performing GDA twice and solving the optimization problem using CCCP. The complexity of GDA is (n^3). The LP problem inside each iteration of CCCP can be solved efficiently. From our experimental results, CCCP converges very fast in less than 10 iterations. So SSGDA and M-SSGDA are efficient under most situations.

Singular Value Decomposition

SVD can be viewed as a method for transforming correlated variables into a set of uncorrelated ones that better expose the various relationships among the original data items. It is a method for identifying and ordering the dimensions along which data points exhibit the most variation. With SVD, it's possible to find the best approximation of the original data points using fewer dimensions. Hence, SVD is used for data reduction.

Singular Value Decomposition factorizes a real or complex matrix. For an $M \times N$ matrix A of rank r there exists a factorization (Singular Value Decomposition = SVD) as follows:

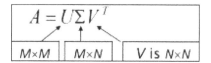

Here the columns of U are orthogonal eigen vectors of AA^T, the columns of V are orthogonal eigen vectors of A^TA and Eigen values $\lambda_1 ... \lambda_r$ of AA^T are the eigen values of A^TA. An illustration of SVD dimensions and sparseness is as given in figure below:

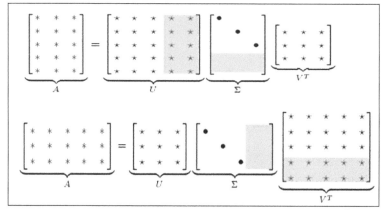

SVD Illustration.

The corresponding singular values are given below:

$$\sigma_i = \sqrt{\lambda_i}$$

$$\sum = diag(\sigma_1 ... \sigma_r) \leftarrow singular\ values$$

Computation of SVD

Any real **m x n** matrix A can be decomposed uniquely:

$$A = UDV^T$$

Here U is m x n and column orthonormal ($U^TU=I$) and D is n x n and diagonal:

$$D = diag(\sigma_1, \sigma_2, ... \sigma_n)$$

σ_i are called singular values of A. It is assumed that $\sigma_1 \geq \sigma_2 \geq ... \geq \sigma_n \geq 0$. V is **n x n** and orthonormal ($VV^T=V^TV=I$). The columns of U are eigenvectors of AA^T:

$$AA^T = UDV^TVDU^T = UD^2U^T$$

The columns of V are eigenvectors of $A^T A$:

$$A^T A = V D U^T U D V^T = V D^2 V$$

If λ_i is an eigenvalue of $A^T A$ (or AA^T), then $\lambda i = \sigma_i^2$.

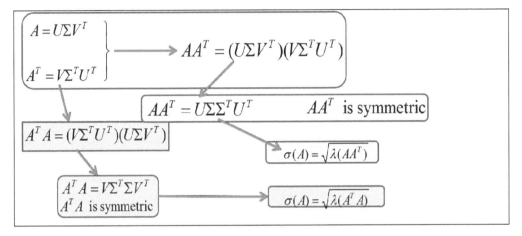

The step in the computation of SVD is given in figure. From figure (b) we see that given the matrix A, we first find $W = A^T A$ and then make the determinant of $(W-\lambda I)=0$ where I is the identity matrix to find the value of the eigen values λ_1 and λ_2 and hence the singular values λ_1 and λ_2. These eigenvectors become column vectors in a matrix ordered by the size of the corresponding eigenvalue. In other words, the eigenvector of the largest eigenvalue is column one, the eigenvector of the next largest eigenvalue is column two, and so forth and so on until we have the eigenvector of the smallest eigenvalue as the last column of our matrix. Finally after appropriate calculations shown in the figure we find the orthonormal basis u_1. Similarly we now we use AA^T to find u_1, u_2 and u_3, the orthonormal basis. Now we write the matrix A= range matrix formed by u_1, u_2 and u_3 x rank matrix of A and the Null (A). Figure shows how the matrix needs to be converted into bi-diagonal and then diagonal to get the SVD.

Example:

$$u_1 = \begin{bmatrix} \frac{1}{\sqrt{2}} \\ \frac{1}{\sqrt{2}} \\ 0 \end{bmatrix} \quad u_2, u_3 \text{ orthonormal basis for Null(AA}^T)$$

$$AA^T = \begin{bmatrix} 2 & 2 & 0 \\ 2 & 2 & 0 \\ 0 & 0 & 0 \end{bmatrix}$$

Range(A) Rank(A)   Null(A)

$$\begin{bmatrix} 1 & 1 \\ 1 & 1 \\ 0 & 0 \end{bmatrix} = \begin{bmatrix} \frac{1}{\sqrt{2}} & \frac{1}{\sqrt{2}} & 0 \\ \frac{1}{\sqrt{2}} & \frac{1}{\sqrt{2}} & 0 \\ 0 & 0 & 1 \end{bmatrix} \begin{bmatrix} 2 & 0 \\ 0 & 0 \\ 0 & 0 \end{bmatrix} \begin{bmatrix} \frac{1}{\sqrt{2}} & \frac{1}{\sqrt{2}} \\ \frac{1}{\sqrt{2}} & \frac{-1}{\sqrt{2}} \end{bmatrix}$$

$$u_2 = \begin{bmatrix} \frac{1}{\sqrt{2}} \\ \frac{-1}{\sqrt{2}} \\ 0 \end{bmatrix} \quad u_3 = \begin{bmatrix} 0 \\ 0 \\ 1 \end{bmatrix}$$

Computation of SVD.

The property of the standard deviation of a square matrix is shown in figure. If **m=n**, then U is n x n and orthonormal ($U^TU=UU^T=I$), D is n x n and diagonal is as before and V is n x n and orthonormal ($VV^T=V^TV=I$). Similarly the properties of eigen values, singular values and determinants of square matrices is shown in figure. Another example of the calculation of singular values is given in figure above.

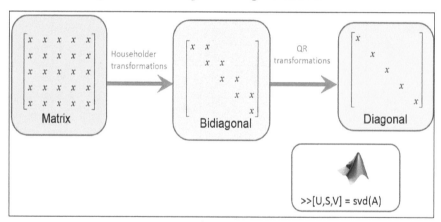

Concept used in SVD calculation.

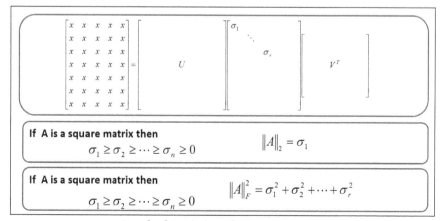

Standard Deviation of a Square Matrix.

If A is a square matrix then,

$$\sigma_1 \geq \sigma_2 \geq ... \geq \sigma_n \geq 0 \qquad \|A\|_2 = \sigma_1$$

If A is a square matrix then,

$$\sigma_1 \geq \sigma_2 \geq ... \geq \sigma_n \geq 0 \qquad \|A\|_F^2 = \sigma_1^2 + \sigma_2^2 + ... + \sigma_r^2$$

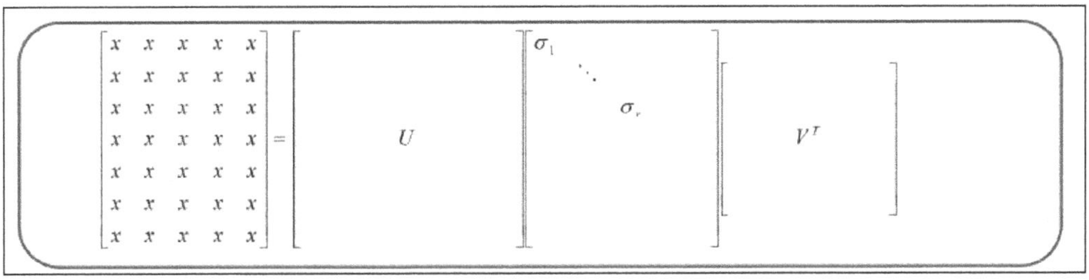

Singular Values of a Square Symmetric Matrix.

If A is a square symmetric matrix then the singular values of A are the absolute values of A are the eigenvalues of A.

$$A = Q \Sigma Q^T = Q |\Sigma| sign(\Sigma) Q^T$$

If A is a square matrix then,

$$|\det(A)| = \prod_{i=1}^{n} \sigma_i$$

Let $A = \begin{bmatrix} 1 & -1 \\ 0 & 1 \\ 1 & 0 \end{bmatrix}$ Thus M=3, N=2. Its SVD is

$$\begin{bmatrix} 0 & 2/\sqrt{6} & 1/\sqrt{3} \\ 1/\sqrt{2} & -1/\sqrt{6} & 1/\sqrt{3} \\ 1/\sqrt{2} & 1/\sqrt{6} & -1/\sqrt{3} \end{bmatrix} \begin{bmatrix} 1 & 0 \\ 0 & \sqrt{3} \\ 0 & 0 \end{bmatrix} \begin{bmatrix} 1/\sqrt{2} & 1/\sqrt{2} \\ 1/\sqrt{2} & -1/\sqrt{2} \end{bmatrix}$$

Typically, the singular values arranged in decreasing order.

Example for Calculation of Singular Values.

Figure gives a table showing the difference between SVD and eigen decomposition.

SVD	Eigen Decomp
Use two Different bases U & V	Uses just one (eigenvectors)
Uses orthonormal bases	Generally is not orthogonal
All matrices (even rectangular)	Not all matrices (even square) (only diagonalizable)

Classification Techniques

There are various types of classification techniques in machine learning, each suited to a specific task and role, and is a part of the supervised machine learning approach. This chapter touches upon the various classification techniques like statistical classification, probabilistic classification, multiclass classification and linear classifier to provide an extensive understanding on the topic.

Statistical classification is the division of data into meaningful categories for analysis. It is possible to apply statistical formulas to data to do this automatically, allowing for large scale data processing in preparation for analysis. Some standardized systems exist for common types of data like results from medical imaging studies. This allows multiple entities to evaluate data with the same metrics so they can compare and exchange information easily.

As researchers and other parties collect data, they can assign it to loose categories on the basis of similar characteristics. They can also develop formulas to classify their data as it comes in, automatically dividing it into specific statistical classifications. As they collect information, researchers may not know very much about their data, which makes it difficult to classify. Formulas can identify important features to use as potential category identifiers.

Processing data requires statistical classification to separate out different kinds of information for analysis and comparison. For instance, in a census, workers should be able to explore multiple parameters to provide a meaningful assessment of the data they collect. Using declarations on census forms, a statistical classification algorithm can separate out different types of households and individuals on the basis of information like age, household configuration, average income, and so forth.

The data collected must be quantitative in nature for statistical analysis to work. Qualitative information can be too subjective. As a result, researchers need to design data collection methods carefully to get information they can actually use. For example, in a clinical trial, observers filling out forms during follow-up examinations could use a scoring rubric to assess patient health. Instead of a qualitative assessment like "the patient looks good," the researcher could assign a score of seven on a scale, which a formula could use to process the data.

Classification is of two types:

- Binary Classification: When we have to categorize given data into 2 distinct classes. Example – On the basis of given health conditions of a person, we have to determine whether the person has a certain disease or not.

- Multiclass Classification: The number of classes is more than 2. For Example – On the basis of data about different species of flowers, we have to determine which specie does our observation belong to.

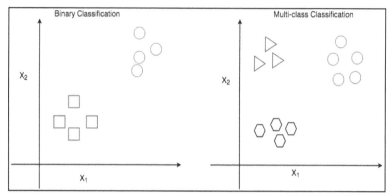

Figure: Binary and Multiclass Classification. Here x1 and x2 are our variables upon which the class is predicted.

Working of Classification

Suppose we have to predict whether a given patient has a certain disease or not, on the basis of 3 variables, called features.

Which means there are two possible outcomes:

1. The patient has the said disease. Basically a result labelled "Yes" or "True".

2. The patient is disease free. A result labelled "No" or "False".

This is a binary classification problem.

We have a set of observations called training data set, which comprises of sample data with actual classification results. We train a model, called Classifier on this data set, and use that model to predict whether a certain patient will have the disease or not.

The outcome, thus now depends upon:

1. How well these features are able to "map" to the outcome.

2. The quality of our data set. By quality I refer to statistical and Mathematical qualities.

3. How well our Classifier generalizes this relationship between the features and the outcome.

4. The values of the x1 and x2.

Following is the generalized block diagram of the classification task.

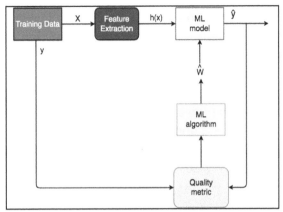

Generalized Classification Block Diagram.

- X: pre-classified data, in the form of a N*M matrix. N is the no. of observations and M is the number of features.

- y: An N-d vector corresponding to predicted classes for each of the N observations.

- Feature Extraction: Extracting valuable information from input X using a series of transforms.

- ML Model: The "Classifier" we'll train.

- y': Labels predicted by the Classifier.

- Quality Metric: Metric used for measuring the performance of the model.

- ML Algorithm: The algorithm that is used to update weights w', which update the model and "learns" iteratively.

Types of Classifiers (Algorithms)

There are various types of classifiers. Some of them are:

- Linear Classifiers: Logistic Regression.

- Tree Based Classifiers: Decision Tree Classifier.

- Support Vector Machines.

- Artificial Neural Networks.

- Bayesian Regression.

- Gaussian Naive Bayes Classifiers.

- Stochastic Gradient Descent (SGD) Classifier.

- Ensemble Methods: Random Forests, AdaBoost, Bagging Classifier, Voting Classifier, ExtraTrees Classifier.

Frequentist Procedures

Early work on statistical classification was undertaken by Fisher, in the context of two-group problems, leading to Fisher's linear discriminant function as the rule for assigning a group to a new observation. This early work assumed that data-values within each of the two groups had a multivariate normal distribution. The extension of this same context to more than two-groups has also been considered with a restriction imposed that the classification rule should be linear. Later work for the multivariate normal distribution allowed the classifier to be nonlinear: several classification rules can be derived based on slight different adjustments of the Mahalanobis distance, with a new observation being assigned to the group whose center has the lowest adjusted distance from the observation.

Bayesian Procedures

Unlike frequentist procedures, Bayesian classification procedures provide a natural way of taking into account any available information about the relative sizes of the sub-populations associated with the different groups within the overall population. Bayesian procedures tend to be computationally expensive and, in the days before Markov chain Monte Carlo computations were developed, approximations for Bayesian clustering rules were devised.

Some Bayesian procedures involve the calculation of group membership probabilities: these can be viewed as providing a more and more informative outcome of a data analysis than a simple attribution of a single group-label to each new observation.

Feature Vectors

Most algorithms describe an individual instance whose category is to be predicted using a feature vector of individual, measurable properties of the instance. Each property is termed a feature, also known in statistics as an explanatory variable (or independent variable, although features may or may not be statistically independent). Features may variously be binary (e.g. "on" or "off"); categorical (e.g. "A", "B", "AB" or "O", for blood type); ordinal (e.g. "large", "medium" or "small"); integer-valued (e.g. the number of occurrences of a particular word in an email); or real-valued (e.g. a measurement of blood pressure). If the instance is an image, the feature values might correspond to the pixels of an image; if the instance is a piece of text, the feature values might be occurrence frequencies of different words. Some algorithms work only in terms of discrete data and require that real-valued or integer-valued data be *discretized* into groups (e.g. less than 5, between 5 and 10, or greater than 10).

Linear Classifiers

A large number of algorithms for classification can be phrased in terms of a linear function that assigns a score to each possible category k by combining the feature vector of an instance with a vector of weights, using a dot product. The predicted category is the one with the highest score. This type of score function is known as a linear predictor function and has the following general form:

$$\text{score}(\mathbf{X}_i, k) = \beta_k \cdot \mathbf{X}_i,$$

where X_i is the feature vector for instance i, β_k is the vector of weights corresponding to category k, and score(X_i, k) is the score associated with assigning instance i to category k. In discrete choice theory, where instances represent people and categories represent choices, the score is considered the utility associated with person i choosing category k.

Algorithms with this basic setup are known as linear classifiers. What distinguishes them is the procedure for determining (training) the optimal weights/coefficients and the way that the score is interpreted.

Examples of such algorithms are

- Logistic regression and Multinomial logistic regression.

- Probit regression.

- The perceptron algorithm.

- Support vector machines.

- Linear discriminant analysis.

Practical Applications of Classification

- Google's self driving car uses deep learning enabled classification techniques which enables it to detect and classify obstacles.

- Spam E-mail filtering is one of the most widespread and well recognized uses of Classification techniques.

- Detecting Health Problems, Facial Recognition, Speech Recognition, Object Detection, Sentiment Analysis all use Classification at their core.

Probabilistic Classification

Probabilistic classifiers and, in particular, the archetypical naive Bayes classifier, are among the most popular classifiers used in the machine learning community and increasingly in many applications. These classifiers are derived from generative probability models which provide a principled way to the study of statistical classification in complex domains such as natural language and visual processing.

The study of probabilistic classification is the study of approximating a joint distribution with a product distribution. Bayes rule is used to estimate the conditional probability of a class label, and then assumptions are made on the model, to decompose this probability into a product of conditional probabilities.

$$Pr\left(y|x\right) = Pr\left(y|x^1, x^2, \ldots x^n\right) = \prod_{i=1}^{n} Pr\left(x^i | x^1, \ldots x^{i-1}, y\right)\frac{Pr\left(y\right)}{Pr\left(x\right)} = \prod_{j=1}^{n'} Pr\left(y^j | y\right)\frac{Pr\left(y\right)}{Pr\left(x\right)},$$

where $x = \left(x^1, \ldots, x^n\right)$ is the observation and the $y^j = g_j\left(x^1, \ldots x^{i-1}, x^i\right)$, for some function g_j, are independent given the class label y.

While the use of Bayes rule is harmless, the final decomposition step introduces independence assumptions, which may not hold in the data. The functions g_j encode the probabilistic assumptions and allow the representation of any Bayesian network, e.g., a Markov model. The most common model used in classification, however, is the naive Bayes model in which $\forall_{j}, g_j\left(x^1, \ldots x^{i-1}, x^i\right) \equiv x^i$. That is, the original attributes are assumed to be independent given the class label.

Although the naive Bayes algorithm makes some unrealistic probabilistic assumptions it has been found to work remarkably well in practice. Roth develops a partial answer to this unexpected behavior using techniques from learning theory. It is shown that naive Bayes and other probabilistic classifiers are all "Linear Statistical Query" classifiers; thus, PAC type guarantees can be given on the performance of the classifier on future, previously unseen data, as a function of its performance on the training data, independently of the probabilistic assumptions made when deriving the classifier.

We consider the standard binary classification problem in a probabilistic setting. In this model one assumes that data elements (x, y) are sampled according to some arbitrary distribution P on $\chi \times \{0, 1\}$. χ (e.g., $\chi = \Re^M$) is the instance space and $y \in \{0, 1\}$ is the label. The goal of the learner is to determine, given a new example $x \in \chi,$, its most likely corresponding label $y(x)$, which is chosen as follows:

$$y(x) = \arg\max_{i \in \{0,1\}} P\left(y = i | x\right) = \arg\max_{i \in \{0,1\}} P\left(x | y = i\right)\frac{P(y = i)}{P(x)}.$$

We define the following distributions over χ: $P_0 = P\left(x | y = 0\right)$ and $P_1 = P\left(x | y = 1\right)$. With this notation, the Bayesian classifier predicts $y = 0$ iff $P_0\left(x\right) > P_1\left(x\right)$.

Types of Classification

Formally, an "ordinary" classifier is some rule, or function, that assigns to a sample x a class label $\hat{y}$:

$$\hat{y} = f(x)$$

The samples come from some set X (e.g., the set of all documents, or the set of all images), while the class labels form a finite set Y defined prior to training.

Probabilistic classifiers generalize this notion of classifiers: instead of functions, they are conditional distributions $\Pr(Y\,|\,X)$, meaning that for a given $x \in X$, they assign probabilities to all $y \in Y$ (and these probabilities sum to one). "Hard" classification can then be done using the optimal decision rule.

$$\hat{y} = \arg\max_{y} \Pr(Y = y\,|\,X)$$

or, in English, the predicted class is that which has the highest probability.

Binary probabilistic classifiers are also called binomial regression models in statistics. In econometrics, probabilistic classification in general is called discrete choice.

Some classification models, such as naive Bayes, logistic regression and multilayer perceptrons (when trained under an appropriate loss function) are naturally probabilistic. Other models such as support vector machines are not, but methods exist to turn them into probabilistic classifiers.

Generative and Conditional Training

Some models, such as logistic regression, are conditionally trained: they optimize the conditional probability $\Pr(Y\,|\,X)$ directly on a training set. Other classifiers, such as naive Bayes, are trained generatively: at training time, the class-conditional distribution $\Pr(X\,|\,Y)$ and the class prior $\Pr(Y)$ are found, and the conditional distribution $\Pr(Y\,|\,X)$ is derived using Bayes' rule.

Probability Calibration

When performing classification you often want not only to predict the class label, but also obtain a probability of the respective label. This probability gives you some kind of confidence on the prediction. Some models can give you poor estimates of the class probabilities and some even do not support probability prediction. The calibration module allows you to better calibrate the probabilities of a given model, or to add support for probability prediction.

Well calibrated classifiers are probabilistic classifiers for which the output of the predict_proba method can be directly interpreted as a confidence level. For instance, a well calibrated (binary) classifier should classify the samples such that among the samples to which it gave a predict_proba value close to 0.8, approximately 80% actually belong to the positive class. The following plot compares how well the probabilistic predictions of different classifiers are calibrated.

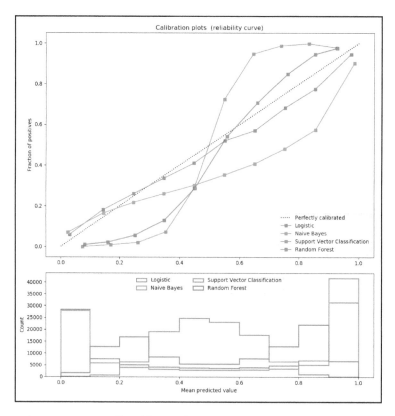

Logistic Regression returns well calibrated predictions by default as it directly optimizes log-loss. In contrast, the other methods return biased probabilities; with different biases per method:

- GaussianNB tends to push probabilities to 0 or 1 (note the counts in the histograms). This is mainly because it makes the assumption that features are conditionally independent given the class, which is not the case in this dataset which contains 2 redundant features.

- Random Forest Classifier shows the opposite behavior: the histograms show peaks at approximately 0.2 and 0.9 probability, while probabilities close to 0 or 1 are very rare. An explanation for this is given by Niculescu-Mizil and Caruana. "Methods such as bagging and random forests that average predictions from a base set of models can have difficulty making predictions near 0 and 1 because variance in the underlying base models will bias predictions that should be near zero or one away from these values. Because predictions are restricted to the interval [0,1], errors caused by variance tend to be one-sided near zero and one. For example, if a model should predict p = 0 for a case, the only way bagging can achieve this is if all bagged trees predict zero. If we add noise to the trees that bagging is averaging over, this noise will cause some trees to predict values larger than 0 for this case, thus moving the average prediction of the bagged ensemble away from 0. We observe this effect most strongly with random forests because the base-level trees trained with random forests have relatively high variance due to feature sub setting." As a result, the calibration curve also referred to as the reliability diagram shows a characteristic sigmoid shape, indicating that the classifier could trust its "intuition" more and return probabilities closer to 0 or 1 typically.

- Linear Support Vector Classification (LinearSVC) shows an even more sigmoid curve as the RandomForestClassifier, which is typical for maximum-margin methods, which focus on hard samples that are close to the decision boundary (the support vectors).

Two approaches for performing calibration of probabilistic predictions are provided: a parametric approach based on Platt's sigmoid model and a non-parametric approach based on isotonic regression (sklearn.isotonic). Probability calibration should be done on new data not used for model fitting. The class CalibratedClassifierCV uses a cross-validation generator and estimates for each split the model parameter on the train samples and the calibration of the test samples. The probabilities predicted for the folds are then averaged. Already fitted classifiers can be calibrated by CalibratedClassifierCV via the parameter cv="prefit". In this case, the user has to take care manually that data for model fitting and calibration are disjoint.

The following images demonstrate the benefit of probability calibration. The first image present a dataset with 2 classes and 3 blobs of data. The blob in the middle contains random samples of each class. The probability for the samples in this blob should be 0.5.

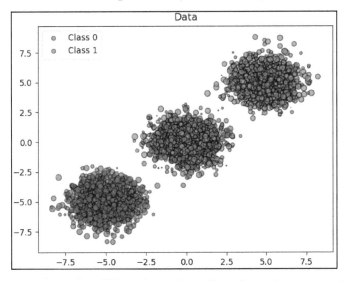

The following image shows on the data above the estimated probability using a Gaussian naive Bayes classifier without calibration, with a sigmoid calibration and with a non-parametric isotonic calibration. One can observe that the non-parametric model provides the most accurate probability estimates for samples in the middle, i.e., 0.5.

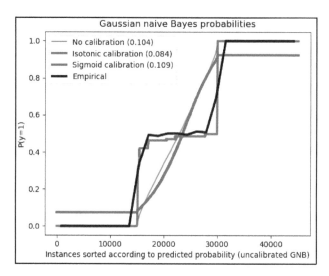

The following experiment is performed on an artificial dataset for binary classification with 100.000 samples (1.000 of them are used for model fitting) with 20 features. Of the 20 features, only 2 are informative and 10 are redundant. The figure shows the estimated probabilities obtained with logistic regression, a linear support-vector classifier (SVC), and linear SVC with both isotonic calibration and sigmoid calibration. The calibration performance is evaluated with Brier score brier_score_loss, reported in the legend (the smaller the better).

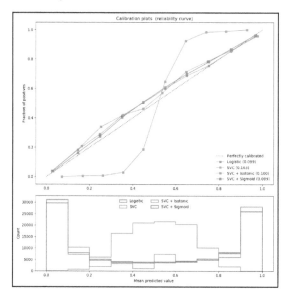

One can observe here that logistic regression is well calibrated as its curve is nearly diagonal. Linear SVC's calibration curve or reliability diagram has a sigmoid curve, which is typical for an under-confident classifier. In the case of LinearSVC, this is caused by the margin property of the hinge loss, which lets the model focus on hard samples that are close to the decision boundary (the support vectors). Both kinds of calibration can fix this issue and yield nearly identical results. The next figure shows the calibration curve of Gaussian naive Bayes on the same data, with both kinds of calibration and also without calibration.

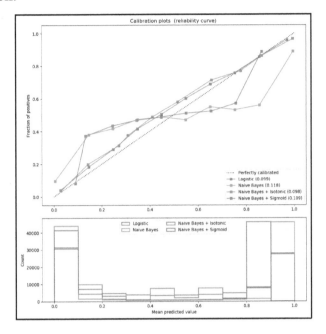

One can see that Gaussian naive Bayes performs very badly but does so in an other way than linear SVC: While linear SVC exhibited a sigmoid calibration curve, Gaussian naive Bayes' calibration curve has a transposed-sigmoid shape. This is typical for an over-confident classifier. In this case, the classifier's overconfidence is caused by the redundant features which violate the naive Bayes assumption of feature-independence.

Calibration of the probabilities of Gaussian naive Bayes with isotonic regression can fix this issue as can be seen from the nearly diagonal calibration curve. Sigmoid calibration also improves the brier score slightly, albeit not as strongly as the non-parametric isotonic calibration. This is an intrinsic limitation of sigmoid calibration, whose parametric form assumes a sigmoid rather than a transposed-sigmoid curve. The non-parametric isotonic calibration model, however, makes no such strong assumptions and can deal with either shape, provided that there is sufficient calibration data. In general, sigmoid calibration is preferable in cases where the calibration curve is sigmoid and where there is limited calibration data, while isotonic calibration is preferable for non-sigmoid calibration curves and in situations where large amounts of data are available for calibration.

Calibrated Classifier CV can also deal with classification tasks that involve more than two classes if the base estimator can do so. In this case, the classifier is calibrated first for each class separately in an one-vs-rest fashion. When predicting probabilities for unseen data, the calibrated probabilities for each class are predicted separately. As those probabilities do not necessarily sum to one, a post processing is performed to normalize them.

The next image illustrates how sigmoid calibration changes predicted probabilities for a 3-class classification problem. Illustrated is the standard 2-simplex, where the three corners correspond to the three classes. Arrows point from the probability vectors predicted by an uncalibrated classifier to the probability vectors predicted by the same classifier after sigmoid calibration on a hold-out validation set. Colors indicate the true class of an instance (red: class 1, green: class 2, blue: class 3).

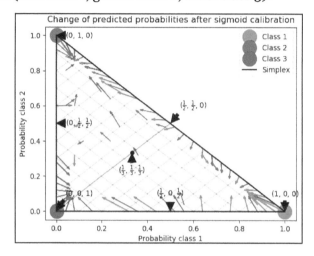

The base classifier is a random forest classifier with 25 base estimators (trees). If this classifier is trained on all 800 training data points, it is overly confident in its predictions and thus incurs a large log-loss. Calibrating an identical classifier, which was trained on 600 data points, with method='sigmoid' on the remaining 200 data points reduces the confidence of the predictions, i.e., moves the probability vectors from the edges of the simplex towards the center:

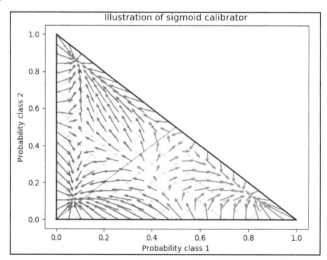

This calibration results in a lower log-loss. An alternative would have been to increase the number of base estimators which would have resulted in a similar decrease in log-loss.

Naive Bayes Classifier

Naive Bayes classifiers are a collection of classification algorithms based on Bayes' Theorem. It is not a single algorithm but a family of algorithms where all of them share a common principle, i.e. every pair of features being classified is independent of each other.

To start with, let us consider a dataset.

Consider a fictional dataset that describes the weather conditions for playing a game of golf. Given the weather conditions, each tuple classifies the conditions as fit("Yes") or unfit("No") for planning golf.

Here is a tabular representation of our dataset.

	OUTLOOK	TEMPERATURE	HUMIDITY	WINDY	PLAY GOLF
0	Rainy	Hot	High	False	No
1	Rainy	Hot	High	True	No
2	Overcast	Hot	High	False	Yes
3	Sunny	Mild	High	False	Yes
4	Sunny	Cool	Normal	False	Yes
5	Sunny	Cool	Normal	True	No
6	Overcast	Cool	Normal	True	Yes
7	Rainy	Mild	High	False	No
8	Rainy	Cool	Normal	False	Yes
9	Sunny	Mild	Normal	False	Yes
10	Rainy	Mild	Normal	True	Yes
11	Overcast	Mild	High	True	Yes
12	Overcast	Hot	Normal	False	Yes
13	Sunny	Mild	High	True	No

The dataset is divided into two parts, namely, feature matrix and the response vector.

- Feature matrix contains all the vectors (rows) of dataset in which each vector consists of the value of dependent features. In above dataset, features are 'Outlook', 'Temperature', 'Humidity' and 'Windy'.

- Response vector contains the value of class variable (prediction or output) for each row of feature matrix. In above dataset, the class variable name is 'Play golf'.

Assumption

The fundamental Naive Bayes assumption is that each feature makes an:

- Independent,
- Equal.

contribution to the outcome.

With relation to our dataset, this concept can be understood as:

- We assume that no pair of features are dependent. For example, the temperature being 'Hot' has nothing to do with the humidity or the outlook being 'Rainy' has no effect on the winds. Hence, the features are assumed to be independent.

- Secondly, each feature is given the same weight (or importance). For example, knowing only temperature and humidity alone can't predict the outcome accurately. None of the attributes is irrelevant and assumed to be contributing equally to the outcome.

Note: The assumptions made by Naive Bayes are not generally correct in real-world situations. In-fact, the independence assumption is never correct but often works well in practice.

Now, before moving to the formula for Naive Bayes, it is important to know about Bayes' theorem.

Bayes' Theorem

Bayes' Theorem finds the probability of an event occurring given the probability of another event that has already occurred. Bayes' theorem is stated mathematically as the following equation:

$$P(A \mid B) = \frac{P(B \mid A)P(A)}{P(B)}$$

where A and B are events and P(B) ? 0.

- Basically, we are trying to find probability of event A, given the event B is true. Event B is also termed as evidence.

- P (A) is the priori of A (the prior probability, i.e. Probability of event before evidence is seen). The evidence is an attribute value of an unknown instance (here, it is event B).

- P (A|B) is a posteriori probability of B, i.e. probability of event after evidence is seen.

Now, with regards to our dataset, we can apply Bayes' theorem in following way:

$$P(y \mid X) = \frac{P(X \mid y)P(y)}{P(X)}$$

where, y is class variable and X is a dependent feature vector (of size n) where:

$$X = (x_1, x_2, x_3, \ldots, x_n)$$

Just to clear, an example of a feature vector and corresponding class variable can be: (refer 1st row of dataset).

X = (Rainy, Hot, High, False)

y = No

So basically, P (X|y) here means, the probability of "Not playing golf" given that the weather conditions are "Rainy outlook", "Temperature is hot", "high humidity" and "no wind".

Naive Assumption

Now, its time to put a naive assumption to the Bayes' theorem, which is independence among the features. So now, we split evidence into the independent parts.

Now, if any two events A and B are independent, then,

P(A,B) = P(A)P(B)

Hence, we reach to the result:

$$P(y \mid x_1,...,x_n) = \frac{P(x_1 \mid y)P(x_2 \mid y)...P(x_n \mid y)P(y)}{P(x_1)P(x_2)...P(x_n)}$$

which can be expressed as:

$$P(y \mid x_1,...,x_n) = \frac{P(y)\prod_{i=1}^{n} P(x_i \mid y)}{P(x_1)P(x_2)...P(x_n)}$$

Now, as the denominator remains constant for a given input, we can remove that term:

$$P(y \mid x_1,...,x_n) \propto P(y)\prod_{i=1}^{n} P(x_i \mid y)$$

.

Now, we need to create a classifier model. For this, we find the probability of given set of inputs for all possible values of the class variable y and pick up the output with maximum probability. This can be expressed mathematically as:

$$y = argmax_y P(y)\prod_{i=1}^{n} P(x_i \mid y)$$

So, finally, we are left with the task of calculating P(y) and P(x_i | y).

Please note that P (y) is also called class probability and P(xi | y) is called conditional probability.

The different naive Bayes classifiers differ mainly by the assumptions they make regarding the distribution of P (x_i | y).

Let us try to apply the above formula manually on our weather dataset. For this, we need to do some pre computations on our dataset.

We need to find P (x_i | y_j) for each x_i in X and y_j in y. All these calculations have been demonstrated in the tables below:

Outlook

	Yes	No	P(yes)	P(no)
Sunny	2	3	2/9	3/5
Overcast	4	0	4/9	0/5
Rainy	3	2	3/9	2/5
Total	9	5	100%	100%

Temperature

	Yes	No	P(yes)	P(no)
Hot	2	2	2/9	2/5
Mild	4	2	4/9	2/5
Cool	3	1	3/9	1/5
Total	9	5	100%	100%

Humidity

	Yes	No	P(yes)	P(no)
High	3	4	3/9	4/5
Normal	6	1	6/9	1/5
Total	9	5	100%	100%

Wind

	Yes	No	P(yes)	P(no)
False	6	2	6/9	2/5
True	3	3	3/9	3/5
Total	9	5	100%	100%

Play		P(Yes)/P(No)
Yes	9	9/14
No	5	5/14
Total	14	100%

So, in the figure above, we have calculated P (x_i | y_j) for each x_i in X and y_j in y manually in the tables 1-4. For example, probability of playing golf given that the temperature is cool, i.e P (temp. = cool | play golf = Yes) = 3/9.

Also, we need to find class probabilities (P(y)) which has been calculated in the table 5. For example, P (play golf = Yes) = 9/14.

So now, we are done with our pre-computations and the classifier is ready!

Let us test it on a new set of features (let us call it today):

today = (Sunny, Hot, Normal, False)

So, probability of playing golf is given by:

$$P(Yes \mid today) = \frac{P(Sunny\ Outlook \mid Yes)P(HotTemperature \mid Yes)P(NormalHumidity \mid Yes)P(NoWind \mid Yes)P(Yes)}{P(today)}$$

and probability to not play golf is given by:

$$P(No \mid today) = \frac{P(Sunny\ Outlook \mid No)P(HotTemperature \mid No)P(NormalHumidity \mid No)P(NoWind \mid No)P(No)}{P(today)}$$

Since, P (today) is common in both probabilities, we can ignore P(today) and find proportional probabilities as:

$$P(Yes \mid today) \propto \frac{2}{9}.\frac{2}{9}.\frac{6}{9}.\frac{6}{9}.\frac{9}{14} \approx 0.0141$$

and

$$P(No \mid today) \propto \frac{3}{5} \cdot \frac{2}{5} \cdot \frac{1}{5} \cdot \frac{2}{5} \cdot \frac{5}{14} \approx 0.0068$$

Now, since

$$P(Yes \mid today) + P(No \mid today) = 1$$

These numbers can be converted into a probability by making the sum equal to 1 (normalization):

$$P(Yes \mid today) = \frac{0.0141}{0.0141 + 0.0068} = 0.67$$

and

$$P(No \mid today) = \frac{0.0068}{0.0141 + 0.0068} = 0.33$$

Since

$$P(Yes \mid today) > P(No \mid today)$$

So, prediction that golf would be played is 'Yes'.

The method that we discussed above is applicable for discrete data. In case of continuous data, we need to make some assumptions regarding the distribution of values of each feature. The different naive Bayes classifiers differ mainly by the assumptions they make regarding the distribution of $P(x_i \mid y)$.

Now, we discuss one of such classifiers here.

Gaussian Naive Bayes Classifier

In Gaussian Naive Bayes, continuous values associated with each feature are assumed to be distributed according to a Gaussian distribution. A Gaussian distribution is also called Normal distribution. When plotted, it gives a bell shaped curve which is symmetric about the mean of the feature values as shown below:

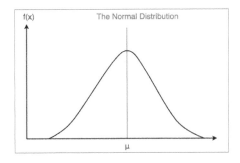

The likelihood of the features is assumed to be Gaussian, hence, conditional probability is given by:

$$P(x_i|y) = \frac{1}{\sqrt{2\pi\sigma_y^2}} exp\left(-\frac{(x_i - \mu y)^2}{2\sigma_y^2}\right)$$

Now, we look at an implementation of Gaussian Naive Bayes classifier using scikit-learn.

```
# load the iris dataset

from sklearn.datasets import load_iris

iris = load_iris()


# store the feature matrix (X) and response vector (y)

X = iris.data

y = iris.target


# splitting X and y into training and testing sets

from sklearn.model_selection import train_test_split

X_train, X_test, y_train, y_test = train_test_split(X, y, test_size=0.4,
random_state=1)


# training the model on training set

from sklearn.naive_bayes import GaussianNB

gnb = GaussianNB()

gnb.fit(X_train, y_train)


# making predictions on the testing set

y_pred = gnb.predict(X_test)


# comparing actual response values (y_test) with predicted response
values (y_pred)

from sklearn import metrics
```

```
print("Gaussian Naive Bayes model accuracy(in %):", metrics.accura-
cy_score(y_test, y_pred)*100)
```

Run on IDE

Output

Gaussian Naive Bayes model accuracy(in %): 95.0

Other popular Naive Bayes classifiers are:

- Multinomial Naive Bayes: Feature vectors represent the frequencies with which certain events have been generated by a multinomial distribution. This is the event model typically used for document classification.

- Bernoulli Naive Bayes: In the multivariate Bernoulli event model, features are independent booleans (binary variables) describing inputs. Like the multinomial model, this model is popular for document classification tasks, where binary term occurrence (i.e. a word occurs in a document or not) features are used rather than term frequencies (i.e. frequency of a word in the document).

Multiclass Classification

In multiclass classification, each record belongs to one of three or more classes, and the algorithm's goal is to construct a function which, given a new data point, will correctly identify into which class the new data point falls.

For example, a multiclass algorithm can determine which parental guideline rating a movie is likely to receive – "PG," "TV-14," "R," "G," etc. – based on patterns it learns from this sample movie dataset:

Title	Rating	Tags	Release Year	User Rating Score
Hannah Montana: The Movie	G	[General Audiences], Suitable for all ages]	2009	56
Hannah Montana: The Movie	G	[General Audiences], Suitable for all ages]	2009	56
Chicken Little	G	[General Audiences], Suitable for all ages]	2005	95
The Smurfs and the Magic Flute	G	[General Audiences], Suitable for all ages]	1976	NA
Zootopia	PG	[Mild thematic elements], [ruude humor], [action]	2016	97
Finding Dory	PG	[Mild thematic elements], [ruude humor], [action]	2016	98
Pete's Dragon	PG	[action], [peril], [brief language]	2016	93
Kubo and the Two Strings	PG	[Thematic elements], [Scary images], [action], [peril]	2016	96
Sherlock	TV-14	[Parents strongly cautioned]	2016	95
Death Note	TV-14	[Parents strongly cautioned]	2006	77
Arrow	TV-14	[Parents strongly cautioned]	2015	96

The movies have also been tagged with descriptions – "General Audience," "Suitable for all ages," etc. This is different than the rating system in that each movie can be described by one or more of the tag categories, which is known as a multi-label classification problem.

Binary to Multiclass

There are multiple ways to decompose the multiclass prediction into multiple binary decisions.

One-versus-all

Let's assume that our black-box algorithm is a linear classifier, and each class can be separated from all the rest labels. If we do this, we are basically decomposing the task to learning k independent binary classifiers, and we know how to do this.

Formally, let D be the set of training examples. For any label I, take elements of D with label I as positive examples and all other elements of D as negative examples. Then, construct a binary classification problem for I. This is a binary learning problem that we can solve. Since there are k possible labels, we are producing k binary classifiers $w_1, w_2, ..., w_k$. Once we have learned the k classifiers, the decision is made by winner takes all (WTA) strategy, such that $f(x) = \arg\max_i w_i^T x$. The "score" $w_i^T x$ (the sigmoid function can be applied on it) can be thought of as the probability that x has label i.

Graphically, consider the data set with three color labels shown in the figure below. Using binary classifiers, we separated the black from the rest, blue from the rest, and green from the rest. Easy.

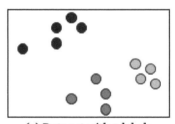

(a) Data set with 3 labels.

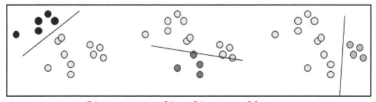

(b) Decomposed into binary problems.

The only caveat is that when some points with a certain label are not linearly separable from the other, like shown in the figure below, this scheme cannot be used. Basically, we are concerned about the expressivity of this paradigm.

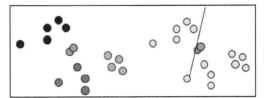

Figure: Red points are not linearly separable from other points.

It is not always possible to learn, because it is not always separable in the way we want. Even though it works well and is the commonly used method, there is no theoretical justification for it.

All-versus-all

Assume that there is a separation between every pair of classes using a binary classifier in the hypothesis space. Then, we can look at all pairs of labels $\left(\binom{k}{2}\right)$ of them)), and for each pair, define a binary learning problem. In each case, for pair (i, j), the positive examples are all examples with label i, and negative examples are those with label j. Now instead of k classifiers as in OvA, we have $\binom{k}{2}$ classifier.

In this case each label gets k_1 votes, and the decision is more involved, because output of binary classifiers may not cohere. To make a decision, an option is to classify example x to take label i if i wins on x more often than any $j = 1, ...,k,$. Alternatively, we can do a tournament. Starting with n/2 pairs, continue with the winners and go down iteratively. Either way, there are potential issues. However, overall, it is a good method.

Figure: Tournament and majority vote.

One-versus-all VS all-versus-all

There is a trade-off between OvA and AvA paradigms. Computationally, to apply AvA, a quadratic number of classifiers have to be trained, while OvA requires linear number of classifiers. AvA has more expressivity, but less examples to learn from. In terms of number of examples, AvA has smaller learning problems. And it makes AvA preferable when ran in dual.

Extension from Binary

This topic discusses strategies of extending the existing binary classifiers to solve multi-class classification problems. Several algorithms have been developed based on neural networks, decision trees, k-nearest neighbors, naive Bayes, support vector machines and Extreme Learning Machines to address multi-class classification problems. These types of techniques can also be called as algorithm adaptation techniques.

Neural Networks

Multilayer perceptrons provide a natural extension to the multi-class problem. Instead of just having one neuron in the output layer, with binary output, one could have N binary neurons leading to multi-class classification. In practice, the last layer of a neural network is usually a softmax function layer, which is the algebraic simplification of N logistic classifiers, normalized per class by the sum of the N-1 other logistic classifiers.

Extreme Learning Machines

Extreme Learning Machines (ELM) is a special case of single hidden layer feed-forward neural networks (SLFNs) where in the input weights and the hidden node biases can be chosen at random. Many variants and developments are made to the ELM for multiclass classification.

k-nearest Neighbours

k-nearest neighbors kNN is considered among the oldest non-parametric classification algorithms. To classify an unknown example, the distance from that example to every other training example is measured. The k smallest distances are identified, and the most represented class by these k nearest neighbors is considered the output class label.

Naive Bayes

Naive Bayes is a successful classifier based upon the principle of maximum a posteriori (MAP). This approach is naturally extensible to the case of having more than two classes, and was shown to perform well in spite of the underlying simplifying assumption of conditional independence.

Decision Trees

Decision trees are a powerful classification technique. The tree tries to infer a split of the training data based on the values of the available features to produce a good generalization. The algorithm can naturally handle binary or multiclass classification problems. The leaf nodes can refer to either of the K classes concerned.

Support Vector Machines

Support vector machines are based upon the idea of maximizing the margin i.e. maximizing the minimum distance from the separating hyper plane to the nearest example.

The basic SVM supports only binary classification, but extensions have been proposed to handle the multiclass classification case as well. In these extensions, additional parameters and constraints are added to the optimization problem to handle the separation of the different classes.

Hierarchical Classification

Hierarchical classification tackles the multi-class classification problem by dividing the output space i.e. into a tree. Each parent node is divided into multiple child nodes and the process is continued until each child node represents only one class. Several methods have been proposed based on hierarchical classification.

Learning Paradigms

Based on learning paradigms, the existing multi-class classification techniques can be classified into batch learning and online learning. Batch learning algorithms require all the data samples to be available beforehand. It trains the model using the entire training data and then predicts the test sample using the found relationship. The online learning algorithms, on the other hand, incrementally build their models in sequential iterations. In iteration t, an online algorithm receives a sample, x_t and predicts its label $\hat{y}_t$ using the current model; the algorithm then receives y_t, the true label of x_t and updates its model based on the sample-label pair: (x_t, y_t). Recently, a new learning paradigm called progressive learning technique has been developed. The progressive learning technique is capable of not only learning from new samples but also capable of learning new classes of data and yet retain the knowledge learnt thus far.

Linear Classifier

A linear classifier does classification decision based on the value of a linear combination of the characteristics. Imagine that the linear classifier will merge into its weights all the characteristics that define a particular class. (Like merge all samples of the class cars together).

This type of classifier works better when the problem is linear separable.

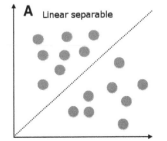
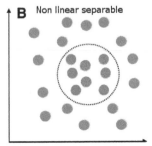

$$f(\vec{x}, \vec{W}, \vec{b}) = \sum j(Wjx_j) + b$$

x: input vector

W: Weight matrix

b: Bias vector

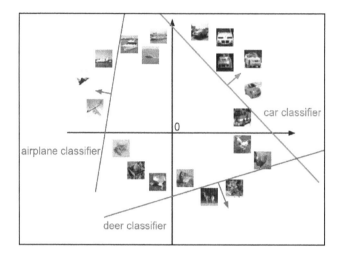

The weight matrix will have one row for every class that needs to be classified, and one column for ever element (feature) of x. On the picture above each line will be represented by a row in our weight matrix.

Weight and Bias Effect

The effect of changing the weight will change the line angle, while changing the bias, will move the line left/right.

Parametric Approach

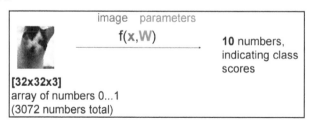

The idea is that out hypothesis/model have parameters that will aid the mapping between the input vectors to a specific class score. The parametric model has two important components:

- Score Function: Is a function f (x,W,b) that will map our raw input vector to a score vector.

- Loss Function: Quantifies how well our current set of weights maps some input x to a expected output y, the loss function is used during training time.

On this approach, the training phase will find us a set of parameters that will change the hypothesis/model to map some input, to some of the output class.

During the training phase, which consist as a optimization problem, the weights (W) and bias (b) are the only thing that we can change.

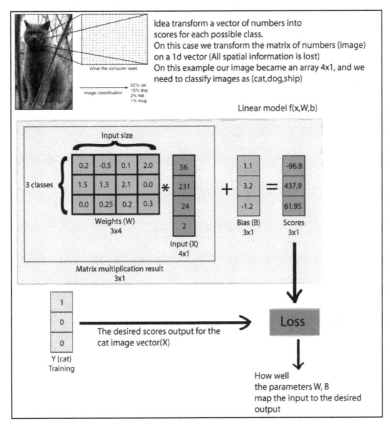

Now some topics that is important on the diagram above:

1. The input image x is stretched to a single dimension vector, this loose spatial information.

2. The weight matrix will have one column for every element on the input.

3. The weight matrix will have one row for every element of the output (on this case 3 labels).

4. The bias will have one row for every element of the output (on this case 3 labels).

5. The loss will receive the current scores and the expected output for it's current input X.

Consider each row of W a kind of pattern match for a specified class. The score for each class is calculated by doing a inner product between the input vector X and the specific row for that class. Ex:

$$score_{cat} = [0.2(56) - 0.5(231) + 0.1(24) + 2(2)] + 1.1 = -96.8$$

Example on Matlab

```
>> W = [0.2 -0.5 0.1 2; 1.5 1.3 2.1 0; 0 0.25 0.2 0.3]

W =

    0.2000   -0.5000    0.1000    2.0000
    1.5000    1.3000    2.1000         0
         0    0.2500    0.2000    0.3000

>> X = [56 231 24 2]'

X =

    56
   231
    24
     2

>> B = [1.1 3.2 -1.2]

B =

    1.1000    3.2000   -1.2000

>> scores = (W*X)+B'

scores =

   -96.8000
   437.9000
    61.9500
```

The image below reshape back the weights to an image, we can see by this image that the training try to compress on each row of W all the variants of the same class.

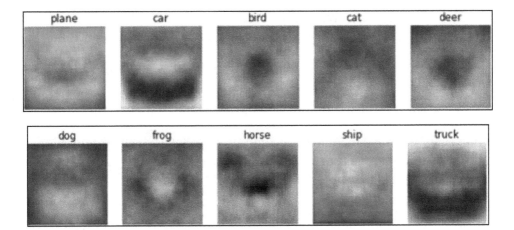

Bias Trick

Some learning libraries implementations, does a trick to consider the bias as part of the weight matrix, the advantage of this approach is that we can solve the linear classification with a single matrix multiplication.

$$f(x,W) = W.x$$

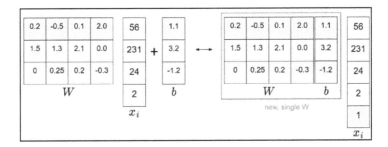

Basically you add an extra row at the end of the input vector, and concatenate a column on the W matrix.

Input and Features

The input vector sometimes called feature vector, is your input data that is sent to the classifier. As the linear classifier does not handle non-linear problems, it is the responsibility of the engineer, process this data and presents it in a form that is separable to the classifier.

The best case scenario is that you have a large number of features, and each of them has a high correlation to the desired output and low correlation between them.

Generative Models vs. Discriminative Models

There are two broad classes of methods for determining the parameters of a linear classifier . They can be generative and discriminative models. Methods of the first class model conditional density functions $P(\vec{x}\,|\,\text{class})$. Examples of such algorithms include:

- Linear Discriminant Analysis (or Fisher's linear discriminant) (LDA)—assumes Gaussian conditional density models.

- Naive Bayes classifier with multinomial or multivariate Bernoulli event models.

The second set of methods includes discriminative models, which attempt to maximize the quality of the output on a training set. Additional terms in the training cost function can easily perform regularization of the final model. Examples of discriminative training of linear classifiers include

- Logistic regression—maximum likelihood estimation of $P(\vec{x}\,|\,\text{class})$ assuming that the observed training set was generated by a binomial model that depends on the output of the classifier.

- Perceptron—an algorithm that attempts to fix all errors encountered in the training set.

- Support vector machine—an algorithm that maximizes the margin between the decision hyper plane and the examples in the training set.

Despite its name, LDA does not belong to the class of discriminative models in this taxonomy. However, its name makes sense when we compare LDA to the other main linear dimensionality reduction algorithm: principal components analysis (PCA). LDA is a supervised learning algorithm that utilizes the labels of the data, while PCA is an unsupervised learning algorithm that ignores the labels. To summarize, the name is a historical artifact.

Discriminative training often yields higher accuracy than modeling the conditional density functions. However, handling missing data is often easier with conditional density models.

All of the linear classifier algorithms listed above can be converted into non-linear algorithms operating on a different input space $\varphi(\vec{x})$, using the kernel trick.

Discriminative Training

Discriminative training of linear classifiers usually proceeds in a supervised way, by means of an optimization algorithm that is given a training set with desired outputs and a loss function that measures the discrepancy between the classifier's outputs and the desired outputs. Thus, the learning algorithm solves an optimization problem of the form:

$$\underset{\mathbf{w}}{\operatorname{argmin}}\ R(\mathbf{w}) + C\sum_{i=1}^{N} L(y_i, \mathbf{w}^\mathsf{T}\mathbf{x}_i)$$

where,

- w is a vector of classifier parameters,

- $L(y_i, w^T x_i)$ is a loss function that measures the discrepancy between the classifier's prediction and the true output y_i for the i'th training example,

- $R(w)$ is a regularization function that prevents the parameters from getting too large (causing overfitting),

- C is a scalar constant (set by the user of the learning algorithm) that controls the balance between the regularization and the loss function.

Popular loss functions include the hinge loss (for linear SVMs) and the log loss (for linear logistic regression). If the regularization function R is convex, then the above is a convex problem. Many algorithms exist for solving such problems; popular ones for linear classification include (stochastic) gradient descent, L-BFGS, coordinate descent and Newton methods.

Perceptron

A perceptron is a simple model of a biological neuron in an artificial neural network. Perceptron is also the name of an early algorithm for supervised learning of binary classifiers.

The perceptron algorithm was designed to classify visual inputs, categorizing subjects into one of two types and separating groups with a line. Classification is an important part of machine learning and image processing. Machine learning algorithms find and classify patterns by many different means. The perceptron algorithm classifies patterns and groups by finding the linear separation between different objects and patterns that are received through numeric or visual input.

The perceptron algorithm was developed at Cornell Aeronautical Laboratory in 1957, funded by the United States Office of Naval Research. The algorithm was the first step planned for a machine implementation for image recognition. The machine, called Mark 1 Perceptron, was physically made up of an array of 400 photocells connected to perceptrons whose weights were recorded in potentiometers, as adjusted by electric motors. The machine was one of the first artificial neural networks ever created.

At the time, the perceptron was expected to be very significant for the development of artificial intelligence (AI). While high hopes surrounded the initial perceptron, technical limitations were soon demonstrated. Single-layer perceptrons can only separate classes if they are linearly separable. Later on, it was discovered that by using multiple layers, perceptrons can classify groups that are not linearly separable, allowing them to solve problems single layer algorithms can't solve.

References

- Venkatesan, Rajasekar; Meng Joo, Er (2016). "A novel progressive learning technique for multi-class classification". Neurocomputing. 207: 310–321. arXiv:1609.00085. doi:10.1016/j.neucom.2016.05.006

- Naive-bayes-classifiers: geeksforgeeks.org, Retrieved 13 July 2020

- Peter Mills (2011). "Efficient statistical classification of satellite measurements". International Journal of Remote Sensing. arXiv:1202.2194. doi:10.1080/01431161.2010.507795

- Getting-started-with-classification: geeksforgeeks.org, Retrieved 26 March 2020

- Har-Peled, S., Roth, D., Zimak, D. (2003) "Constraint Classification for Multiclass Classification and Ranking." In: Becker, B., Thrun, S., Obermayer, K. (Eds) Advances in Neural Information Processing Systems 15: Proceedings of the 2002 Conference, MIT Press. ISBN 0-262-02550-7

- What-is-statistical-classification: wisegeek.com, Retrieved 09 April 2020

## 5

Theories of Machine Learning

Many theories on machine learning have been put forward to determine the best approach to develop complex artificially intelligent systems which can learn and perform tasks without any human intervention. Theories like the computational learning theory, statistical learning theory, adaptive resonance theory, Hebbian theory, etc. are all part of this endeavor and are thoroughly covered in this chapter.

Computational Learning Theory

Computational learning theory is a branch of theoretical computer science that formally studies how to design computer programs that are capable of learning and identifies the computational limits of learning by machines Historically researchers in the artificial intelligence community have judged learning algorithms empirically according to their performance on sample problems While such evaluations provide much useful information and insight often it is hard using such evaluations to make meaningful comparisons among competing learning algorithms.

Computational learning theory provides a formal framework in which to precisely formulate and address questions regarding the performance of different learning algorithms so that careful comparisons of both the predictive power and the computational efficiency of alternative learning algorithms can be made Three key aspects that must be formalized are the way in which the learner interacts with its environment the definition of successfully completing the learning task and a formal definition of efficiency of both data usage sample complexityand processing time complexity It is important to remember that the theoretical learning models studied are abstractions from reallife problems Thus close connections with experimentalists are useful to help validate or modify these abstractions so that the theoretical results help to explain or predict empirical performance In this direction computational learning theory research has predict empirical performance In this direction computational learning theory research .

Theoretical results in machine learning mainly deal with a type of inductive learning called supervised learning. In supervised learning, an algorithm is given samples that are labeled in some useful way. For example, the samples might be descriptions of mushrooms, and the labels could be whether or not the mushrooms are edible. The algorithm takes these previously labeled samples and uses them to induce a classifier. This classifier is a function that assigns labels to samples including samples that have never been previously seen by the algorithm. The goal of the supervised learning algorithm is to optimize some measure of performance such as minimizing the number of mistakes made on new samples.

In addition to performance bounds, computational learning theory studies the time complexity and feasibility of learning.. In computational learning theory, a computation is considered feasible if it can be done in polynomial time. There are two kinds of time complexity results:

- Positive results – Showing that a certain class of functions is learnable in polynomial time.

- Negative results – Showing that certain classes cannot be learned in polynomial time.

Negative results often rely on commonly believed, but yet unproven assumptions, such as:

- Computational complexity – P ≠ NP (the P versus NP problem);

- Cryptographic – One-way functions exist.

There are several different approaches to computational learning theory. These differences are based on making assumptions about the inference principles used to generalize from limited data. This includes different definitions of probability and different assumptions on the generation of samples. The different approaches include:

- Exact learning, proposed by Dana Angluin;

- Probably approximately correct learning (PAC learning), proposed by Leslie Valiant.

- VC theory, proposed by Vladimir Vapnik and Alexey Chervonenkis.

- Bayesian inference.

- Algorithmic learning theory, from the work of E. Mark Gold.

- Online machine learning, from the work of Nick Littlestone.

Computational learning theory has led to several practical algorithms. For example, PAC theory inspired boosting, VC theory led to support vector machines, and Bayesian inference led to belief networks (by Judea Pearl).

Statistical Learning Theory

The main goal of statistical learning theory is to provide a framework for studying the problem of inference, that is of gaining knowledge, making predictions, making decisions or constructing models from a set of data. This is studied in a statistical framework that is there are assumptions of statistical nature about the underlying phenomena.

Indeed, a theory of inference should be able to give a formal definition of words like learning, generalization, over fitting, and also to characterize the performance of learning algorithms so that, ultimately, it may help design better learning algorithms.

There are thus two goals: make things more precise and derive new or improved algorithms.

Learning and Inference

What is under study here is the process of inductive inference which can roughly be summarized as the following steps:

1. Observe a phenomenon.

2. Construct a model of that phenomenon.

3. Make predictions using this model.

Of course, this definition is very general and could be taken more or less as the goal of Natural Sciences. The goal of Machine Learning is to actually automate this process and the goal of Learning Theory is to formalize it.

We consider a special case of the above process, which is the supervised learning framework for pattern recognition. In this framework, the data consists of instance-label pairs, where the label is either +1 or −1. Given a set of such pairs, a learning algorithm constructs a function mapping instances to labels. This function should be such that it makes few mistakes when predicting the label of unseen instances.

Of course, given some training data, it is always possible to build a function that fits exactly the data. But, in the presence of noise, this may not be the best thing to do as it would lead to a poor performance on unseen instances (this is usually referred to as over fitting).

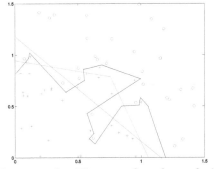

Figure: Trade-off between fit and complexity.

The general idea behind the design of learning algorithms is thus to look for regularities (in a sense to be defined later) in the observed phenomenon (i.e. training data). These can then be generalized from the observed past to the future. Typically, one would look, in a collection of possible models, for one which fits well the data, but at the same time is as simple as possible. This immediately raises the question of how to measure and quantify simplicity of a model (i.e. a {−1, +1}-valued function).

It turns out that there are many ways to do so, but no best one. For example in Physics, people tend to prefer models which have a small number of constants and that correspond to simple mathematical formulas. Often, the length of description of a model in a coding language can be an indication of its complexity. In classical statistics, the number of free parameters of a model is usually a measure of its complexity. Surprisingly as it may seem, there is no universal way of measuring simplicity (or its counterpart complexity) and the choice of a specific measure inherently depends on the problem at hand. It is actually in this choice that the designer of the learning algorithm introduces knowledge about the specific phenomenon under study.

This lack of universally best choice can actually be formalized in what is called the No Free Lunch theorem, which in essence says that, if there is no assumption on how the past (i.e. training data) is related to the future (i.e. test data), prediction is impossible. Even more, if there is no a priori restriction on the possible phenomena that are expected, it is impossible to generalize and there is thus no better algorithm (any algorithm would be beaten by another one on some phenomenon).

Hence the need to make assumptions, like the fact that the phenomenon we observe can be explained by a simple model. However, as we said, simplicity is not an absolute notion, and this leads to the statement that data cannot replace knowledge, or in pseudo-mathematical terms:

$$\text{Generalization} = \text{Data} + \text{Knowledge}.$$

We assume that data are an i.i.d. sample of n pairs $\left\{ (X_t, Y_t) \right\}_{t=1}^{n} \in (X \times Y)^n$. A learning algorithm (or, a prediction rule) is a mapping $\hat{Y} : (X \times Y)^n \to D$,, where $D = y^X$ is the space of all measurable functions $x \to y$. We either write $\hat{y}(x; X^n, Y^n)$ to make the dependence on data explicit, or simply $\hat{y}(x)$ if the dependence is understood. Let P denote the set of all distributions on $x \times y$ Consider the case of regression with squared loss. For the distribution-free setting of Statistical Learning Theory, define the minimax value is:

$$vx^{iid,sq}(F,n) \triangleq \inf_{\hat{y}} \sup_{P \in p} \left\{ \mathbb{E}\left(\hat{y}(x)-y\right)^2 - \inf_{f \in F} \mathbb{E}\left(f(x)-y\right)^2 \right\}$$

$$= \inf_{\hat{y}} \sup_{P \in p, f \in F} \left\{ \mathbb{E}\left(\hat{y}(x)-y\right) - \mathbb{E}\left(f(x)-y\right)^2 \right\}$$

where the expected value in the first term is over n + 1 i.i.d. random variables (X1,

Y1),..., (Xn, Yn), (X, Y). Note that the supremum ranges over all distributions on X × Y. The minimax objective $vx^{iid,sq}(F,n)$ is defined above in terms of predictive risk relative to the risk of a reference class F. Alternatively, it can be re-written as follows:

$$v^{iid,sq}(F,n) \triangleq \inf_{\hat{y}} \sup_{P \in p} \left\{ \mathbb{E}\|\hat{y}-f_P\|^2 - \inf_{f \in F}\|f-f_P\|^2 \right\}$$

$$= \inf_{\hat{y}} \sup_{P \in p, f \in F} \left\{ \mathbb{E}\|\hat{y}-f_P\|^2 - \|f-f_P\|^2 \right\}$$

Where $f_P(a) = \mathbb{E}[Y|X=a]$ is the mean function associated with P, and the norm $\|.\| = \|.\|_{L_2}(P_X)$. Recalling that $\|g\|^2_{L_2(P_X)} = \int g^2(x)P_X(dx) = \mathbb{E}g^2(X)$, we can easily verify the equivalence of (5.7) and (5.8). For absolute loss, let us define the analogue of (5.7) as:

$$vx^{iid,sq}(F,n) \triangleq \inf_{\hat{y}} \sup_{P \in p} \left\{ \mathbb{E}|\hat{y}(x)-y| - \inf_{f \in F} \mathbb{E}|f(x)-y| \right\}$$

and for general losses as:

$$v^{iid}(F,n) \triangleq \inf_{\hat{y}} \sup_{P \in p} \left\{ \mathbb{E}l(\hat{y}(x,y)) - \inf_{f \in F} \mathbb{E}l(f,(x,y)) \right\}$$

Let us now consider the distribution-dependent PAC framework for classification and write down its minimax value:

$$v^{pac}(F,n) \triangleq \inf_{\hat{y}} \sup_{P_f} P(\hat{y}(x) \neq f(x)) = \inf_{\hat{y}} \sup_{P_f} \mathbb{E}|\hat{y}(x)-f(x)|$$

Where P_f ranges over distributions given by $P_X \times P^f_{Y|X}$ with $P_X \times P^f_{Y|X=a} = \delta_{f(a)}$ for $f \in F$ a class of {0, 1}-valued functions. In the label noise scenario, the distribution $P^f_{Y|X=a}$ a puts some mass on 1− f (a).

As we go forward, it is important to think of $v(F,n)$ as a measure of complexity of F. If F = {f} contains only one function, the values defined above are zero since we can simply set $\hat{y} = f$. On the opposite end of the spectrum, the complexity V(Y X, n) of the set of all possible functions is, in general, impossible to make small. One goal of this course is to understand how this value fares for function classes between these two extremes, and to understand what other (easier-to-grasp) measures of complexity of F are related to V(F, n).

Adaptive Resonance Theory

This network was developed by Stephen Grossberg and Gail Carpenter in 1987. It is based on competition and uses unsupervised learning model. Adaptive Resonance Theory (ART) networks, as the name suggests, is always open to new learning (adaptive) without losing the old patterns (resonance). Basically, ART network is a vector classifier which accepts an input vector and classifies it into one of the categories depending upon which of the stored pattern it resembles the most.

Operating Principal

The main operation of ART classification can be divided into the following phases –

- Recognition phase – The input vector is compared with the classification presented at every node in the output layer. The output of the neuron becomes "1" if it best matches with the classification applied, otherwise it becomes "0".

- Comparison phase – In this phase, a comparison of the input vector to the comparison layer vector is done. The condition for reset is that the degree of similarity would be less than vigilance parameter.

- Search phase – In this phase, the network will search for reset as well as the match done in the above phases. Hence, if there would be no reset and the match is quite good, then the classification is over. Otherwise, the process would be repeated and the other stored pattern must be sent to find the correct match.

ART1

It is a type of ART, which is designed to cluster binary vectors. We can understand about this with the architecture of it.

Architecture of ART1

It consists of the following two units –

Computational Unit

Components of computational units are as follows –

- Input unit (F1 layer) – It further has the following two portions –

  ○ F1(a) layer (Input portion) – In ART1, there would be no processing in this portion rather than having the input vectors only. It is connected to F1(b) layer (interface portion).

  ○ F1(b) layer (Interface portion) – This portion combines the signal from the input portion with that of F2 layer. F1(b) layer is connected to F2 layer through bottom up weights bij and F2layer is connected to F1(b) layer through top down weights tji.

- Cluster Unit (F2 layer) – This is a competitive layer. The unit having the largest net input is selected to learn the input pattern. The activation of all other cluster unit are set to 0.

- Reset Mechanism – The work of this mechanism is based upon the similarity between the top-down weight and the input vector. Now, if the degree of this similarity is less than the vigilance parameter, then the cluster is not allowed to learn the pattern and a rest would happen.

Supplement Unit

Actually the issue with Reset mechanism is that the layer F2 must have to be inhibited under certain conditions and must also be available when some learning happens. That is why two supplemental units namely, G1 and G2 are added along with reset unit, R. They are called gain control units. These units receive and send signals to the other units present in the network. '+' indicates an excitatory signal, while '–' indicates an inhibitory signal.

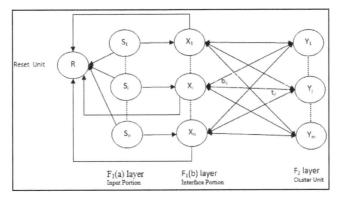

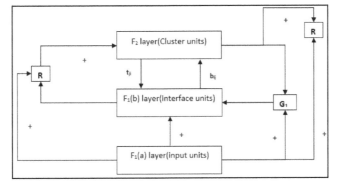

Parameters used

Following parameters are used –

- n – Number of components in the input vector
- m – Maximum number of clusters that can be formed
- bij – Weight from F1(b) to F2 layer, i.e. bottom-up weights
- tji – Weight from F2 to F1(b) layer, i.e. top-down weights

- ρ – Vigilance parameter
- ||x|| – Norm of vector x

Algorithm

Step 1 – Initialize the learning rate, the vigilance parameter, and the weights as follows:

$$\alpha > 1 \text{ and } 0 < \rho \leq 1$$

$$0 < b_{ij}(0) < \frac{\alpha}{\alpha - 1 + n} \text{ and } t_{ij}(0) = 1$$

Step 2 – Continue step 3-9, when the stopping condition is not true.

Step 3 – Continue step 4-6 for every training input.

Step 4 – Set activations of all F1(a) and F1 units as follows:

$$F2 = 0 \text{ and } F1(a) = \text{input vectors}$$

Step 5 – Input signal from F1(a) to F1(b) layer must be sent like:

$$s_i = x_i$$

Step 6 – For every inhibited F2 node:

$$y_j = \sum_i b_{ij} x_i \text{ the condition is yj} \neq -1$$

Step 7 – Perform step 8-10, when the reset is true.

Step 8 – Find J for yJ ≥ yj for all nodes j.

Step 9 – Again calculate the activation on F1(b) as follows:

$$x_i = sitJi$$

Step 10 – Now, after calculating the norm of vector x and vector s, we need to check the reset condition as follows:

If ||x||/ ||s|| < vigilance parameter ρ, then inhibit node J and go to step 7.

Else If ||x||/ ||s|| ≥ vigilance parameter ρ, then proceed further.

Step 11 – Weight updating for node J can be done as follows:

$$b_{ij}(new) = \frac{\alpha x_i}{\alpha - 1 + \ddot{u} \; x \;\mid}$$

$$t_{ij}(new) = x_i$$

Step 12 – The stopping condition for algorithm must be checked and it may be as follows:

- Do not have any change in weight.

- Reset is not performed for units.
- Maximum number of epochs reached.

Hebbian Theory

Hebbian theory is a theoretical type of cell activation model in artificial neural networks that assesses the concept of "synaptic plasticity" or dynamic strengthening or weakening of synapses over time according to input factors.

Hebbian theory is also known as Hebbian learning, Hebb's rule or Hebb's postulate.

Hebbian theory is named after Donald Hebb, a neuroscientist from Nova Scotia who wrote "The Organization of Behavior" in 1949, which has been part of the basis for the development of artificial neural networks.

When someone learns something new, the neurons within the brain begin to adapt to the processes that are required. This is a basic mechanism of synaptic plasticity, which is described through the Hebbian theory.

How neurons operate and link together creates a trend that begins the skill-building process within the brain. When they fire, then they tend to be wired together in some way. Through the Hebbian theory, that wiring is described as a process of causality. Many neurons will fire simultaneously during the learning process.

These connections form to become engrams. Those engrams become patterns of learning. Those patterns will then eventually turn into practical knowledge that can be used for multiple purposes.

Mirror Neurons and the Hebbian Theory

The learning process that is described through Hebbian theory and the synaptic plasticity involved is also the foundation of how mirror neurons are able to form within the engrams that are eventually created by the patterns of firing. A mirror neuron fires when an action must be performed or when an individual hears or sees a similar action being taken that is similar.

These neurons show how the "learning by osmosis" skill, or watching and then doing, can develop within living beings. The neurons activate by seeing the skill being performed, then activate once again when the skills are being observed. This process reinforces the building patterns of the engrams, establishing information additions in various conditions.

It is possible for all 5 traditional senses to create their own engrams that interlock with each other, creating mirror neurons that fire in different ways, based on the perspective of the individual sense. Watching someone perform a skill would be different from hearing someone perform a skill, for example.

And when individuals perform the skill on their own, the sense of touch reflects the movements being performed and continues to build neuron "neighborhoods" that help the information be retained for future reference.

Hopfield Model

Hopfield model is an associative memory model using the Hebb's rule for all possible pairs ij with binary units. The state variable xi of the neuron i takes on either on of the two possible values: 1 or -1, which corresponds to the firing state or not firing state, respectively.

$$S_i(t+1) := \operatorname{sgn}\left(\sum_j w_{ij} S_i(t) - \mu_i\right)$$

Where sgn is the sign function defined as follows:

$$\operatorname{sgn}(x) = \begin{cases} 1 & if\, x \geq 0 \\ -1 & if\, x < 0 \end{cases}$$

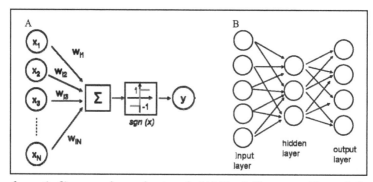

Figure: The schematic diagram of neural network. (A) Hopfield neuron. The unit fires if the weighted sum $\Sigma j\ wijSj$ of the inputs reaches or exceeds the threshold μi. (B) An example of three layer perceptron.

Drawbacks of Hebb's Rule

Though being simple, the classical Hebb's rule has some disadvantages. Depending the application area of neural network, some drawbacks are tolerable but some need improvement. Generally speaking, for the purpose of data processing and statistical analysis, the speed and power of computation are valued more than the resemblance between the model and the physiological realism. On the other hand, for unraveling the memory formation mechanism and harvesting the emerging properties of biological network, the models need to be built upon a certain degree of biophysical basis.

Stability of Hebbian Network

For classical Hebb's rule, there is no algorithm for synapses to get weaker and no upper bound that limits how strong the connectivity can get. Therefore, it is intrinsically unstable. To overcome the stability problem, Bienenstock, Cooper, and Munro proposed an omega shaped learning rule called BCM rule. The general BCM improves Hebb's rule and takes the following form:

$$\frac{dw_{ij}}{dt} = \varphi(x_i).x_j - k_w.w_{ij}$$

There are two main differences between these two rules: the decay of synaptic weight with a rate constant kw and the nonlinear dependence of synaptic weight with respect to postsynaptic activities. The nonlinearity was described by the postsynaptic activation function $\varphi(x)$. As shown in figure, the activation function is negative for xi under threshold value θw but grows positive once the postsynaptic activity becomes larger than θw.

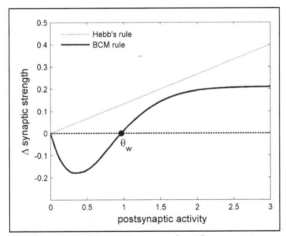

Figure: The activation function of synaptic strength with respect to postsynaptic activity. Hebb's rule poses linear dependence of synaptic strength on postsynaptic activity while BCM rule sets nonlinear omega-shaped dependence. The x-axis corresponds to postsynaptic activity, xi and the y-axis represents the activation function, $\varphi(x)$.

The Simplification of Neuronal Activities

Under external stimulation, neurons fire and emit a series of pulses instead of a simple output level. In Hebb's rule, only a single value xi is assigned to the neuron i to represent its activity. Yet the simplification results into the loss of information such as the threshold and tendency of firing as well as the detailed change in the short-term and the long-term plasticity.

The variety and emerging properties may be the results of differentiated neurons. The network of these specialized neurons with individual attributes gives rise to bountiful functionality.

The Inability to Model Spike Timing Dependence

It has been experimentally shown that the change in synaptic plasticity depends upon the relative spike timing between presynaptic and postsynaptic neurons. Spike timing dependence has become an important experimental protocol in eliciting change in synaptic plasticity since its discovery. Although the role of temporal order was suggested in the original statement of Hebb's rule, the time window requirement is not incorporated in the equations.

Algorithms in Machine Learning

Machine learning algorithms are programs that adjust themselves to perform better as they are exposed to more data. They automatically create models of data and change how they process data over time. There are many types of machine learning algorithms and each one is thoroughly examined and analyzed to provide a complete understanding of this subject.

Expectation–maximization Algorithm

In statistics, an expectation–maximization (EM) algorithm is an iterative method to find maximum likelihood or maximum a posteriori (MAP) estimates of parameters in statistical models, where the model depends on unobserved latent variables. The EM iteration alternates between performing an expectation (E) step, which creates a function for the expectation of the log-likelihood evaluated using the current estimate for the parameters, and a maximization (M) step, which computes parameters maximizing the expected log-likelihood found on the E step. These parameter-estimates are then used to determine the distribution of the latent variables in the next E step.

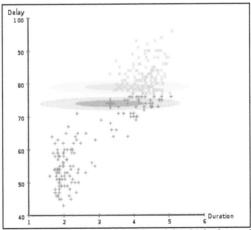

EM clustering of Old Faithful eruption data. The random initial model (which, due to the different scales of the axes, appears to be two very flat and wide spheres) is fit to the observed data. In the first iterations, the model changes substantially, but then converges to the two modes of the geyser.

History

The EM algorithm was explained and given its name in a classic 1977 paper by Arthur Dempster, Nan Laird, and Donald Rubin. They pointed out that the method had been "proposed many times in special circumstances" by earlier authors. A very detailed treatment of the EM method for exponential families was published by Rolf Sundberg in his thesis and several papers following his collaboration with Per Martin-Löf and Anders Martin-Löf. The Dempster-Laird-Rubin paper in

1977 generalized the method and sketched a convergence analysis for a wider class of problems. Regardless of earlier inventions, the innovative Dempster-Laird-Rubin paper in the *Journal of the Royal Statistical Society* received an enthusiastic discussion at the Royal Statistical Society meeting with Sundberg calling the paper "brilliant". The Dempster-Laird-Rubin paper established the EM method as an important tool of statistical analysis.

The convergence analysis of the Dempster-Laird-Rubin paper was flawed and a correct convergence analysis was published by C.F. Jeff Wu in 1983. Wu's proof established the EM method's convergence outside of the exponential family, as claimed by Dempster-Laird-Rubin.

Introduction

The EM algorithm is used to find (locally) maximum likelihood parameters of a statistical model in cases where the equations cannot be solved directly. Typically these models involve latent variables in addition to unknown parameters and known data observations. That is, either missing values exist among the data, or the model can be formulated more simply by assuming the existence of further unobserved data points. For example, a mixture model can be described more simply by assuming that each observed data point has a corresponding unobserved data point, or latent variable, specifying the mixture component to which each data point belongs.

Finding a maximum likelihood solution typically requires taking the derivatives of the likelihood function with respect to all the unknown values, the parameters and the latent variables, and simultaneously solving the resulting equations. In statistical models with latent variables, this is usually impossible. Instead, the result is typically a set of interlocking equations in which the solution to the parameters requires the values of the latent variables and vice versa, but substituting one set of equations into the other produces an unsolvable equation.

The EM algorithm proceeds from the observation that the following is a way to solve these two sets of equations numerically. One can simply pick arbitrary values for one of the two sets of unknowns, use them to estimate the second set, then use these new values to find a better estimate of the first set, and then keep alternating between the two until the resulting values both converge to fixed points. It's not obvious that this will work at all, but it can be proven that in this context it does, and that the derivative of the likelihood is (arbitrarily close to) zero at that point, which in turn means that the point is either a maximum or a saddle point. In general, multiple maxima may occur, with no guarantee that the global maximum will be found. Some likelihoods also have singularities in them, i.e., nonsensical maxima. For example, one of the *solutions* that may be found by EM in a mixture model involves setting one of the components to have zero variance and the mean parameter for the same component to be equal to one of the data points.

Description

Given the statistical model which generates a set $\mathbf{X}$ of observed data, a set of unobserved latent data or missing values $\mathbf{Z}$, and a vector of unknown parameters θ, along with a likelihood function $L(\theta; X, Z) = p(X, Z \mid \theta)$, the maximum likelihood estimate (MLE) of the unknown parameters is determined by the marginal likelihood of the observed data.

$$L(\theta; X) = p(X \mid \theta) = \int p(X, Z \mid \theta) dZ$$

However, this quantity is often intractable (e.g. if $\mathbf{Z}$ is a sequence of events, so that the number of values grows exponentially with the sequence length, making the exact calculation of the sum extremely difficult).

The EM algorithm seeks to find the MLE of the marginal likelihood by iteratively applying these two steps:

Expectation step (E step): Calculate the expected value of the log likelihood function, with respect to the conditional distribution of $\mathbf{Z}$ given $\mathbf{X}$ under the current estimate of the parameters $\theta^{(t)}$:

$$Q(\theta \mid \theta^{(t)}) = E_{\mathbf{Z} \mid \mathbf{X}, \theta^{(t)}} \left[\log L(\theta; \mathbf{X}, \mathbf{Z}) \right]$$

Maximization step (M step): Find the parameter that maximizes this quantity:

$$\theta^{(t+1)} = \underset{\theta}{\arg\max} \ Q(\theta \mid \theta^{(t)})$$

In typical models to which EM is applied:

1. The observed data points $\mathbf{X}$ may be discrete (taking values in a finite or countably infinite set) or continuous (taking values in an uncountably infinite set). Associated with each data point may be a vector of observations.

2. The missing values (aka latent variables) $\mathbf{Z}$ are discrete, drawn from a fixed number of values, and with one latent variable per observed data point.

3. The parameters are continuous, and are of two kinds: Parameters that are associated with all data points, and those associated with a specific value of a latent variable (i.e., associated with all data points which corresponding latent variable has that value).

However, it is possible to apply EM to other sorts of models.

The motive is as follows. If the value of the parameters θ is known, usually the value of the latent variables $\mathbf{Z}$ can be found by maximizing the log-likelihood over all possible values of $\mathbf{Z}$, either simply by iterating over $\mathbf{Z}$ or through an algorithm such as the Viterbi algorithm for hidden Markov models. Conversely, if we know the value of the latent variables $\mathbf{Z}$, we can find an estimate of the parameters θ fairly easily, typically by simply grouping the observed data points according to the value of the associated latent variable and averaging the values, or some function of the values, of the points in each group. This suggests an iterative algorithm, in the case where both θ and $\mathbf{Z}$ are unknown:

1. First, initialize the parameters θ to some random values.

2. Compute the best value for $\mathbf{Z}$ given these parameter values.

3. Then, use the just-computed values of $\mathbf{Z}$ to compute a better estimate for the parameters θ. Parameters associated with a specific value of $\mathbf{Z}$ will use only those data points which associated latent variable has that value.

4. Iterate steps 2 and 3 until convergence.

The algorithm as just described monotonically approaches a local minimum of the cost function, and is commonly called *hard EM*. The k-means algorithm is an example of this class of algorithms.

However, somewhat better methods exist. Rather than making a hard choice for $\mathbf{Z}$ given the current parameter values and averaging only over the set of data points associated with some value of $\mathbf{Z}$, instead, determine the probability of each possible value of $\mathbf{Z}$ for each data point, and then use the probabilities associated with some value of $\mathbf{Z}$ to compute a weighted average over the whole set of data points. The resulting algorithm is commonly called *soft EM*, and is the type of algorithm normally associated with EM. The counts used to compute these weighted averages are called *soft counts* (as opposed to the *hard counts* used in a hard-EM-type algorithm such as k-means). The probabilities computed for $\mathbf{Z}$ are posterior probabilities and are what is computed in the E step. The soft counts used to compute new parameter values are what is computed in the M step.

Properties

Speaking of an expectation (E) step is a bit of a misnomer. What is calculated in the first step are the fixed, data-dependent parameters of the function Q. Once the parameters of Q are known, it is fully determined and is maximized in the second (M) step of an EM algorithm.

Although an EM iteration does increase the observed data (i.e., marginal) likelihood function, no guarantee exists that the sequence converges to a maximum likelihood estimator. For multimodal distributions, this means that an EM algorithm may converge to a local maximum of the observed data likelihood function, depending on starting values. A variety of heuristic or metaheuristic approaches exist to escape a local maximum, such as random-restart hill climbing (starting with several different random initial estimates $\theta^{(t)}$), or applying simulated annealing methods.

EM is especially useful when the likelihood is an exponential family: the E step becomes the sum of expectations of sufficient statistics, and the M step involves maximizing a linear function. In such a case, it is usually possible to derive closed-form expression updates for each step, using the Sundberg formula (published by Rolf Sundberg using unpublished results of Per Martin-Löf and Anders Martin-Löf).

The EM method was modified to compute maximum a posteriori (MAP) estimates for Bayesian inference in the original paper by Dempster, Laird, and Rubin.

Other methods exist to find maximum likelihood estimates, such as gradient descent, conjugate gradient, or variants of the Gauss–Newton algorithm. Unlike EM, such methods typically require the evaluation of first and/or second derivatives of the likelihood function.

Proof of Correctness

Expectation-maximization works to improve $Q(\theta \mid \theta^{(t)})$ rather than directly improving $\log p(X \mid \theta)$. Here is shown that improvements to the former imply improvements to the latter.

For any Z with non-zero probability $p(Z \mid X, \theta)$, we can write:

$$\log p(X \mid \theta) = \log p(X, Z \mid \theta) - \log p(Z \mid X, \theta).$$

We take the expectation over possible values of the unknown data $\mathbf{Z}$ under the current parameter estimate $\theta^{(t)}$ by multiplying both sides by $p(Z \mid X, \theta^{(t)})$ and summing (or integrating) over $\mathbf{Z}$. The left-hand side is the expectation of a constant, so we get:

$$\log p(X \mid \theta) = \sum_{Z} p(Z \mid X, \theta^{(t)}) \log p(X, Z \mid \theta) - \sum_{Z} p(Z \mid X, \theta^{(t)}) \log p(Z \mid X, \theta)$$
$$= Q(\theta \mid \theta^{(t)}) + H(\theta \mid \theta^{(t)}),$$

where $H(\theta \mid \theta^{(t)})$ is defined by the negated sum it is replacing. This last equation holds for any value of θ including $\theta = \theta^{(t)}$:

$$\log p(X \mid \theta^{(t)}) = Q(\theta^{(t)} \mid \theta^{(t)}) + H(\theta^{(t)} \mid \theta^{(t)})$$

and subtracting this last equation from the previous equation gives:

$$\log p(X \mid \theta) - \log p(X \mid \theta^{(t)}) = Q(\theta \mid \theta^{(t)}) - Q(\theta^{(t)} \mid \theta^{(t)}) + H(\theta \mid \theta^{(t)}) - H(\theta^{(t)} \mid \theta^{(t)})$$

However, Gibbs' inequality tells us that $H(\theta \mid \theta^{(t)}) \geq H(\theta^{(t)} \mid \theta^{(t)})$, so we can conclude that:

$$\log p(X \mid \theta) - \log p(X \mid \theta^{(t)}) \geq Q(\theta \mid \theta^{(t)}) - Q(\theta^{(t)} \mid \theta^{(t)}).$$

In words, choosing θ to improve $Q(\theta \mid \theta^{(t)})$ beyond $Q(\theta^{(t)} \mid \theta^{(t)})$ can not cause $\log p(X \mid \theta)$ to decrease below $\log p(X \mid \theta^{(t)})$, and so the marginal likelihood of the data is non-decreasing.

As a Maximization-maximization Procedure

The EM algorithm can be viewed as two alternating maximization steps, that is, as an example of coordinate ascent. Consider the function:

$$F(q, \theta) := E_q[\log L(\theta; x, Z)] + H(q),$$

where q is an arbitrary probability distribution over the unobserved data z and $H(q)$ is the entropy of the distribution q. This function can be written as:

$$F(q, \theta) = -D_{KL}\left(q \,\middle\|\, p_{Z|X}(\cdot \mid x; \theta)\right) + \log L(\theta; x),$$

where $p_{Z|X}(\cdot \mid x; \theta)$ is the conditional distribution of the unobserved data given the observed data x and D_{KL} is the Kullback–Leibler divergence.

Then the steps in the EM algorithm may be viewed as:

Expectation step: Choose q to maximize F:

$$q^{(t)} = \operatorname{argmax}_q F(q, \theta^{(t)})$$

Maximization step: Choose θ to maximize F:

$$\theta^{(t+1)} = \operatorname{argmax}_\theta F(q^{(t)}, \theta)$$

Applications

EM is frequently used for data clustering in machine learning and computer vision. In natural language processing, two prominent instances of the algorithm are the Baum-Welch algorithm for hidden Markov models, and the inside-outside algorithm for unsupervised induction of probabilistic context-free grammars.

In psychometrics, EM is almost indispensable for estimating item parameters and latent abilities of item response theory models.

With the ability to deal with missing data and observe unidentified variables, EM is becoming a useful tool to price and manage risk of a portfolio.

The EM algorithm (and its faster variant ordered subset expectation maximization) is also widely used in medical image reconstruction, especially in positron emission tomography and single photon emission computed tomography.

In structural engineering, the Structural Identification using Expectation Maximization (STRIDE) algorithm is an output-only method for identifying natural vibration properties of a structural system using sensor data.

Filtering and Smoothing EM Algorithms

A Kalman filter is typically used for on-line state estimation and a minimum-variance smoother may be employed for off-line or batch state estimation. However, these minimum-variance solutions require estimates of the state-space model parameters. EM algorithms can be used for solving joint state and parameter estimation problems.

Filtering and smoothing EM algorithms arise by repeating this two-step procedure:

E-step

> Operate a Kalman filter or a minimum-variance smoother designed with current parameter estimates to obtain updated state estimates.

M-step

> Use the filtered or smoothed state estimates within maximum-likelihood calculations to obtain updated parameter estimates.

Suppose that a Kalman filter or minimum-variance smoother operates on measurements of a single-input-single-output system that possess additive white noise. An updated measurement noise variance estimate can be obtained from the maximum likelihood calculation:

$$\hat{\sigma}_v^2 = \frac{1}{N} \sum_{k=1}^{N} (z_k - \hat{x}_k)^2$$

where $\hat{x}_k$ are scalar output estimates calculated by a filter or a smoother from N scalar measurements z_k. The above update can also be applied to updating a Poisson measurement noise intensity. Similarly, for a first-order auto-regressive process, an updated process noise variance estimate can be calculated by,

$$\hat{\sigma}_w^2 = \frac{1}{N}\sum_{k=1}^{N}(\hat{x}_{k+1} - \hat{F}\hat{x}_k)^2$$

where $\hat{x}_k$ and $\hat{x}_{k+1}$ are scalar state estimates calculated by a filter or a smoother. The updated model coefficient estimate is obtained via:

$$\hat{F} = \frac{\sum_{k=1}^{N}\left(\hat{x}_{k+1} - \hat{F}''\hat{x}_k\right)}{\sum_{k=1}^{N}\hat{x}_k^2}.$$

The convergence of parameter estimates such as those above are well studied.

Variants

A number of methods have been proposed to accelerate the sometimes slow convergence of the EM algorithm, such as those using conjugate gradient and modified Newton's methods (Newton–Raphson). Also, EM can be used with constrained estimation methods.

Expectation conditional maximization (ECM) replaces each M step with a sequence of conditional maximization (CM) steps in which each parameter θ_i is maximized individually, conditionally on the other parameters remaining fixed.

This idea is further extended in *generalized expectation maximization (GEM)* algorithm, in which is sought only an increase in the objective function *F* for both the E step and M step as described in the As a maximization-maximization procedure section. GEM is further developed in a distributed environment and shows promising results.

It is also possible to consider the EM algorithm as a subclass of the MM (Majorize/Minimize or Minorize/Maximize, depending on context) algorithm, and therefore use any machinery developed in the more general case.

α-EM Algorithm

The Q-function used in the EM algorithm is based on the log likelihood. Therefore, it is regarded as the log-EM algorithm. The use of the log likelihood can be generalized to that of the α-log likelihood ratio. Then, the α-log likelihood ratio of the observed data can be exactly expressed as equality by using the Q-function of the α-log likelihood ratio and the α-divergence. Obtaining this Q-function is a generalized E step. Its maximization is a generalized M step. This pair is called the α-EM algorithm which contains the log-EM algorithm as its subclass. Thus, the α-EM algorithm by Yasuo Matsuyama is an exact generalization of the log-EM algorithm. No computation of gradient or Hessian matrix is needed. The α-EM shows faster convergence than the log-EM algorithm by choosing an appropriate α. The α-EM algorithm leads to a faster version of the Hidden Markov model estimation algorithm α-HMM.

Relation to Variational Bayes Methods

EM is a partially non-Bayesian, maximum likelihood method. Its final result gives a probability distribution over the latent variables (in the Bayesian style) together with a point estimate for θ (either a maximum likelihood estimate or a posterior mode). A fully Bayesian version of this may be wanted, giving a probability distribution over θ and the latent variables. The Bayesian approach to inference is simply to treat θ as another latent variable. In this paradigm, the distinction between the E and M steps disappears. If using the factorized Q approximation as described above (variational Bayes), solving can iterate over each latent variable (now including θ) and optimize them one at a time. Now, k steps per iteration are needed, where k is the number of latent variables. For graphical models this is easy to do as each variable's new Q depends only on its Markov blanket, so local message passing can be used for efficient inference.

Geometric Interpretation

In information geometry, the E step and the M step are interpreted as projections under dual affine connections, called the e-connection and the m-connection; the Kullback–Leibler divergence can also be understood in these terms.

Examples

Gaussian Mixture

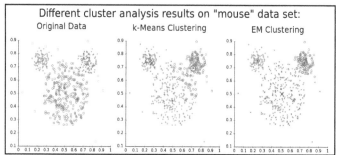

Comparison of k-means and EM on artificial Data visualized with ELKI. Using the Variances,
the EM algorithm can describe the normal distributions exact, while k-Means splits the data in Voronoi-Cells.
The Cluster center is visualized by the lighter, bigger Symbol.

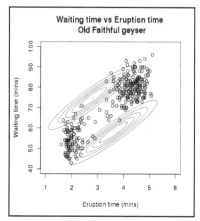

Demonstration of the EM algorithm fitting a two component Gaussian mixture
model to the Old Faithful dataset. The algorithm steps through from a random initialization to convergence.

Let $\mathbf{x} = (\mathbf{x}_1, \mathbf{x}_2, \ldots, \mathbf{x}_n)$ be a sample of n independent observations from a mixture of two multivariate normal distributions of dimension d, and let $\mathbf{z} = (z_1, z_2, \ldots, z_n)$ be the latent variables that determine the component from which the observation originates.

$$X_i \mid (Z_i = 1) \sim \mathcal{N}_d(\mu_1, \Sigma_1) \text{ and } X_i \mid (Z_i = 2) \sim \mathcal{N}_d(\mu_2, \Sigma_2)$$

where

$$P(Z_i = 1) = \tau_1 \text{ and } P(Z_i = 2) = \tau_2 = 1 - \tau_1$$

The aim is to estimate the unknown parameters representing the *mixing* value between the Gaussians and the means and covariances of each:

$$\theta = (\tau, \mu_1, \mu_2, \Sigma_1, \Sigma_2)$$

where the incomplete-data likelihood function is:

$$L(\theta; x) = \prod_{i=1}^{n} \sum_{j=1}^{2} \tau_j \, f(x_i; \mu_j, \Sigma_j),$$

and the complete-data likelihood function is:

$$L(\theta; x, z) = p(x, z \mid \theta) = \prod_{i=1}^{n} \prod_{j=1}^{2} [f(x_i; \mu_j, \Sigma_j) \tau_j]^{\mathbb{I}(z_i = j)}$$

or

$$L(\theta; x, z) = \exp\left\{ \sum_{i=1}^{n} \sum_{j=1}^{2} \mathbb{I}(z_i = j) \left[\log \tau_j - \tfrac{1}{2} \log |\Sigma_j| - \tfrac{1}{2}(x_i - \mu_j)^\top \Sigma_j^{-1}(x_i - \mu_j) - \tfrac{d}{2}\log(2\pi) \right] \right\}.$$

where $\mathbb{I}$ is an indicator function and f is the probability density function of a multivariate normal.

To see the last equality, then for each i all indicators $\mathbb{I}(z_i = j)$ are equal to zero, except for one which is equal to one. The inner sum thus reduces to one term.

E Step

Given our current estimate of the parameters $\theta^{(t)}$, the conditional distribution of the Z_i is determined by Bayes theorem to be the proportional height of the normal density weighted by τ:

$$T_{j,i}^{(t)} := P(Z_i = j \mid X_i = x_i; \theta^{(t)}) = \frac{\tau_j^{(t)} \, f(x_i; \mu_j^{(t)}, \Sigma_j^{(t)})}{\tau_1^{(t)} \, f(x_i; \mu_1^{(t)}, \Sigma_1^{(t)}) + \tau_2^{(t)} \, f(x_i; \mu_2^{(t)}, \Sigma_2^{(t)})}.$$

These are called the "membership probabilities" which are normally considered the output of the E step (although this is not the Q function of below).

This E step corresponds with this function for Q:

$$Q(\theta \mid \theta^{(t)}) = E_{Z|X, \theta^{(t)}}[\log L(\theta; x, Z)]$$

$$= E_{Z|X, \theta^{(t)}}[\log \prod_{i=1}^{n} L(\theta; x_i, z_i)]$$

$$= E_{Z|X,\theta^{(t)}} \left[\sum_{i=1}^{n} \log L(\theta; x_i, z_i) \right]$$

$$= \sum_{i=1}^{n} E_{Z|X;\theta^{(t)}} \left[\log L(\theta; x_i, z_i) \right]$$

$$= \sum_{i=1}^{n} \sum_{j=1}^{2} P(Z_i = j \mid X_i = x_i; \theta^{(t)}) \log L(\theta_j; x_i, z_i)$$

$$= \sum_{i=1}^{n} \sum_{j=1}^{2} T_{j,i}^{(t)} \left[\log \tau_j - \tfrac{1}{2} \log |\Sigma_j| - \tfrac{1}{2}(x_i - \mu_j)^\top \Sigma_j^{-1}(x_i - \mu_j) - \tfrac{d}{2} \log(2\pi) \right]$$

This full conditional expectation does not need to be calculated in one step, because τ and μ/Σ appear in separate linear terms and can thus be maximized independently.

M Step

$Q(\theta|\theta^{(t)})$ being quadratic in form means that determining the maximizing values of θ is relatively straightforward. Also, τ, (μ_1, Σ_1) and (μ_2, Σ_2) may all be maximized independently since they all appear in separate linear terms.

To begin, consider τ, which has the constraint $\tau_1 + \tau_2 = 1$:

$$\tau^{(t+1)} = \underset{\tau}{\operatorname{argmax}}\ Q(\theta|\theta^{(t)})$$

$$= \underset{\tau}{\operatorname{argmax}} \left\{ \left[\sum_{i=1}^{n} T_{1,i}^{(t)} \right] \log \tau_1 + \left[\sum_{i=1}^{n} T_{2,i}^{(t)} \right] \log \tau_2 \right\}$$

This has the same form as the MLE for the binomial distribution, so:

$$\tau_j^{(t+1)} = \frac{\sum_{i=1}^{n} T_{j,i}^{(t)}}{\sum_{i=1}^{n} (T_{1,i}^{(t)} + T_{2,i}^{(t)})} = \frac{1}{n} \sum_{i=1}^{n} T_{j,i}^{(t)}.$$

For the next estimates of (μ_1, Σ_1):

$$(\mu_1^{(t+1)}, \Sigma_1^{(t+1)}) = \underset{\mu_1, \Sigma_1}{\operatorname{argmax}}\ Q(\theta|\theta^{(t)})$$

$$= \underset{\mu_1, \Sigma_1}{\operatorname{argmax}} \sum_{i=1}^{n} T_{1,i}^{(t)} \left\{ -\tfrac{1}{2} \log |\Sigma_1| - \tfrac{1}{2}(x_i - \mu_1)^\top \Sigma_1^{-1}(x_i - \mu_1) \right\}$$

This has the same form as a weighted MLE for a normal distribution, so:

$$\mu_2^{(t+1)} = \frac{\sum_{i=1}^{n} T_{2,i}^{(t)} x_i}{\sum_{i=1}^{n} T_{2,i}^{(t)}} \quad \text{and} \quad \Sigma_1^{(t+1)} = \frac{\sum_{i=1}^{n} T_{1,i}^{(t)} (x_i - \mu_1^{(t+1)})(x_i - \mu_1^{(t+1)})^\top}{\sum_{i=1}^{n} T_{1,i}^{(t)}}$$

and, by symmetry:

$$\mu_2^{(t+1)} = \frac{\sum_{i=1}^{n} T_{2,i}^{(t)} x_i}{\sum_{i=1}^{n} T_{2,i}^{(t)}} \text{ and } \Sigma_2^{(t+1)} = \frac{\sum_{i=1}^{n} T_{2,i}^{(t)} (x_i - \mu_2^{(t+1)})(x_i - \mu_2^{(t+1)})^{\top}}{\sum_{i=1}^{n} T_{2,i}^{(t)}}.$$

Termination

Conclude the iterative process if $E_{Z|\theta^{(t)},x}[\log L(\theta^{(t)}; x, Z)] \leq E_{Z|\theta^{(t-1)},x}[\log L(\theta^{(t-1)}; x, Z)] + \epsilon$ for ϵ below some preset threshold.

Generalization

The algorithm illustrated above can be generalized for mixtures of more than two multivariate normal distributions.

Truncated and Censored Regression

The EM algorithm has been implemented in the case where an underlying linear regression model exists explaining the variation of some quantity, but where the values actually observed are censored or truncated versions of those represented in the model. Special cases of this model include censored or truncated observations from one normal distribution.

Alternatives

EM typically converges to a local optimum, not necessarily the global optimum, with no bound on the convergence rate in general. It is possible that it can be arbitrarily poor in high dimensions and there can be an exponential number of local optima. Hence, a need exists for alternative methods for guaranteed learning, especially in the high-dimensional setting. Alternatives to EM exist with better guarantees for consistency, which are termed *moment-based approaches* or the so-called *spectral techniques*. Moment-based approaches to learning the parameters of a probabilistic model are of increasing interest recently since they enjoy guarantees such as global convergence under certain conditions unlike EM which is often plagued by the issue of getting stuck in local optima. Algorithms with guarantees for learning can be derived for a number of important models such as mixture models, HMMs etc. For these spectral methods, no spurious local optima occur, and the true parameters can be consistently estimated under some regularity conditions.

Forward–backward Algorithm

The forward–backward algorithm is an inference algorithm for hidden Markov models which computes the posterior marginals of all hidden state variables given a sequence of observations/emissions $o_{1:t} := o_1, \ldots, o_t$, i.e. it computes, for all hidden state variables $X_k \in \{X_1, \ldots, X_t\}$, the distribution $P(X_k \mid o_{1:t})$. This inference task is usually called *smoothing*. The algorithm makes use of the principle of dynamic programming to compute efficiently the values that are required to obtain the posterior marginal distributions in two passes. The first pass goes forward in time while the second goes backward in time; hence the name *forward–backward algorithm*.

The term *forward–backward algorithm* is also used to refer to any algorithm belonging to the general class of algorithms that operate on sequence models in a forward–backward manner.

Overview

In the first pass, the forward–backward algorithm computes a set of forward probabilities which provide, for all $k \in \{1,\ldots,t\}$, the probability of ending up in any particular state given the first k observations in the sequence, i.e. $P(X_k \mid o_{1:k})$. In the second pass, the algorithm computes a set of backward probabilities which provide the probability of observing the remaining observations given any starting point k, i.e. $P(o_{k+1:t} \mid X_k)$. These two sets of probability distributions can then be combined to obtain the distribution over states at any specific point in time given the entire observation sequence:

$$P(X_k \mid o_{1:t}) = P(X_k \mid o_{1:k}, o_{k+1:t}) \propto P(o_{k+1:t} \mid X_k)P(o_{1:k}, X_k)$$

The last step follows from an application of the Bayes' rule and the conditional independence of $o_{k+1:t}$ and $o_{1:k}$ given X_k.

As outlined above, the algorithm involves three steps:

- Computing forward probabilities.

- Computing backward probabilities.

- Computing smoothed values.

The forward and backward steps may also be called "forward message pass" and "backward message pass" - these terms are due to the *message-passing* used in general belief propagation approaches. At each single observation in the sequence, probabilities to be used for calculations at the next observation are computed. The smoothing step can be calculated simultaneously during the backward pass. This step allows the algorithm to take into account any past observations of output for computing more accurate results.

The forward–backward algorithm can be used to find the most likely state for any point in time. It cannot, however, be used to find the most likely sequence of states.

Forward Probabilities

The following description will use matrices of probability values rather than probability distributions, although in general the forward-backward algorithm can be applied to continuous as well as discrete probability models.

We transform the probability distributions related to a given hidden Markov model into matrix notation as follows. The transition probabilities $\mathbf{P}(X_t \mid X_{t-1})$ of a given random variable X_t representing all possible states in the hidden Markov model will be represented by the matrix $\mathbf{T}$

where the column index i will represent the target state and the row index j represents the start state. A transition from row-vector state π_t to the incremental row-vector state π_{t+1} is written as $\pi_{t+1} = \pi_t T$. The example below represents a system where the probability of staying in the same state after each step is 70% and the probability of transitioning to the other state is 30%. The transition matrix is then:

$$\mathbf{T} = \begin{pmatrix} 0.7 & 0.3 \\ 0.3 & 0.7 \end{pmatrix}$$

In a typical Markov model we would multiply a state vector by this matrix to obtain the probabilities for the subsequent state. In a hidden Markov model the state is unknown, and we instead observe events associated with the possible states. An event matrix of the form:

$$\mathbf{B} = \begin{pmatrix} 0.9 & 0.1 \\ 0.2 & 0.8 \end{pmatrix}$$

provides the probabilities for observing events given a particular state. In the above example, event 1 will be observed 90% of the time if we are in state 1 while event 2 has a 10% probability of occurring in this state. In contrast, event 1 will only be observed 20% of the time if we are in state 2 and event 2 has an 80% chance of occurring. Given an arbitrary row-vector describing the state of the system (π), the probability of observing event j is then:

$$\mathbf{P}(O = j) = \sum_i \pi_i b_{j,i}$$

This can be represented in matrix form by multiplying the state row-vector (π) by an observation matrix ($\mathbf{O}_j = \mathrm{diag}(b_{*,o_j})$) containing only diagonal entries. Each entry is the probability of the observed event given each state. Continuing the above example, an observation of tevent 1 would be:

$$\mathbf{O}_1 = \begin{pmatrix} 0.9 & 0.0 \\ 0.0 & 0.2 \end{pmatrix}$$

This allows us to calculate the new unnormalized probabilities state vector π' through Bayes rule, weighting by the likelihood that each element of π generated event 1 as:

$$\pi' = \pi \mathbf{O}_1$$

We can now make this general procedure specific to our series of observations. Assuming an initial state vector π_0, (which can be optimized as a parameter through repetitions of the forward-back procedure), we begin with:

$$f_{0:0} = \pi_0 T O_{o(0)}$$

This process can be carried forward with additional observations using:

$$\mathbf{f}_{0:t} = \mathbf{f}_{0:t-1}\mathbf{TO}_{o(t)}$$

This value is the forward unnormalized probability vector. The i'th entry of this vector provides:

$$f_{0:t}(i) = P(o_1, o_2, \ldots, o_t, X_t = x_i \mid \pi)$$

Typically, we will normalize the probability vector at each step so that its entries sum to 1. A scaling factor is thus introduced at each step such that:

$$\hat{\mathbf{f}}_{0:t} = c_t^{-1}\hat{\mathbf{f}}_{0:t-1}\mathbf{TO}_{o(t)}$$

where $\hat{\mathbf{f}}_{0:t-1}$ represents the scaled vector from the previous step and c_t represents the scaling factor that causes the resulting vector's entries to sum to 1. The product of the scaling factors is the total probability for observing the given events irrespective of the final states:

$$P(o_1, o_2, \ldots, o_t \mid \pi) = \prod_{s=1}^{t} c_s$$

This allows us to interpret the scaled probability vector as:

$$\hat{f}_{0:t}(i) = \frac{f_{0:t}(i)}{\prod_{s=1}^{t} c_s} = \frac{P(o_1, o_2, \ldots, o_t, X_t = x_i \mid \pi)}{P(o_1, o_2, \ldots, o_t \mid \pi)} = P(X_t = x_i \mid o_1, o_2, \ldots, o_t, \pi)$$

We thus find that the product of the scaling factors provides us with the total probability for observing the given sequence up to time t and that the scaled probability vector provides us with the probability of being in each state at this time.

Backward Probabilities

A similar procedure can be constructed to find backward probabilities. These intend to provide the probabilities:

$$\mathbf{b}_{t:T}(i) = P(o_{t+1}, o_{t+2}, \ldots, o_T \mid X_t = x_i)$$

That is, we now want to assume that we start in a particular state ($X_t = x_i$), and we are now interested in the probability of observing all future events from this state. Since the initial state is assumed as given (i.e. the prior probability of this state = 100%), we begin with:

$$\mathbf{b}_{T:T} = [1\,1\,1\ldots]^T$$

Notice that we are now using a column vector while the forward probabilities used row vectors. We can then work backwards using:

$$\mathbf{b}_{t-1:T} = \mathbf{TO}_t\mathbf{b}_{t:T}$$

While we could normalize this vector as well so that its entries sum to one, this is not usually done. Noting that each entry contains the probability of the future event sequence given a particular initial state, normalizing this vector would be equivalent to applying Bayes' theorem to find the likelihood of each initial state given the future events (assuming uniform priors for the final state vector). However, it is more common to scale this vector using the same c_t constants used in the forward probability calculations. $\mathbf{b}_{T:T}$ is not scaled, but subsequent operations use:

$$\hat{\mathbf{b}}_{t-1:T} = c_t^{-1}\mathbf{TO}_t\hat{\mathbf{b}}_{t:T}$$

where $\hat{\mathbf{b}}_{t:T}$ represents the previous, scaled vector. This result is that the scaled probability vector is related to the backward probabilities by:

$$\hat{\mathbf{b}}_{t:T}(i) = \frac{\mathbf{b}_{t:T}(i)}{\prod\limits_{s=t+1}^{T} c_s}$$

This is useful because it allows us to find the total probability of being in each state at a given time, t, by multiplying these values:

$$\gamma_t(i) = P(X_t = x_i \mid o_1, o_2, \ldots, o_T, \pi) = \frac{P(o_1, o_2, \ldots, o_T, X_t = x_i \mid \pi)}{P(o_1, o_2, \ldots, o_T \mid \pi)} = \frac{f_{0:t}(i) \cdot b_{t:T}(i)}{\prod\limits_{s=1}^{T} c_s} = \hat{f}_{0:t}(i) \cdot \hat{b}_{t:T}(i)$$

To understand this, we note that $\mathbf{f}_{0:t}(i) \cdot \mathbf{b}_{t:T}(i)$ provides the probability for observing the given events in a way that passes through state x_i at time t. This probability includes the forward probabilities covering all events up to time t as well as the backward probabilities which include all future events. This is the numerator we are looking for in our equation, and we divide by the total probability of the observation sequence to normalize this value and extract only the probability that $X_t = x_i$. These values are sometimes called the "smoothed values" as they combine the forward and backward probabilities to compute a final probability.

The values $\gamma_t(i)$ thus provide the probability of being in each state at time t. As such, they are useful for determining the most probable state at any time. It should be noted, however, that the term "most probable state" is somewhat ambiguous. While the most probable state is the most likely to be correct at a given point, the sequence of individually probable states is not likely to be the most probable sequence. This is because the probabilities for each point are calculated independently of each other. They do not take into account the transition probabilities between states, and it is thus possible to get states at two moments (t and t+1) that are both most probable at those time points but which have very little probability of occurring together, i.e. $\mathbf{P}(X_t = x_i, X_{t+1} = x_j) \neq \mathbf{P}(X_t = x_i)\mathbf{P}(X_{t+1} = x_j)$. The most probable sequence of states that produced an observation sequence can be found using the Viterbi algorithm.

Example

This example takes as its basis the umbrella world in Russell & Norvig 2010 Chapter 15 pp. 566 in which we would like to infer the weather given observation of a man either carrying or not carrying an umbrella. We assume two possible states for the weather: state 1 = rain, state 2 = no rain.

We assume that the weather has a 70% chance of staying the same each day and a 30% chance of changing. The transition probabilities are then:

$$\mathbf{T} = \begin{pmatrix} 0.7 & 0.3 \\ 0.3 & 0.7 \end{pmatrix}$$

We also assume each state generates 2 events: event 1 = umbrella, event 2 = no umbrella. The conditional probabilities for these occurring in each state are given by the probability matrix:

$$\mathbf{B} = \begin{pmatrix} 0.9 & 0.1 \\ 0.2 & 0.8 \end{pmatrix}$$

We then observe the following sequence of events: {umbrella, umbrella, no umbrella, umbrella, umbrella} which we will represent in our calculations as:

$$\mathbf{O}_1 = \begin{pmatrix} 0.9 & 0.0 \\ 0.0 & 0.2 \end{pmatrix} \mathbf{O}_2 = \begin{pmatrix} 0.9 & 0.0 \\ 0.0 & 0.2 \end{pmatrix} \mathbf{O}_3 = \begin{pmatrix} 0.1 & 0.0 \\ 0.0 & 0.8 \end{pmatrix} \mathbf{O}_4 = \begin{pmatrix} 0.9 & 0.0 \\ 0.0 & 0.2 \end{pmatrix} \mathbf{O}_5 = \begin{pmatrix} 0.9 & 0.0 \\ 0.0 & 0.2 \end{pmatrix}$$

Note that $\mathbf{O}_3$ differs from the others because of the "no umbrella" observation.

In computing the forward probabilities we begin with:

$$\mathbf{f}_{0:0} = \begin{pmatrix} 0.5 & 0.5 \end{pmatrix}$$

which is our prior state vector indicating that we don't know which state the weather is in before our observations. While a state vector should be given as a row vector, we will use the transpose of the matrix so that the calculations below are easier to read. Our calculations are then written in the form:

$$(\hat{\mathbf{f}}_{0:t})^{\mathrm{T}} = c^{-1}\mathbf{O}_t(\mathbf{T})^{\mathrm{T}}(\hat{\mathbf{f}}_{0:t-1})^{\mathrm{T}}$$

instead of:

$$\hat{\mathbf{f}}_{0:t} = c^{-1}\hat{\mathbf{f}}_{0:t-1}\mathbf{T}\mathbf{O}_t$$

Notice that the transformation matrix is also transposed, but in our example the transpose is equal to the original matrix. Performing these calculations and normalizing the results provides:

$$(\hat{\mathbf{f}}_{0:1})^{\mathrm{T}} = c_1^{-1} \begin{pmatrix} 0.9 & 0.0 \\ 0.0 & 0.2 \end{pmatrix} \begin{pmatrix} 0.7 & 0.3 \\ 0.3 & 0.7 \end{pmatrix} \begin{pmatrix} 0.5000 \\ 0.5000 \end{pmatrix} = c_1^{-1} \begin{pmatrix} 0.4500 \\ 0.1000 \end{pmatrix} = \begin{pmatrix} 0.8182 \\ 0.1818 \end{pmatrix}$$

$$(\hat{\mathbf{f}}_{0:2})^{\mathrm{T}} = c_2^{-1} \begin{pmatrix} 0.9 & 0.0 \\ 0.0 & 0.2 \end{pmatrix} \begin{pmatrix} 0.7 & 0.3 \\ 0.3 & 0.7 \end{pmatrix} \begin{pmatrix} 0.8182 \\ 0.1818 \end{pmatrix} = c_2^{-1} \begin{pmatrix} 0.5645 \\ 0.0745 \end{pmatrix} = \begin{pmatrix} 0.8834 \\ 0.1166 \end{pmatrix}$$

$$(\hat{\mathbf{f}}_{0:3})^{\mathrm{T}} = c_3^{-1} \begin{pmatrix} 0.1 & 0.0 \\ 0.0 & 0.8 \end{pmatrix} \begin{pmatrix} 0.7 & 0.3 \\ 0.3 & 0.7 \end{pmatrix} \begin{pmatrix} 0.8834 \\ 0.1166 \end{pmatrix} = c_3^{-1} \begin{pmatrix} 0.0653 \\ 0.2772 \end{pmatrix} = \begin{pmatrix} 0.1907 \\ 0.8093 \end{pmatrix}$$

$$(\hat{\mathbf{f}}_{0:4})^{\mathrm{T}} = c_4^{-1} \begin{pmatrix} 0.9 & 0.0 \\ 0.0 & 0.2 \end{pmatrix} \begin{pmatrix} 0.7 & 0.3 \\ 0.3 & 0.7 \end{pmatrix} \begin{pmatrix} 0.1907 \\ 0.8093 \end{pmatrix} = c_4^{-1} \begin{pmatrix} 0.3386 \\ 0.1247 \end{pmatrix} = \begin{pmatrix} 0.7308 \\ 0.2692 \end{pmatrix}$$

$$(\hat{\mathbf{f}}_{0:5})^{\mathrm{T}} = c_5^{-1} \begin{pmatrix} 0.9 & 0.0 \\ 0.0 & 0.2 \end{pmatrix} \begin{pmatrix} 0.7 & 0.3 \\ 0.3 & 0.7 \end{pmatrix} \begin{pmatrix} 0.7308 \\ 0.2692 \end{pmatrix} = c_5^{-1} \begin{pmatrix} 0.5331 \\ 0.0815 \end{pmatrix} = \begin{pmatrix} 0.8673 \\ 0.1327 \end{pmatrix}$$

For the backward probabilities we start with:

$$\mathbf{b}_{5:5} = \begin{pmatrix} 1.0 \\ 1.0 \end{pmatrix}$$

We are then able to compute (using the observations in reverse order and normalizing with different constants):

$$\hat{\mathbf{b}}_{4:5} = \alpha \begin{pmatrix} 0.7 & 0.3 \\ 0.3 & 0.7 \end{pmatrix} \begin{pmatrix} 0.9 & 0.0 \\ 0.0 & 0.2 \end{pmatrix} \begin{pmatrix} 1.0000 \\ 1.0000 \end{pmatrix} = \alpha \begin{pmatrix} 0.6900 \\ 0.4100 \end{pmatrix} = \begin{pmatrix} 0.6273 \\ 0.3727 \end{pmatrix}$$

$$\hat{\mathbf{b}}_{3:5} = \alpha \begin{pmatrix} 0.7 & 0.3 \\ 0.3 & 0.7 \end{pmatrix} \begin{pmatrix} 0.9 & 0.0 \\ 0.0 & 0.2 \end{pmatrix} \begin{pmatrix} 0.6273 \\ 0.3727 \end{pmatrix} = \alpha \begin{pmatrix} 0.4175 \\ 0.2215 \end{pmatrix} = \begin{pmatrix} 0.6533 \\ 0.3467 \end{pmatrix}$$

$$\hat{\mathbf{b}}_{2:5} = \alpha \begin{pmatrix} 0.7 & 0.3 \\ 0.3 & 0.7 \end{pmatrix} \begin{pmatrix} 0.1 & 0.0 \\ 0.0 & 0.8 \end{pmatrix} \begin{pmatrix} 0.6533 \\ 0.3467 \end{pmatrix} = \alpha \begin{pmatrix} 0.1289 \\ 0.2138 \end{pmatrix} = \begin{pmatrix} 0.3763 \\ 0.6237 \end{pmatrix}$$

$$\hat{\mathbf{b}}_{1:5} = \alpha \begin{pmatrix} 0.7 & 0.3 \\ 0.3 & 0.7 \end{pmatrix} \begin{pmatrix} 0.9 & 0.0 \\ 0.0 & 0.2 \end{pmatrix} \begin{pmatrix} 0.3763 \\ 0.6237 \end{pmatrix} = \alpha \begin{pmatrix} 0.2745 \\ 0.1889 \end{pmatrix} = \begin{pmatrix} 0.5923 \\ 0.4077 \end{pmatrix}$$

$$\hat{\mathbf{b}}_{0:5} = \alpha \begin{pmatrix} 0.7 & 0.3 \\ 0.3 & 0.7 \end{pmatrix} \begin{pmatrix} 0.9 & 0.0 \\ 0.0 & 0.2 \end{pmatrix} \begin{pmatrix} 0.5923 \\ 0.4077 \end{pmatrix} = \alpha \begin{pmatrix} 0.3976 \\ 0.2170 \end{pmatrix} = \begin{pmatrix} 0.6469 \\ 0.3531 \end{pmatrix}$$

Finally, we will compute the smoothed probability values. These result also must be scaled so that its entries sum to 1 because we did not scale the backward probabilities with the c_t's found earlier. The backward probability vectors above thus actually represent the likelihood of each state at time t given the future observations. Because these vectors are proportional to the actual backward probabilities, the result has to be scaled an additional time.

$$(\gamma_0)^{\mathrm{T}} = \alpha \begin{pmatrix} 0.5000 \\ 0.5000 \end{pmatrix} \circ \begin{pmatrix} 0.6469 \\ 0.3531 \end{pmatrix} = \alpha \begin{pmatrix} 0.3235 \\ 0.1765 \end{pmatrix} = \begin{pmatrix} 0.6469 \\ 0.3531 \end{pmatrix}$$

$$(\gamma_1)^{\mathrm{T}} = \alpha \begin{pmatrix} 0.8182 \\ 0.1818 \end{pmatrix} \circ \begin{pmatrix} 0.5923 \\ 0.4077 \end{pmatrix} = \alpha \begin{pmatrix} 0.4846 \\ 0.0741 \end{pmatrix} = \begin{pmatrix} 0.8673 \\ 0.1327 \end{pmatrix}$$

$$(\gamma_2)^{\mathrm{T}} = \alpha \begin{pmatrix} 0.8834 \\ 0.1166 \end{pmatrix} \circ \begin{pmatrix} 0.3763 \\ 0.6237 \end{pmatrix} = \alpha \begin{pmatrix} 0.3324 \\ 0.0728 \end{pmatrix} = \begin{pmatrix} 0.8204 \\ 0.1796 \end{pmatrix}$$

$$(\gamma_3)^{\mathrm{T}} = \alpha \begin{pmatrix} 0.1907 \\ 0.8093 \end{pmatrix} \circ \begin{pmatrix} 0.6533 \\ 0.3467 \end{pmatrix} = \alpha \begin{pmatrix} 0.1246 \\ 0.2806 \end{pmatrix} = \begin{pmatrix} 0.3075 \\ 0.6925 \end{pmatrix}$$

$$(\gamma_4)^{\mathrm{T}} = \alpha \begin{pmatrix} 0.7308 \\ 0.2692 \end{pmatrix} \circ \begin{pmatrix} 0.6273 \\ 0.3727 \end{pmatrix} = \alpha \begin{pmatrix} 0.4584 \\ 0.1003 \end{pmatrix} = \begin{pmatrix} 0.8204 \\ 0.1796 \end{pmatrix}$$

$$(\gamma_5)^{\mathrm{T}} = \alpha \begin{pmatrix} 0.8673 \\ 0.1327 \end{pmatrix} \circ \begin{pmatrix} 1.0000 \\ 1.0000 \end{pmatrix} = \alpha \begin{pmatrix} 0.8673 \\ 0.1327 \end{pmatrix} = \begin{pmatrix} 0.8673 \\ 0.1327 \end{pmatrix}$$

Notice that the value of γ_0 is equal to $\hat{\mathbf{b}}_{0:5}$ and that γ_5 is equal to $\hat{\mathbf{f}}_{0:5}$. This follows naturally because both $\hat{\mathbf{f}}_{0:5}$ and $\hat{\mathbf{b}}_{0:5}$ begin with uniform priors over the initial and final state vectors (respectively) and take into account all of the observations. However, γ_0 will only be equal to $\hat{\mathbf{b}}_{0:5}$ when our initial state vector represents a uniform prior (i.e. all entries are equal). When this is not the case $\hat{\mathbf{b}}_{0:5}$ needs to be combined with the initial state vector to find the most likely initial state. We thus find that the forward probabilities by themselves are sufficient to calculate the most likely final state. Similarly, the backward probabilities can be combined with the initial state vector to provide the most probable initial state given the observations. The forward and backward probabilities need only be combined to infer the most probable states between the initial and final points.

The calculations above reveal that the most probable weather state on every day except for the third one was "rain." They tell us more than this, however, as they now provide a way to quantify the probabilities of each state at different times. Perhaps most importantly, our value at γ_5 quantifies our knowledge of the state vector at the end of the observation sequence. We can then use this to predict the probability of the various weather states tomorrow as well as the probability of observing an umbrella.

Performance

The brute-force procedure for the solution of this problem is the generation of all possible N^{T} state sequences and calculating the joint probability of each state sequence with the observed series of events. This approach has time complexity $O(T \cdot N^{\mathrm{T}})$, where T is the length of sequences and N is the number of symbols in the state alphabet. This is intractable for realistic problems, as the number of possible hidden node sequences typically is extremely high. However, the forward–backward algorithm has time complexity $O(N^2 T)$.

An enhancement to the general forward-backward algorithm, called the Island algorithm, trades smaller memory usage for longer running time, taking $O(N^2 T \log T)$ time and $O(N \log T)$ memory. On a computer with an unlimited number of processors, this can be reduced to $O(N^2 T)$ total time, while still taking only $O(N \log T)$ memory.

In addition, algorithms have been developed to compute $\mathbf{f}_{0:t+1}$ efficiently through online smoothing such as the fixed-lag smoothing (FLS) algorithm Russell & Norvig 2010.

Pseudocode

```
Backward(guessState, sequenceIndex):

    if sequenceIndex is past the end of the sequence, return 1

    if (guessState, sequenceIndex) has been seen before, return saved
result

    result = 0

    for each neighboring state n:

        result = result + (transition probability from guessState to

                        n given observation element at sequenceIndex)

                    * Backward(n, sequenceIndex+1)

    save result for (guessState, sequenceIndex)

    return result
```

Python Example

Given HMM (just like in Viterbi algorithm) represented in the Python programming language:

```python
states = ('Healthy', 'Fever')
end_state = 'E'

observations = ('normal', 'cold', 'dizzy')

start_probability = {'Healthy': 0.6, 'Fever': 0.4}


transition_probability = {
   'Healthy' : {'Healthy': 0.69, 'Fever': 0.3, 'E': 0.01},
   'Fever'   : {'Healthy': 0.4, 'Fever': 0.59, 'E': 0.01},
   }


emission_probability = {
   'Healthy' : {'normal': 0.5, 'cold': 0.4, 'dizzy': 0.1},
   'Fever'   : {'normal': 0.1, 'cold': 0.3, 'dizzy': 0.6},
   }
```

We can write implementation like this:

```
def fwd_bkw(observations, states, start_prob, trans_prob, emm_prob, end_
st):

    # forward part of the algorithm

    fwd = []

    f_prev = {}

    for i, observation_i in enumerate(observations):

        f_curr = {}

        for st in states:

            if i == 0:

                # base case for the forward part

                prev_f_sum = start_prob[st]

            else:

                prev_f_sum = sum(f_prev[k]*trans_prob[k][st] for k in
states)


            f_curr[st] = emm_prob[st][observation_i] * prev_f_sum


        fwd.append(f_curr)

        f_prev = f_curr


    p_fwd = sum(f_curr[k] * trans_prob[k][end_st] for k in states)


    # backward part of the algorithm

    bkw = []

    b_prev = {}

    for i, observation_i_plus in enumerate(reversed(observations[1:]+(-
None,))):

        b_curr = {}
```

```
        for st in states:

            if i == 0:

                # base case for backward part

                b_curr[st] = trans_prob[st][end_st]

            else:

                b_curr[st] = sum(trans_prob[st][l] * emm_prob[l][obser-
vation_i_plus] * b_prev[l] for l in states)


        bkw.insert(0,b_curr)

        b_prev = b_curr


    p_bkw = sum(start_prob[l] * emm_prob[l][observations] * b_curr[l] for
l in states)


    # merging the two parts
    posterior = []
    for i in range(len(observations)):

        posterior.append({st: fwd[i][st] * bkw[i][st] / p_fwd for st in
states})


    assert p_fwd == p_bkw

    return fwd, bkw, posterior
```

The function fwd_bkw takes the following arguments: x is the sequence of observations, e.g. ['normal', 'cold', 'dizzy']; states is the set of hidden states; a_0 is the start probability; a are the transition probabilities; and e are the emission probabilities.

For simplicity of code, we assume that the observation sequence x is non-empty and that a[i][j] and e[i][j] is defined for all states i,j.

In the running example, the forward-backward algorithm is used as follows:

```
def example():

    return fwd_bkw(observations,
```

```
                        states,

                        start_probability,

                        transition_probability,

                        emission_probability,

                        end_state)
>>> for line in example():
...     print(*line)
...
```

{'Healthy': 0.3, 'Fever': 0.04000000000000001} {'Healthy': 0.0892, 'Fever': 0.03408} {'Healthy': 0.007518, 'Fever': 0.02812031999999997}

{'Healthy': 0.0010418399999999998, 'Fever': 0.00109578} {'Healthy':
0.00249, 'Fever': 0.00394} {'Healthy': 0.01, 'Fever': 0.01}

{'Healthy':   0.8770110375573259,   'Fever':   0.1229889624426741}
{'Healthy': 0.623228030950954, 'Fever': 0.3767719690490461} {'Healthy':
0.2109527048413057, 'Fever': 0.7890472951586943}

Structured kNN

The Structured k-Nearest Neighbours is a machine learning algorithm that generalizes the k-Nearest Neighbors (kNN) classifier. Whereas the kNN classifier supports binary classification, multiclass classification and regression, the Structured kNN (SkNN) allows training of a classifier for general structured output labels.

As an example, a sample instance might be a natural language sentence, and the output label is an annotated parse tree. Training a classifier consists of showing pairs of correct sample and output label pairs. After training, the structured kNN model allows one to predict for new sample instances the corresponding output label; that is, given a natural language sentence, the classifier can produce the most likely parse tree.

Training

As a training set SkNN accepts sequences of elements with defined class labels. Type of elements does not matter, the only condition is the existence of metric function that defines a distance between each pair of elements of a set.

SkNN is based on idea of creating a graph, each node of which represents class label. There is an edge between a pair of nodes iff there is a sequence of two elements in training set with corresponding classes. Thereby the first step of SkNN training is the construction of described graph from training sequences. There are two special nodes in the graph corresponding to an end and a beginning of sentences. If sequence starts with class `C`, the edge between node `START` and node `C` should be created.

Like a regular kNN, the second part of the training of SkNN consists only of storing the elements of trained sequence in special way. Each element of training sequences is stored in node related to the class of previous element in sequence. Every first element is stored in node `START`.

Inference

Labelling of input sequences in SkNN consists in finding sequence of transitions in graph, starting from node `START`, which minimises overall cost of path. Each transition corresponds to a single element of input sequence and visa versa. As a result, label of element is determined as target node label of the transition. Cost of the path is defined as sum of all its transitions, and the cost of transition from node `A` to node `B` is a distance from current input sequence element to the nearest element of class `B`, stored in node `A`. Searching of optimal path may be performed using modified Viterbi algorithm. Unlike the original one, the modified algorithm instead of maximizing the product of probabilities minimizes the sum of the distances.

Wake-sleep Algorithm

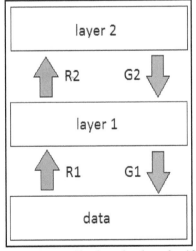

Layers of the neural network. R, G are weights used by the wake-sleep algorithm to modify data inside the layers.

The wake-sleep algorithm is an unsupervised learning algorithm for a stochastic multilayer neural network. The algorithm adjusts the parameters so as to produce a good density estimator. There are two learning phases, the "wake" phase and the "sleep" phase, which are performed alternately. It was first designed as a model for brain functioning using variational Bayesian learning. After that, the algorithm was adapted to machine learning. It can be viewed as a way to train a Helmholtz Machine

Description

The wake-sleep algorithms is visualized as a stack of layers containing representations of data.

Layers above represent data from the layer below it. Actual data is placed below the bottom layer, causing layers on top of it to become gradually more abstract. Between each pair of layers there is a recognition weight and generative weight, which are trained to improve reliability during the algorithm runtime.

The wake-sleep algorithm is convergent and can be stochastic if alternated appropriately.

Training

Training consists of two phases – the "wake" phase and the "sleep" phase.

The "Wake" Phase

Neurons are fired by recognition connections (from what would be input to what would be output). Generative connections (leading from outputs to inputs) are then modified to increase probability that they would recreate the correct activity in the layer below – closer to actual data from sensory input.

The "Sleep" Phase

The process is reversed in the "sleep" phase – neurons are fired by generative connections while recognition connections are being modified to increase probability that they would recreate the correct activity in the layer above – further to actual data from sensory input.

Potential Risks

Variational Bayesian learning is based on probabilities. There is a chance that an approximation is performed with mistakes, damaging further data representations. Another downside pertains to complicated or corrupted data samples, making it difficult to infer a representational pattern.

The wake-sleep algorithm has been suggested not to be powerful enough for the layers of the inference network in order to recover a good estimator of the posterior distribution of latent variables.

Manifold Alignment

Manifold alignment is a class of machine learning algorithms that produce projections between sets of data, given that the original data sets lie on a common manifold. The concept was first introduced as such by Ham, Lee, and Saul in 2003, adding a manifold constraint to the general problem of correlating sets of high-dimensional vectors.

Overview

Manifold alignment assumes that disparate data sets produced by similar generating processes will share a similar underlying manifold representation. By learning projections from each original space to the shared manifold, correspondences are recovered and knowledge from one domain can be transferred to another. Most manifold alignment techniques consider only two data sets, but the concept extends to arbitrarily many initial data sets.

Consider the case of aligning two data sets, X and Y, with $X_i \in \mathbb{R}^m$ and $Y_i \in \mathbb{R}^n$.

Manifold alignment algorithms attempt to project both X and Y into a new d-dimensional space such that the projections both minimize distance between corresponding points and preserve the local manifold structure of the original data. The projection functions are denoted:

$$\phi_X : \mathbb{R}^m \to \mathbb{R}^d$$

$$\phi_Y : \mathbb{R}^n \to \mathbb{R}^d$$

Let W represent the binary correspondence matrix between points in X and Y:

$$W_{i,j} = \begin{cases} 1 & \text{if } X_i \leftrightarrow Y_j \\ 0 & \text{otherwise} \end{cases}$$

Let S_X and S_Y represent pointwise similarities within data sets. This is usually encoded as the heat kernel of the adjacency matrix of a k-nearest neighbor graph.

Finally, introduce a coefficient $0 \le \mu \le 1$, which can be tuned to adjust the weight of the 'preserve manifold structure' goal, versus the 'minimize corresponding point distances' goal.

With these definitions in place, the loss function for manifold alignment can be written:

$$\arg\min_{\phi_X, \phi_Y} \mu \sum_{i,j} \left\| \phi_X(X_i) - \phi_X(X_j) \right\|^2 S_{X,i,j} + \mu \sum_{i,j} \left\| \phi_Y(Y_i) - \phi_Y(Y_j) \right\|^2 S_{Y,i,j}$$

$$+ (1-\mu) \sum_{i,j} \| \phi_X(X_i) - \phi_Y(Y_j) \|^2 W_{i,j}$$

Solving this optimization problem is equivalent to solving a generalized eigenvalue problem using the graph laplacian of the joint matrix, G:

$$G = \begin{bmatrix} \mu S_X & (1-\mu)W \\ (1-\mu)W^T & \mu S_Y \end{bmatrix}$$

Inter-data Correspondences

The algorithm described above requires full pairwise correspondence information between input data sets; a supervised learning paradigm. However, this information is usually difficult or impossible to obtain in real world applications. Recent work has extended the core manifold alignment algorithm to semi-supervised, unsupervised, and multiple-instance settings.

One-step vs. Two-step Alignment

The algorithm described above performs a "one-step" alignment, finding embeddings for both data sets at the same time. A similar effect can also be achieved with "two-step" alignments, following a slightly modified procedure:

- Project each input data set to a lower-dimensional space independently, using any of a variety of dimension reduction algorithms.

- Perform linear manifold alignment on the embedded data, holding the first data set fixed, mapping each additional data set onto the first's manifold. This approach has the benefit of decomposing the required computation, which lowers memory overhead and allows parallel implementations.

Instance-level vs. Feature-level Projections

Manifold alignment can be used to find linear (feature-level) projections, or nonlinear (instance-level) embeddings. While the instance-level version generally produces more accurate alignments, it sacrifices a great degree of flexibility as the learned embedding is often difficult to parameterize. Feature-level projections allow any new instances to be easily embedded in the manifold space, and projections may be combined to form direct mappings between the original data representations. These properties are especially important for knowledge-transfer applications.

Applications

Manifold alignment is suited to problems with several corpora that lie on a shared manifold, even when each corpus is of a different dimensionality. Many real-world problems fit this description, but traditional techniques are not able to take advantage of all corpora at the same time. Manifold alignment also facilitates transfer learning, in which knowledge of one domain is used to jump-start learning in correlated domains.

Applications of manifold alignment include:

- Cross-language information retrieval / automatic translation:

  - By representing documents as vector of word counts, manifold alignment can recover the mapping between documents of different languages.

  - Cross-language document correspondence is relatively easy to obtain, especially from multi-lingual organizations like the European Union.

- Transfer learning of policy and state representations for reinforcement learning.

- Alignment of protein NMR structures.

Randomized Weighted Majority Algorithm

The randomized weighted majority algorithm is an algorithm in machine learning theory. It improves the mistake bound of the weighted majority algorithm.

Imagine that every morning before the stock market opens, we get a prediction from each of our "experts" about whether the stock market will go up or down. Our goal is to somehow combine this set of predictions into a single prediction that we then use to make a buy or sell decision for the day. The RWMA gives us a way to do this combination such that our prediction record will be nearly as good as that of the single best expert in hindsight.

Motivation

In machine learning, the weighted majority algorithm (WMA) is a meta-learning algorithm which "predicts from expert advice". It is not a randomized algorithm:

```
initialize all experts to weight 1.

for each round:

    poll all the experts and predict based on a weighted majority vote
of their predictions.

    cut in half the weights of all experts that make a mistake.
```

Suppose there are n experts and the best expert makes m mistakes. The weighted majority algorithm (WMA) makes at most $2.4(\log_2 n + m)$ mistakes, which is not a very good bound. We can do better by introducing randomization.

Randomized Weighted Majority Algorithm (RWMA)

The nonrandomized weighted majority algorithm (WMA) only guarantees an upper bound of $2.4(\log_2 n + m)$, which is problematic for highly error-prone experts (e.g. the best expert still makes a mistake 20% of the time.) Suppose we do $N = 100$ rounds using $n = 10$ experts. If the best expert makes $m = 20$ mistakes, we can only guarantee an upper bound of $2.4(\log_2 10 + 20) \approx 56$ on our number of mistakes.

As this is a known limitation of WMA, attempts to improve this shortcoming have been explored in order to improve the dependence on m. Instead of predicting based on majority vote, the weights are used as probabilities: hence the name randomized weighted majority. If w_i is the weight of expert i, let $W = \sum_i w_i$. We will follow expert i with probability $\frac{w_i}{W}$. The goal is to bound the worst-case expected number of mistakes, assuming that the adversary (the world) has to select one of the answers as correct before we make our coin toss. Why is this better in the worst case? Idea: the worst case for the deterministic algorithm (weighted majority algorithm) was when the weights split 50/50. But, now it is not so bad since we also have a 50/50 chance of getting it right. Also, to trade-off between dependence on m and $\log_2 n$, we will generalize to multiply by $\beta < 1$, instead of necessarily by $\frac{1}{2}$.

Analysis

At the t-th round, define F_t to be the fraction of weight on the wrong answers. so, F_t is the probability we make a mistake on the t-th round. Let M denote the total number of mistakes we made so far. Furthermore, we define $E[M] = \sum_t F_t$, using the fact that expectation is additive. On the t

-th round, W becomes $W(1-(1-\beta)F_t)$. Reason: on F_t fraction, we are multiplying by β. So, $W_{final} = n*(1-(1-\beta)F_1)*(1-(1-\beta)F_2)$.

Let's say that m is the number of mistakes of the best expert so far. We can use the inequality $W \geq \beta^m$. Now we solve. First, take the natural log of both sides. We get: $m\ln\beta \leq \ln(n) + \sum_t \ln(1-(1-\beta)F_t)$, Simplify:

$$\ln(1-x) = -x - \frac{x^2}{2} - \frac{x^3}{3} - ..., \text{ So,}$$

$$\ln(1-(1-\beta)F_t) < -(1-\beta)F_t.$$

$$m\ln\beta \leq \ln(n) - (1-\beta)*\sum_t F_t$$

Now, use $E[M] = \sum_t F_t$, and the result is:

$$E[M] \leq \frac{m\ln(1/\beta) + \ln(n)}{1-\beta}$$

Let's see if we made any progress:

If $\beta = \frac{1}{2}$, we get, $1.39m + 2\ln(n)$.

if $\beta = \frac{3}{4}$, we get, $1.15m + 4\ln(n)$.

so we can see we made progress. Roughly, of the form $(1+\epsilon)*m + \epsilon^{-1}*\ln(n)$.

Uses of Randomized Weighted Majority Algorithm (RWMA)

The Randomized Weighted Majority Algorithm can be used to combine multiple algorithms in which case RWMA can be expected to perform nearly as well as the best of the original algorithms in hindsight.

Furthermore, one can apply the Randomized Weighted Majority Algorithm in situations where experts are making choices that cannot be combined (or can't be combined easily). For example, RWMA can be applied to repeated game-playing or the online shortest path problem. In the online shortest path problem, each expert is telling you a different way to drive to work. You pick one path using RWMA. Later you find out how well you would have done using all of the suggested paths and penalize appropriately. To do this right, we want to generalize from "losses" of 0 or 1 to losses in [0,1]. The goal is to have an expected loss not much larger than the loss of the best expert. We can generalize the RWMA by applying a penalty of β^{loss} (i.e. two losses of one half result in the same weight as one loss of 1 and one loss of 0).

Extensions

- Multi-armed bandit problem.

- Efficient algorithm for some cases with many experts.

- Sleeping experts/"specialists" setting.

k-nearest Neighbors Algorithm

In pattern recognition, the k-nearest neighbors algorithm (k-NN) is a non-parametric method used for classification and regression. In both cases, the input consists of the k closest training examples in the feature space. The output depends on whether k-NN is used for classification or regression:

- In *k-NN classification*, the output is a class membership. An object is classified by a majority vote of its neighbors, with the object being assigned to the class most common among its k nearest neighbors (k is a positive integer, typically small). If $k = 1$, then the object is simply assigned to the class of that single nearest neighbor.

- In *k-NN regression*, the output is the property value for the object. This value is the average of the values of its k nearest neighbors.

k-NN is a type of instance-based learning, or lazy learning, where the function is only approximated locally and all computation is deferred until classification. The k-NN algorithm is among the simplest of all machine learning algorithms.

Both for classification and regression, it can be useful to assign weight to the contributions of the neighbors, so that the nearer neighbors contribute more to the average than the more distant ones. For example, a common weighting scheme consists in giving each neighbor a weight of $1/d$, where d is the distance to the neighbor.

The neighbors are taken from a set of objects for which the class (for k-NN classification) or the object property value (for k-NN regression) is known. This can be thought of as the training set for the algorithm, though no explicit training step is required.

A peculiarity of the k-NN algorithm is that it is sensitive to the local structure of the data. The algorithm is different than k-means, another popular machine learning technique.

Statistical Setting

Suppose we have pairs $(X, Y), (X_1, Y_1), \ldots, (X_n, Y_n)$ taking values in $\mathbb{R}^d \times \{1, 2\}$, where Y is the class label of X, so that $X \mid Y = r \sim P_r$ for $r = 1, 2$ (and probability distributions P_r). Given some norm $\|\cdot\|$ on $\mathbb{R}^d$ and a point $x \in \mathbb{R}^d$, let $(X_{(1)}, Y_{(1)}), \ldots, (X_{(n)}, Y_{(n)})$ be a reordering of the training data such that $\| X_{(1)} - x \| \leq \ldots \leq \| X_{(n)} - x \|$.

Algorithm

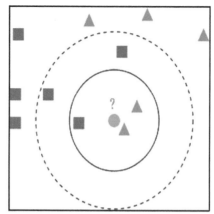

Example of k-NN classification. The test sample (green circle) should be classified either to the first class of blue squares or to the second class of red triangles. If $k = 3$ (solid line circle) it is assigned to the second class because there are 2 triangles and only 1 square inside the inner circle. If $k = 5$ (dashed line circle) it is assigned to the first class (3 squares vs. 2 triangles inside the outer circle).

The training examples are vectors in a multidimensional feature space, each with a class label. The training phase of the algorithm consists only of storing the feature vectors and class labels of the training samples.

In the classification phase, k is a user-defined constant, and an unlabeled vector (a query or test point) is classified by assigning the label which is most frequent among the k training samples nearest to that query point.

A commonly used distance metric for continuous variables is Euclidean distance. For discrete variables, such as for text classification, another metric can be used, such as the overlap metric (or Hamming distance). In the context of gene expression microarray data, for example, k-NN has also been employed with correlation coefficients such as Pearson and Spearman. Often, the classification accuracy of k-NN can be improved significantly if the distance metric is learned with specialized algorithms such as Large Margin Nearest Neighbor or Neighbourhood components analysis.

A drawback of the basic "majority voting" classification occurs when the class distribution is skewed. That is, examples of a more frequent class tend to dominate the prediction of the new example, because they tend to be common among the k nearest neighbors due to their large number. One way to overcome this problem is to weight the classification, taking into account the distance from the test point to each of its k nearest neighbors. The class (or value, in regression problems) of each of the k nearest points is multiplied by a weight proportional to the inverse of the distance from that point to the test point. Another way to overcome skew is by abstraction in data representation. For example, in a self-organizing map (SOM), each node is a representative (a center) of a cluster of similar points, regardless of their density in the original training data. K-NN can then be applied to the SOM.

Parameter Selection

The best choice of k depends upon the data; generally, larger values of k reduce the effect of noise on the classification, but make boundaries between classes less distinct. A good k can be selected by various heuristic techniques. The special case where the class is predicted to be the class of the closest training sample (i.e. when $k = 1$) is called the nearest neighbor algorithm.

The accuracy of the k-NN algorithm can be severely degraded by the presence of noisy or irrelevant features, or if the feature scales are not consistent with their importance. Much research effort has been put into selecting or scaling features to improve classification. A particularly popular approach is the use of evolutionary algorithms to optimize feature scaling. Another popular approach is to scale features by the mutual information of the training data with the training classes.

In binary (two class) classification problems, it is helpful to choose k to be an odd number as this avoids tied votes. One popular way of choosing the empirically optimal k in this setting is via bootstrap method.

The 1-nearest Neighbour Classifier

The most intuitive nearest neighbour type classifier is the one nearest neighbour classifier that assigns a point x to the class of its closest neighbour in the feature space, that is $C_n^{1nn}(x) = Y_{(1)}$.

As the size of training data set approaches infinity, the one nearest neighbour classifier guarantees an error rate of no worse than twice the Bayes error rate (the minimum achievable error rate given the distribution of the data).

The Weighted Nearest Neighbour Classifier

The k-nearest neighbour classifier can be viewed as assigning the k nearest neighbours a weight $1/k$ and all others 0 weight. This can be generalised to weighted nearest neighbour classifiers. That is, where the ith nearest neighbour is assigned a weight w_{ni}, with $\sum_{i=1}^{n} w_{ni} = 1$. An analogous result on the strong consistency of weighted nearest neighbour classifiers also holds.

Let C_n^{wnn} denote the weighted nearest classifier with weights $\{w_{ni}\}_{i=1}^{n}$. Subject to regularity conditions on to class distributions the excess risk has the following asymptotic expansion:

$$\mathcal{R}_{\mathcal{R}}(C_n^{wnn}) - \mathcal{R}_{\mathcal{R}}(C^{Bayes}) = \left(B_1 s_n^2 + B_2 t_n^2\right)\{1 + o(1)\}$$

for constants B_1 and B_2 where $s_n^2 = \sum_{i=1}^{n} w_{ni}^2$ and $t_n = n^{-2/d} \sum_{i=1}^{n} w_{ni}\{i^{1+2/d} - (i-1)^{1+2/d}\}$.

The optimal weighting scheme $\{w_{ni}^*\}_{i=1}^{n}$, that balances the two terms in the display above, is given as follows: set $k^* = \lfloor Bn^{\frac{4}{d+4}} \rfloor$,

$$w_{ni}^* = \frac{1}{k^*}\left[1 + \frac{d}{2} - \frac{d}{2k^{*2/d}}\{i^{1+2/d} - (i-1)^{1+2/d}\}\right] \text{ for } i = 1, 2, \ldots, k^* \text{ and}$$

$w_{ni}^* = 0$ for $i = k^* + 1, \ldots, n$.

With optimal weights the dominant term in the asymptotic expansion of the excess risk is $\mathcal{O}(n^{-\frac{4}{d+4}})$. Similar results are true when using a bagged nearest neighbour classifier.

Properties

k-NN is a special case of a variable-bandwidth, kernel density "balloon" estimator with a uniform kernel.

The naive version of the algorithm is easy to implement by computing the distances from the test example to all stored examples, but it is computationally intensive for large training sets. Using an appropriate nearest neighbor search algorithm makes *k*-NN computationally tractable even for large data sets. Many nearest neighbor search algorithms have been proposed over the years; these generally seek to reduce the number of distance evaluations actually performed.

k-NN has some strong consistency results. As the amount of data approaches infinity, the two-class *k*-NN algorithm is guaranteed to yield an error rate no worse than twice the Bayes error rate (the minimum achievable error rate given the distribution of the data). Various improvements to the *k*-NN speed are possible by using proximity graphs.

For multi-class *k*-NN classification, Cover and Hart (1967) prove an upper bound error rate of:

$$R^* \le R_{kNN} \le R^*(2 - MR^*/(M-1))$$

where R^* is the Bayes error rate (which is the minimal error rate possible), R_{kNN} is the *k*-NN error rate, and M is the number of classes in the problem. For $M = 2$ and as the Bayesian error rate R^* approaches zero, this limit reduces to "not more than twice the Bayesian error rate".

Error Rates

There are many results on the error rate of the *k* nearest neighbour classifiers. The *k*-nearest neighbour classifier is strongly (that is for any joint distribution on (X, Y)) consistent provided $k := k_n$ diverges and k_n / n converges to zero as $n \to \infty$.

Let C_n^{knn} denote the *k* nearest neighbour classifier based on a training set of size *n*. Under certain regularity conditions, the excess risk yields the following asymptotic expansion:

$$\mathcal{R}_{\mathcal{R}}(C_n^{knn}) - \mathcal{R}_{\mathcal{R}}(C^{Bayes}) = \left\{ B_1 \frac{1}{k} + B_2 \left(\frac{k}{n} \right)^{4/d} \right\} \{1 + o(1)\},$$

for some constants B_1 and B_2.

The choice $k^* = \lfloor Bn^{\frac{4}{d+4}} \rfloor$ offers a trade off between the two terms in the above display, for which the k^*-nearest neighbour error converges to the Bayes error at the optimal (minimax) rate $\mathcal{O}(n^{-\frac{4}{d+4}})$.

Metric Learning

The K-nearest neighbor classification performance can often be significantly improved through (supervised) metric learning. Popular algorithms are neighbourhood components analysis and large margin nearest neighbor. Supervised metric learning algorithms use the label information to learn a new metric or pseudo-metric.

Feature Extraction

When the input data to an algorithm is too large to be processed and it is suspected to be redundant (e.g. the same measurement in both feet and meters) then the input data will be transformed into a reduced representation set of features (also named features vector). Transforming the input data into the set of features is called feature extraction. If the features extracted are carefully chosen it is expected that the features set will extract the relevant information from the input data in order to perform the desired task using this reduced representation instead of the full size input. Feature extraction is performed on raw data prior to applying k-NN algorithm on the transformed data in feature space.

An example of a typical computer vision computation pipeline for face recognition using k-NN including feature extraction and dimension reduction pre-processing steps (usually implemented with OpenCV):

1. Haar face detection.

2. Mean-shift tracking analysis.

3. PCA or Fisher LDA projection into feature space, followed by k-NN classification.

Dimension Reduction

For high-dimensional data (e.g., with number of dimensions more than 10) dimension reduction is usually performed prior to applying the k-NN algorithm in order to avoid the effects of the curse of dimensionality.

The curse of dimensionality in the k-NN context basically means that Euclidean distance is unhelpful in high dimensions because all vectors are almost equidistant to the search query vector (imagine multiple points lying more or less on a circle with the query point at the center; the distance from the query to all data points in the search space is almost the same).

Feature extraction and dimension reduction can be combined in one step using principal component analysis (PCA), linear discriminant analysis (LDA), or canonical correlation analysis (CCA) techniques as a pre-processing step, followed by clustering by k-NN on feature vectors in reduced-dimension space. In machine learning this process is also called low-dimensional embedding.

For very-high-dimensional datasets (e.g. when performing a similarity search on live video streams, DNA data or high-dimensional time series) running a fast approximate k-NN search using locality sensitive hashing, "random projections", "sketches" or other high-dimensional similarity search techniques from the VLDB toolbox might be the only feasible option.

Decision Boundary

Nearest neighbor rules in effect implicitly compute the decision boundary. It is also possible to compute the decision boundary explicitly, and to do so efficiently, so that the computational complexity is a function of the boundary complexity.

Data Reduction

Data reduction is one of the most important problems for work with huge data sets. Usually, only some of the data points are needed for accurate classification. Those data are called the *prototypes* and can be found as follows:

- Select the *class-outliers*, that is, training data that are classified incorrectly by k-NN (for a given k).

- Separate the rest of the data into two sets: (i) the prototypes that are used for the classification decisions and (ii) the *absorbed points* that can be correctly classified by k-NN using prototypes. The absorbed points can then be removed from the training set.

Selection of Class-outliers

A training example surrounded by examples of other classes is called a class outlier. Causes of class outliers include:

- Random error.

  Insufficient training examples of this class (an isolated example appears instead of a cluster).

- Missing important features (the classes are separated in other dimensions which we do not know).

- Too many training examples of other classes (unbalanced classes) that create a "hostile" background for the given small class.

Class outliers with k-NN produce noise. They can be detected and separated for future analysis. Given two natural numbers, $k > r > 0$, a training example is called a (k,r)NN class-outlier if its k nearest neighbors include more than r examples of other classes.

CNN for Data Reduction

Condensed nearest neighbor (CNN, the *Hart algorithm*) is an algorithm designed to reduce the data set for k-NN classification. It selects the set of prototypes U from the training data, such that 1NN with U can classify the examples almost as accurately as 1NN does with the whole data set.

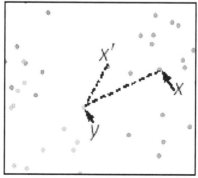

Calculation of the border ratio.

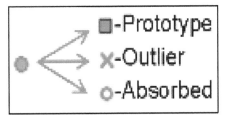

Three types of points: prototypes, class-outliers, and absorbed points.

Given a training set X, CNN works iteratively:

1. Scan all elements of X, looking for an element x whose nearest prototype from U has a different label than x.

2. Remove x from X and add it to U.

3. Repeat the scan until no more prototypes are added to U.

Use U instead of X for classification. The examples that are not prototypes are called "absorbed" points.

It is efficient to scan the training examples in order of decreasing border ratio. The border ratio of a training example x is defined as:

$$a(x) = \frac{\|x'-y\|}{\|x-y\|}$$

where $\|x-y\|$ is the distance to the closest example y having a different color than x, and $\|x'-y\|$ is the distance from y to its closest example x' with the same label as x.

The border ratio is in the interval $[0,1]$ because $\|x'-y\|$ never exceeds $\|x-y\|$. This ordering gives preference to the borders of the classes for inclusion in the set of prototypes U. A point of a different label than x is called external to x. The calculation of the border ratio is illustrated by the figure. The data points are labeled by colors: the initial point is x and its label is red. External points are blue and green. The closest to x external point is y. The closest to y red point is x'. The border ratio $a(x) = \|x'-y\| / \|x-y\|$ is the attribute of the initial point x.

Below is an illustration of CNN in a series of figures. There are three classes (red, green and blue). Fig. a initially there are 60 points in each class. Fig. b shows the 1NN classification map: each pixel is classified by 1NN using all the data. Fig. c shows the 5NN classification map. White areas correspond to the unclassified regions, where 5NN voting is tied (for example, if there are two green, two red and one blue points among 5 nearest neighbors). Fig. d shows the reduced data set. The crosses are the class-outliers selected by the (3,2)NN rule (all the three nearest neighbors of these instances belong to other classes); the squares are the prototypes, and the empty circles are the absorbed points. The left bottom corner shows the numbers of the class-outliers, prototypes and absorbed points for all three classes. The number of prototypes varies from 15% to 20% for different classes in this example. Fig. e shows that the 1NN classification map with the prototypes is very similar to that with the initial data set. The figures were produced using the Mirkes applet.

- CNN model reduction for k-NN classifiers.

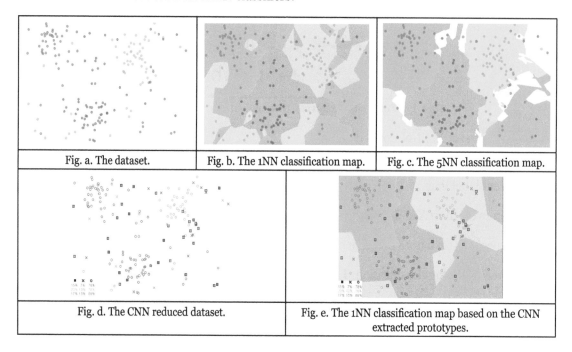

Fig. a. The dataset.	Fig. b. The 1NN classification map.	Fig. c. The 5NN classification map.
Fig. d. The CNN reduced dataset.		Fig. e. The 1NN classification map based on the CNN extracted prototypes.

k-NN Regression

In k-NN regression, the k-NN algorithm is used for estimating continuous variables. One such algorithm uses a weighted average of the k nearest neighbors, weighted by the inverse of their distance. This algorithm works as follows:

1. Compute the Euclidean or Mahalanobis distance from the query example to the labeled examples.

2. Order the labeled examples by increasing distance.

3. Find a heuristically optimal number k of nearest neighbors, based on RMSE. This is done using cross validation.

4. Calculate an inverse distance weighted average with the k-nearest multivariate neighbors.

k-NN outlier

The distance to the kth nearest neighbor can also be seen as a local density estimate and thus is also a popular outlier score in anomaly detection. The larger the distance to the k-NN, the lower the local density, the more likely the query point is an outlier. Although quite simple, this outlier model, along with another classic data mining method, local outlier factor, works quite well also in comparison to more recent and more complex approaches, according to a large scale experimental analysis.

Validation of Results

A confusion matrix or "matching matrix" is often used as a tool to validate the accuracy of k-NN classification. More robust statistical methods such as likelihood-ratio test can also be applied.

Boosting

Boosting is a machine learning ensemble meta-algorithm for primarily reducing bias, and also variance in supervised learning, and a family of machine learning algorithms which convert weak learners to strong ones. Boosting is based on the question posed by Kearns and Valiant (1988, 1989): Can a set of weak learners create a single strong learner? A weak learner is defined to be a classifier which is only slightly correlated with the true classification (it can label examples better than random guessing). In contrast, a strong learner is a classifier that is arbitrarily well-correlated with the true classification.

Robert Schapire's affirmative answer in a 1990 paper to the question of Kearns and Valiant has had significant ramifications in machine learning and statistics, most notably leading to the development of boosting.

When first introduced, the *hypothesis boosting problem* simply referred to the process of turning a weak learner into a strong learner. "Informally, [the hypothesis boosting] problem asks whether an efficient learning algorithm [...] that outputs a hypothesis whose performance is only slightly better than random guessing [i.e. a weak learner] implies the existence of an efficient algorithm that outputs a hypothesis of arbitrary accuracy [i.e. a strong learner]." Algorithms that achieve hypothesis boosting quickly became simply known as "boosting". Freund and Schapire's arcing (Adapt[at]ive Resampling and Combining), as a general technique, is more or less synonymous with boosting.

Boosting Algorithms

While boosting is not algorithmically constrained, most boosting algorithms consist of iteratively learning weak classifiers with respect to a distribution and adding them to a final strong classifier. When they are added, they are typically weighted in some way that is usually related to the weak learners' accuracy. After a weak learner is added, the data are reweighted: examples that are misclassified gain weight and examples that are classified correctly lose weight (some boosting algorithms actually decrease the weight of repeatedly misclassified examples, e.g., boost by majority and BrownBoost). Thus, future weak learners focus more on the examples that previous weak learners misclassified.

There are many boosting algorithms. The original ones, proposed by Robert Schapire (a recursive majority gate formulation) and Yoav Freund (boost by majority), were not adaptive and could not take full advantage of the weak learners. However, Schapire and Freund then developed AdaBoost, an adaptive boosting algorithm that won the prestigious Gödel Prize.

Only algorithms that are provable boosting algorithms in the probably approximately correct learning formulation can accurately be called *boosting algorithms*. Other algorithms that are similar in spirit to boosting algorithms are sometimes called "leveraging algorithms", although they are also sometimes incorrectly called boosting algorithms.

The main variation between many boosting algorithms is their method of weighting training data points and hypotheses. AdaBoost is very popular and perhaps the most significant historically as it was the first algorithm that could adapt to the weak learners. However, there are many more recent algorithms such as LPBoost, TotalBoost, BrownBoost, xgboost, MadaBoost, LogitBoost, and others. Many boosting algorithms fit into the AnyBoost framework, which shows that boosting performs gradient descent in function space using a convex cost function.

Object Categorization

Given images containing various known objects in the world, a classifier can be learned from them to automatically categorize the objects in future images. Simple classifiers built based on some image feature of the object tend to be weak in categorization performance. Using boosting methods for object categorization is a way to unify the weak classifiers in a special way to boost the overall ability of categorization.

Problem of Object Categorization

Object categorization is a typical task of computer vision which involves determining whether or not an image contains some specific category of object. The idea is closely related with recognition, identification, and detection. Appearance based object categorization typically contains feature extraction, learning a classifier, and applying the classifier to new examples. There are many ways to represent a category of objects, e.g. from shape analysis, bag of words models, or local descriptors such as SIFT, etc. Examples of supervised classifiers are Naive Bayes classifier, SVM, mixtures of Gaussians, neural network, etc. However, research has shown that object categories and their locations in images can be discovered in an unsupervised manner as well.

Status Quo for Object Categorization

The recognition of object categories in images is a challenging problem in computer vision, especially when the number of categories is large. This is due to high intra class variability and the need for generalization across variations of objects within the same category. Objects within one category may look quite different. Even the same object may appear unalike under different viewpoint, scale, and illumination. Background clutter and partial occlusion add difficulties to recognition as well. Humans are able to recognize thousands of object types, whereas most of the existing object recognition systems are trained to recognize only a few, e.g., human face, car, simple objects, etc. Research has been very active on dealing with more categories and enabling incremental additions of new categories and although the general problem remains unsolved, several multi-category objects detectors (number of categories around 20) for clustered scenes have been developed. One means is by feature sharing and boosting.

Boosting for Binary Categorization

AdaBoost can be used for face detection as an example of binary categorization. The two categories are faces versus background. The general algorithm is as follows:

- Form a large set of simple features.

- Initialize weights for training images.

- For T rounds,

- ◦ Normalize the weights.

- ◦ For available features from the set, train a classifier using a single feature and evaluate the training error.

- ◦ Choose the classifier with the lowest error.

- ◦ Update the weights of the training images: increase if classified wrongly by this classifier, decrease if correctly.

- Form the final strong classifier as the linear combination of the T classifiers (coefficient larger if training error is small).

After boosting, a classifier constructed from 200 features could yield a 95% detection rate under a 10^{-5} false positive rate.

Another application of boosting for binary categorization is a system which detects pedestrians using patterns of motion and appearance. This work is the first to combine both motion information and appearance information as features to detect a walking person. It takes a similar approach as the face detection work of Viola and Jones.

Boosting for Multi-class Categorization

Compared with binary categorization, multi-class categorization looks for common features that can be shared across the categories at the same time. They turn to be more generic edge like features. During learning, the detectors for each category can be trained jointly. Compared with training separately, it generalizes better, needs less training data, and requires less number of features to achieve same performance.

The main flow of the algorithm is similar to the binary case. What is different is that a measure of the joint training error shall be defined in advance. During each iteration the algorithm chooses a classifier of a single feature (features which can be shared by more categories shall be encouraged). This can be done via converting multi-class classification into a binary one (a set of categories versus the rest), or by introducing a penalty error from the categories which do not have the feature of the classifier.

In the paper "Sharing visual features for multiclass and multiview object detection", A. Torralba et al. used GentleBoost for boosting and showed that when training data is limited, learning via sharing features does a much better job than no sharing, given same boosting rounds. Also, for a given performance level, the total number of features required (and therefore the run time cost of the classifier) for the feature sharing detectors, is observed to scale approximately logarithmically with the number of class, i.e., slower than linear growth in the non-sharing case. Similar results are shown in the paper "Incremental learning of object detectors using a visual shape alphabet", yet the authors used AdaBoost for boosting.

Criticism

In 2008 Phillip Long (at Google) and Rocco A. Servedio (Columbia University) published a paper at the 25th International Conference for Machine Learning suggesting that many of these algorithms are probably flawed. They conclude that "convex potential boosters cannot withstand random classification noise," thus making the applicability of such algorithms for real world, noisy data sets questionable. The paper shows that if any fraction of the training data is mis-labeled, the boosting algorithm tries extremely hard to correctly classify these training examples, and fails to produce a model with accuracy better than 1/2. This result does not apply to branching program based boosters but does apply to AdaBoost, LogitBoost, and others.

Bootstrap Aggregating

Bootstrap aggregating, also called bagging, is a machine learning ensemble meta-algorithm designed to improve the stability and accuracy of machine learning algorithms used in statistical classification and regression. It also reduces variance and helps to avoid overfitting. Although it is usually applied to decision tree methods, it can be used with any type of method. Bagging is a special case of the model averaging approach.

History

Bagging (Bootstrap aggregating) was proposed by Leo Breiman in 1994 to improve the classification by combining classifications of randomly generated training sets.1994.

Description of the Technique

Given a standard training set D of size n, bagging generates m new training sets D_i, each of size n', by sampling from D uniformly and with replacement. By sampling with replacement, some observations may be repeated in each D_i. If $n'=n$, then for large n the set D_i is expected to have the fraction $(1 - 1/e)$ ($\approx$63.2%) of the unique examples of D, the rest being duplicates. This kind of sample is known as a bootstrap sample. The m models are fitted using the above m bootstrap samples and combined by averaging the output (for regression) or voting (for classification).

Bagging leads to "improvements for unstable procedures" (Breiman, 1996), which include, for example, artificial neural networks, classification and regression trees, and subset selection in linear regression (Breiman, 1994). An interesting application of bagging showing improvement in preimage learning is provided here. On the other hand, it can mildly degrade the performance of stable methods such as K-nearest neighbors (Breiman, 1996).

Example: Ozone Data

To illustrate the basic principles of bagging, below is an analysis on the relationship between ozone and temperature (data from Rousseeuw and Leroy (1986), analysis done in R).

The relationship between temperature and ozone in this data set is apparently non-linear, based on the scatter plot. To mathematically describe this relationship, LOESS smoothers (with span 0.5) are used. Instead of building a single smoother from the complete data set, 100 bootstrap samples of the data were drawn. Each sample is different from the original data set, yet resembles it in distribution and variability. For each bootstrap sample, a LOESS smoother was fit. Predictions from these 100 smoothers were then made across the range of the data. The first 10 predicted smooth fits appear as grey lines in the figure below. The lines are clearly very *wiggly* and they overfit the data - a result of the span being too low.

By taking the average of 100 smoothers, each fitted to a subset of the original data set, we arrive at one bagged predictor (red line). Clearly, the mean is more stable and there is less overfit.

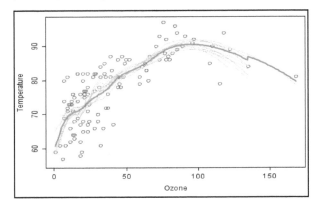

References

- Belkin, M; P Niyogi (2003). "Laplacian eigenmaps for dimensionality reduction and data representation" (PDF). Neural Computation. 15: 1373–1396. doi:10.1162/089976603321780317

- Stuart Russell and Peter Norvig (2010). Artificial Intelligence A Modern Approach 3rd Edition. Upper Saddle River, New Jersey: Pearson Education/Prentice-Hall. ISBN 978-0-13-604259-4

- Ikeda, Shiro; Amari, Shun-ichi; Nakahara, Hiroyuki. "Convergence of The Wake-Sleep Algorithm" (PDF). The Institute of Statistical Mathematics. Retrieved 11, May 2020

- Toussaint GT (April 2005). "Geometric proximity graphs for improving nearest neighbor methods in instance-based learning and data mining". International Journal of Computational Geometry and Applications. 15 (2): 101–150. doi:10.1142/S0218195905001622

- Maei, Hamid Reza (2007-01-25). "Wake-sleep algorithm for representational learning". University of Montreal. Retrieved 29, June 2020

Permissions

Index

Printed in the USA
CPSIA information can be obtained
at www.ICGtesting.com
JSHW051357221024
72173JS00006B/1309

9 781639 873333